DARK INTERPRETER

The Discourse of Romanticism

DARK INTERPRETER
The Discourse of Romanticism

Tilottama Rajan

CORNELL UNIVERSITY PRESS

ITHACA AND LONDON

First published 1980 by Cornell University Press.
Published in the United Kingdom by Cornell University Press Ltd.,
2-4 Brook Street, London W1Y 1AA.

International Standard Book Number 0-8014-1292-7
Library of Congress Catalog Card Number 80-14476
Printed in the United States of America
Librarians: Library of Congress cataloging information appears on the last page of the book.

Suffering is a mightier agency in the hands of nature, as a Demiurgus creating the intellect, than most people are aware of.

The truth I heard often in sleep from the lips of the Dark Interpreter. Who is he? He is a shadow, reader, but a shadow with whom you must suffer me to make you acquainted.... A nature which is profound... cannot be awakened sometimes without afflictions that go to the very foundations, heaving, stirring, yet finally harmonizing; and it is in such cases that the Dark Interpreter does his work, revealing the worlds of pain and agony and woe possible to man—possible even to the innocent spirit of a child.

—De Quincey, *Suspiria de Profundis*

3 6 6 7

Contents

Acknowledgments

Unlike the Romantics, who consented to be educated in illusion before they discovered its limitations, I began with an automatic sense of irony toward a group of poets whom I assumed to be sensitive only to daffodils. It took me some time to recognize that the Romantics were more modern than I had thought, and that their refusal to cross the threshold into modernism was a choice and not a failure. For this insight I am particularly grateful to Milton Wilson. In ways of which he is probably unaware, his undergraduate course on the Romantics taught me to respect a group of poets whom I had intended as victims of my deconstructive energies. The opportunity to teach in conjunction with Cyrus Hamlin provided me with much-needed intellectual stimulus at a crucial stage in the formulation of this book, and confirmed for me the importance of German critical theory for an understanding of Romanticism. Both my parents have provided encouragement (personal and intellectual) at important points, and my father, Professor B. Rajan, has been particularly helpful in suggesting revisions. I am grateful, finally, to the University of Toronto, which awarded the A. S. P. Woodhouse Prize to an earlier version of this book, submitted as my doctoral dissertation.

TILOTTAMA RAJAN

London, Ontario

DARK INTERPRETER

The Discourse of Romanticism

Introduction

The work of art, according to Hegel, is "something made, produced by a man who has taken it into his imagination . . . and issued it by his own activity out of his imagination."[1] Hegel's statement about the purely formal or epistemological ideality of the work of art indicates why the ideals of the Romantic movement are so closely bound up with a belief in the transforming power of aesthetic activity, urged by Shelley and Schiller among others.[2] Art, as the power to invent, is paradigmatic of man's capacity to take existence itself into his mind and rewrite it according to the images of desire. Indeed the historical and etymological connection of the term "Romanticism" with "romance" points to a view of literature as an idealizing rather than a mimetic activity, a mode of consciousness that envisions the unreal and the possible across the barrier of the actual. Yet implicit in this belief that the mind can create the unreal must be a doubt as to the reality of a mental creation. Poetic language, as Paul de Man comments, is intentional in structure: because it is a product of consciousness rather than a reflection of external nature, it shares in the noth-

[1]G. W. F. Hegel, *Aesthetics: Lectures on Fine Art* (1835), trans. T. M. Knox (Oxford: Clarendon, 1975), I, 162.
[2]I refer to Shelley's "A Defence of Poetry" and Schiller's letters *On the Aesthetic Education of Man*. Among critics who have argued for the centrality of imagination to Romantic utopianism are M. H. Abrams (*Natural Supernaturalism: Tradition and Revolution in Romantic Literature* [New York: Norton, 1971], pp. 117ff.), Northrop Frye (*A Study of English Romanticism* [New York: Random House, 1968], pp. 20ff.), Ernest Lee Tuveson (*The Imagination as a Means of Grace* [Berkeley and LosAngeles: University of California Press, 1960]), and Harold Bloom (*The Visionary Company* [New York: Doubleday, 1961], p. xiv; "The Internalization of Quest Romance," in *The Ringers in The Tower* [Chicago: University of Chicago Press, 1971], pp. 13-36).

ingness of consciousness rather than in the substantiality of things. As an attempt to transcend its own nothingness, the poetic image is doomed in advance, because it is "always constitutive, able to posit regardless of presence but, by the same token, unable to give a foundation to what it posits except as an intent of consciousness."[3] It is against this knowledge that we must read the Romantic attempt to deny the gap between fiction and actuality through an aesthetics which claims the identity of beauty and truth or mind and nature. We associate with the Romantics (particularly Coleridge and Schelling) a belief in the unity of consciousness and nature which, in turn, leads to an organic view of poetry as a natural and therefore real construct. But this view emerges as an essentially defensive reaction to an insight into the intentionality of poetic language which is present even in such writers as Coleridge and Schelling.

Even the more idealistic theorists of the period are not unaware that experience contradicts the language of affirmation. Jean-Paul Richter, who tries to argue for the identity of mimesis and idealization in the face of an obvious discrepancy between mental representations and things as they are, suggests that art is not just an imitation but a "corrective" imitation of reality. Poetry, according to him, "should neither destroy nor repeat but decipher reality":

> Poetry represents that highest life which is eternally lacking in all our reality . . . she paints the future drama on the curtain of eternity. She is no flat mirror of the present, but the magic mirror of the time which is not yet. . . . We return to the principle of poetic imitation. If

[3]Paul de Man, "The Intentional Structure of the Romantic Image," in *Romanticism and Consciousness,* ed. Harold Bloom (New York: Norton, 1970), p. 69. The notion of intentionality was originated by Brentano and Husserl, but de Man's use of the term probably derives from Sartre. In defining consciousness itself as "intentional" (i.e., as consciousness *of* something from which it is separated by the act of having to conceive this thing) Sartre emphasizes that consciousness is a *nothing* or lack in relation to the being outside itself. In applying this concept to the image, he notes that "an image, too, is an image *of* something," and is not the thing itself from which it is divided by the act of having to image it (*Imagination: A Psychological Critique* [1936], trans. Forrest Williams [Ann Arbor: University of Michigan Press, 1972], p. 133). For a further discussion of the idea that language can only *intend* and cannot *incarnate* what it describes, see Sartre, *The Psychology of Imagination* (1940), trans. Bernard Frechtman (New York: Washington Square Press, 1968), p. 5; and also *Imagination,* p. 4.

in poetic imitation the copy contains more than the original or even produces its opposite—pleasure from poetic sorrow, for example— this occurs because a double nature is being imitated: an outer and an inner one, *each the mirror of the other.*[4]

But there is in this argument, which bases itself on the doubleness of reality, a hiatus which invites us to deconstruct or see through the confident claim for the authority of poetic idealization. Jean-Paul begins by distinguishing an "inner" from an "outer" and merely apparent reality. He then manages to assume the monistic identity of the actual and the ideal, when in fact he has already used a dualistic separation of the two to restore figuratively a beauty which is clearly not present in life. The deliberate blurring of a vocabulary of transcendence into one of immanence allows him to conceal the extent to which he doubts the reality of his own idealism. To define literature as a decipherment rather than a straightforward imitation is already to constitute the Romantic text on two levels. It is to introduce a lacuna between historical appearance and eschatological innocence that may equally well become a lacuna between aesthetic appearance and existential reality.

It is often assumed (for instance by M. H. Abrams, Northrop Frye, and Ernest Lee Tuveson) that the high claims made for imagination as the guarantor of man's innocence over his corruption constitute what is truly revolutionary in the Romantic movement. In transferring the creative initiative from God to man, and in replacing revelation with imagination, the Romantics are thought to have overthrown a Christian pessimism which denied man direct access to the ideal. But in fact, a case can be made for saying that it is precisely this claim of a natural supernaturalism based on the imagination which is the most conservative element in a literature that stands on the edge of modernism, in a universe already recognized as discontinuous rather than organic. The Romantic rhetoric of affirmation avoids breaking with the past, and simply restates with reference to imagination the optimistic humanism urged by the Enlightenment with reference to reason.

[4]Jean-Paul Richter, *Horn of Oberon: Jean-Paul Richter's "School for Aesthetics"* (1812), trans. Margaret R. Hale (Detroit: Wayne State University Press, 1973), pp. 309, 24. Italics mine.

The compensatory, conservative nature of Romantic sacraments such as the marriage between mind and nature or the identity of beauty and truth is nowhere more evident than in Wordsworth. In both *The Prelude* and *The Excursion* he turns away from the disruptive horror disclosed by the French Revolution to a nature that exists in the past, even though he concedes in the latter poem that his vision of an organic universe may be a fiction of what never was ("Preface" to *The Excursion*, ll. 50–51).[5] In *The Prelude* itself the mythical status of this nature, and hence the compensatory motivation of the mind that imagines it, are repeatedly denied by an argument which speaks of the pastoral communion with nature as something "impaired" and then "restored," remembered and not imagined. But the poem also deconstructs its own assumptions by associating nature itself with the cataclysms of historical experience, which are described in natural metaphors of flood and deluge that make chaos and discontinuity at least as primary as organic unity (x.81–83). Paradoxically it is such recognitions, rather than the post-Enlightenment faith in human perfectibility through a secular conversion of the patterns of providence into those of aesthetic theodicy, which prove to be the truly subversive element in Romanticism.

My concern is not with the Romantic awareness of temporality, or of what Heidegger calls *Geworfenheit*. It is more specifically with the effect of this awareness on Romantic poems, considered reflexively as works that are trying to come to terms with the status of their own discourse, and hence with the function of man's imagination in relation to external reality. At certain critical points the Romantics deconstruct their own affirmative postulates. Jacques Derrida uses the term "deconstruction" to indicate the procedure of textual analysis by which the critic dismantles or takes apart the paraphrasable meaning of a text, in order to disclose within that text the gaps in logic which reveal the author's subconscious awareness of or commitment to a system of assumptions opposite to the one he explicitly endorses. Crucial to this procedure is the assumption that the text itself provides us with the tools we are to use in deconstructing it. To deconstruct a text is thus to assume

---

[5]Unless otherwise indicated, all references to Romantic poems supplied in the text are to the collected editions listed in the Selected List of Works Cited.

that it is a disunified and contradictory structure tacitly involved in contesting its own meaning. The radicalism of deconstructive criticism in relation to other theories of multiple meaning such as the New Criticism has been well described by Derrida's translator, Gayatri Spivak, who notes that Cleanth Brooks equates complexity with a polysemy that does not disrupt the organic unity of the text. In a deconstruction, on the contrary, the critic attempts to "spot the point where a text covers up" its own self-contestation and hence sees "the text coming undone as a structure of concealment, revealing its self-transgression, its undecidability." She emphasizes that it is not a question "simply of locating a moment of ambiguity or irony ultimately incorporated into the text's system of unified meaning but rather a moment that genuinely threatens to collapse that system".[6] Such a moment occurs in the passage by Jean-Paul already cited.

Deconstructive criticism assumes not only that texts are self-negating from a thematic point of view, but also that they betray a semiotic anxiety about the tendency of literature to put what it

---

[6]Jacques Derrida, *Of Grammatology* (1967), trans. Gayatri Spivak (Baltimore: The Johns Hopkins University Press, 1976), pp. lxxiii–lxxv. Deconstruction holds that language is inherently self-undermining and that the text is a self-consuming artifact. It thus sets itself in opposition to almost the entire past tradition of semiotics, which Derrida labels *logocentric* because it invests language with the authority to signify truth. The logocentric tradition assumes that language has the capacity to "make present" the truth which it "re-presents" through linguistic signs, and that this direct correspondence between the signifier and the thing signified is guaranteed either by some transcendent source or (as in Romanticism) by the true voice of feeling. In a literary sense, it is thus possible to speak of a logocentric *poetics of presence,* which assumes that literature can make present that which it signifies, can make real that which it imagines. In contrast, Derrida argues that language is a product of *différance,* and cannot be viewed logocentrically: the prime characteristic of language is that the signifier does not make present the thing signified, and that words are thus the *deferral* rather than the communication of a truth which they indicate but simultaneously undermine. In a literary sense, the consequence of Derrida's view of language would be a *poetics of absence,* in which the text would be a perpetual contesting and canceling of its own meaning, and hence a projection of its own nothingness.

Derrida's use of a deconstructive method of criticism arises from his general characterization of language as *différance* rather than *logos;* I make no such assumptions about the structure of language, and hence do not see deconstruction as a method valid with reference to all texts. Self-contestation is not an inherent feature of literary works, and deconstruction is a critical procedure applicable only to those texts which do contest their own meaning. There are, in other words, logocentric poems, although they do not fall within the range of this study.

says in doubt. There is nothing new about the view that the Romantics had doubts about their own imaginative logocentrism. But the status accorded these doubts in much of the most influential criticism is intermediate rather than terminal, and such criticism therefore does not call into question the view that the Romantics ultimately saw imagination as a transcending act. Bloom[7] and Frye emphasize the mythopoeic and visionary drive of Romantic language even in defeat. Abrams sees dejection and angst as a vital part of a dialectic of contraries which is meant to transcend rather than end in opposition. He does not regard Romantic poetry as what Schiller called a "naive" poetry, the product of a state of unorganized innocence. But he does see the typical Romantic work as capable of absorbing its own doubts without becoming discontinuous with its own assumptions. He does, therefore, tend to see the poetry of the period as committed to the "organized" or complex naiveté envisioned by Schiller as occurring in the future through a Coleridgean reconciliation of opposites in a dynamic unity.

Abrams, of course, is concerned more with the phenomenology of consciousness than with the status of discourse. But insofar as he makes assumptions about discourse, he remains committed to a logocentric reading of Romanticism derived from a philosophy of organicism. It is not unlikely that in determining the role of doubt within the dialectic of hope, he has in mind a model of the text which derives from the New Critical view of the poem as a complex harmony: an organic structure whose unity is strengthened rather than undermined by the presence of irony, ambiguity, and paradox. Such a view of poetry, because it makes the poet into the great reconciler, sustains rather than questions the constructive authority of imagination. While de Man may be wrong in arguing that *no* poetry can survive the self-contestation of irony and remain logocentric, the difficulty he senses about the potential contradiction between organic and ironic views of the poem seems valid with reference to *Romantic* poetry:

> As it refines its interpretations more and more, American criticism does not discover a single meaning, but a plurality of significations

[7]Harold Bloom, *Shelley's Mythmaking* (1959; rpt. Ithaca: Cornell University Press, 1969).

that can be radically opposed to each other. Instead of revealing a continuity affiliated with the coherence of the natural world, it takes us into a discontinuous world of reflective irony and ambiguity. ... This unitarian criticism finally becomes a criticism of ambiguity, an ironic reflection on the absence of the unity it had postulated.[8]

Critics such as Abrams and Earl Wasserman, in other words, take into account the darker side of Romanticism, but do not always recognize how far these elements threaten traditional Romantic postulates. The darker elements in Romantic works are not a part of their organic unity, but rather threaten to collapse this unity.

What is equally important from the point of view of this study is that Abrams finds in German philosophy a theoretical support for an idealism not always carried to its dialectical completion by the poets. He therefore regards as an anachronism the readings of those critics who "looking back at earlier literature through the gloomy contemporary perspective ... [argue] that Romantic writers could not really have meant what they claimed, hence that they must have been self-divided, or even unconsciously committed to the negations of the positives they so confidently asserted."[9] My own argument arises, in part, from a sense that the definitions of discourse developed by modern theorists such as Derrida, Heidegger, Sartre, and de Man[10] can already be found in the work of certain Romantic theorists, and that a deconstructive reading of Romantic poems is historically valid to the same degree as is a logocentric reading. But more important, the model of discourse eventually developed by the Romantic countertradition discussed in the next chapter, while fundamentally different from the one attributed to the Romantic period by critics such as Abrams and Frye, is also significantly different from the one developed by a criticism directed to the deconstruction of logocentric humanism. In other words, the current debate between organicist and deconstructionist critics over the nature of Romanticism was originally waged by the Romantics themselves and was not resolved in favor of either side. Thus it is Schiller,

[8]De Man, *Blindness and Insight: Essays in the Rhetoric of Contemporary Criticism* (New York: Oxford University Press, 1971), p. 28.
[9]Abrams, *Natural Supernaturalism,* p. 446.
[10]See Appendix A for further discussion of the relation of Derrida and de Man to Heidegger and Sartre.

Schopenhauer, and Nietzsche who can provide us with a vocabulary with which to interpret a wide variety of Romantic poems, considered as allegories of the aesthetic act and the operations it performs. This vocabulary, while theoretically autonomous in its potential applicability outside the Romantic period, shares with the vocabulary derived by Abrams from Hegel and Schelling the advantage of being historically grounded within it.

Earlier criticism of Romantic poetry emphasized the validity of the period's transcendental claims for art, without giving full weight to the self-questioning consequent upon the fact that the history of Romantic poetry is that of "a syntax that proved inadequate to the demands placed upon it."[11] From the discontinuity Bostetter noted between an overly optimistic (even if complex) concept of art and a basic fidelity to the facts of existence arises a series of self-frustrating literary structures which German Romantic theorists characterize as ironic or sentimental. But contrary to Bostetter, the Romantic encounter between the theory of art and the poetry of experience is formative as well as frustrating. Poems such as *The Fall of Hyperion* and *The Triumph of Life* are involved in questioning the aesthetic assumptions with which they begin, and in moving toward a concept of art which permits the liberation, for conscious use by the poet, of areas of experience that had previously to be repressed or sublimated in accordance with a more naive view of the function of imagination. On the other hand, it is incorrect to argue that Romanticism is, from its inception, a movement of self-demystification. Paul de Man, who deduces a conscious aesthetic of failure from Romantic choices of literary forms, tends to minimize two related problems. He underestimates the degree to which Romantic poetry is conditioned by the period's belief in art as a transcending act to *evade* sentimentally the recognition of its own temporality. He also does not consider the extent to which such evasion, which distinguishes Romantic writers from modern writers such as Samuel Beckett and prevents Romantic texts from achieving pure irony, is a double-edged phenomenon. The Romantic evasion of the temporality of art is not just an act of bad faith, but ultimately a

[11]Edward Bostetter, *The Romantic Ventriloquists: Wordsworth, Coleridge, Shelley, Keats, Byron* (1963; revised ed. Seattle: University of Washington Press, 1975), p. 5.

gesture that raises legitimate questions about the productive role of illusion in life.

The attempt of Romantic poetry to revise its sense of its own goals and limits is thus a complicated one. Serge Doubrovsky suggests that the "function of literature in every age" may be "precisely to constitute itself within the philosophy that is always more fundamental, more inward, more closely linked to human experience than the 'official' metaphysic of that same age."[12] What is offered in this book is, to some extent, a "deconstruction" of the official Romantic metaphysic of the imagination (endorsed by such modern critics as Abrams and Frye), and an argument that Romantic texts are themselves involved in probing beneath the assumptions about their own language which they incorporate as their surface content. From this point of view, the history of Romantic poetry and aesthetics can be seen as the gradual bringing to light of a counterplot within the apparently utopian narrative of Romantic desire, through the confrontation of recognitions initially hidden in the subtexts rather than the texts of works.[13] But it is also necessary to recognize that the text cannot simply be replaced by a subtext, and that the official content of a work does not cease to exist because it is undermined from within. It is because the doubts buried in subtexts are not necessarily "truer" than the affirmations urged in texts that Romanticism is less decisive in its commitment to self-irony than de Man sometimes supposes.[14] The limitations of deconstruction as a method

[12]Serge Doubrovsky, *The New Criticism in France* (1966), trans. Derek Coltman (Chicago: University of Chicago Press, 1973), p. 279.

[13]The word "subtext" was first used by Stanislavski to indicate that part of a play which is not made explicit in the dialogue, but emerges between the lines. I use the word in a slightly different sense, to indicate a subversive and repressed text which is not consistent with the explicit text, in relation to which it stands as the subconscious to the conscious. I assume first that the subtext is not something that a reader infers from between the lines but something which can be found *in* the words of a poem, and second that the author is not wholly in control of his subtext. Where he is in control of a "second" text within the poem, I would use the term "countertext" or "co-text."

[14]To be fair, de Man does sometimes recognize the "tenacious self-mystification" of Romantic writers with regard to "the truths that come to light in the last quarter of the eighteenth century" ("The Rhetoric of Temporality," in *Interpretation: Theory and Practice,* ed. Charles Singleton [Baltimore: The Johns Hopkins University Press, 1969], p. 191). But latterly he has seemed to view this tendency of Romanticism to relapse into illusions it sees through as something inherent in

of approaching Romantic poetry arise not only from its limitations as a critical position rather than a temporary critical tactic, but also from the Romantic poet's sense of the limits of demystification as an attitude to life.

Two texts not discussed subsequently may serve to illustrate the problematical duality of surface and depth present in Romantic conceptions of aesthetic discourse. The text which eventually became Book I of *The Excursion* began as a short, bare narrative of unrelieved distress. Wordsworth added to it a pantheistic gloss so different from the substance of the poem that at one point (in the D version) he was compelled to split his text into two separate poems, "The Ruined Cottage" and "The Pedlar." The providential vision of nature that emerges from "The Pedlar" reinterprets and sublimates the vision of nature as a bleak, amoral force, similar to Shelley's "Power," which emerges from "The Ruined Cottage." Coleridge's *Rime of the Ancient Mariner* is similarly a work whose stylistically hybrid quality throws into relief a fault or break in the poem's inner space, which divides idealization from truth. The gloss (added in 1817) is an attempt to ameliorate the much earlier narrative through a selective mimesis of the latter, which excludes its ambiguities and horrors, makes the mariner's return to the soul's own country seem more certain than it is, and absorbs purgatory into theodicy. In the cases of both Wordsworth and Coleridge, there is a contradiction between argument and narrative: the text includes a subtext which can be used to take it apart. And in both cases, the chronological priority of this subtext reveals the genesis of an affirmative rhetoric in an anxiety it cannot wholly dismiss.

This peculiar coexistence of one discourse with another that radically contradicts it can be explained only as a result of inconsistent views of how poetry ought to represent the world it depicts. The naturalistic narrative of "The Ruined Cottage" is a product

---

language, which cannot deconstruct except in relation to something constructed. Thus Romanticism, according to him, is not divided between text and subtext. "[It] is not a demystification. It is demystified from the start," as is all language (*Blindness and Insight*, p. 18). I would see the tendency mentioned above as something specific to Romanticism: an upsurge of the idealistic impulse, rather than simply an intermission in the drama of irony. That is to say, I would give the self-mystificatory tendencies in Romanticism more importance than does de Man.

of the belief that poetry should be mimetic, while the psychological biography of the Pedlar is written with a sense that the function of a narrator is correctively to idealize experience by pretending to be innocent of it. That Wordsworth was not unaware of this dichotomy is evident from the fact that he kept revising the text in such a way as to bring out the very heteronomy between the idealistic and mimetic aspects of discourse which he tries to hide. It is also evident from the fact that he elevates the naive figure of the Pedlar to the status of a guide, yet denies his discourse the confirming authority of the first-person narrative used in *The Prelude,* and thus skeptically distances the reader from a "retelling" or "representation" of experience that may be perceived as unreliable. In Coleridge's poem, similarly, the gloss claims for language the power of transcending life. Yet this power is constantly put in question by the fact that the act of speech as it appears in the narrative itself is an act of disclosure and not of idealization: a retelling in which the Mariner must return obsessively into the very core of darkness he is supposed to have mastered.

Coleridge's inclusion of two texts (the gloss and the narrative) thematizes the process by which art "represents" experience, and exposes a lacuna between aesthetic form and existential content that exists less obviously in the texts discussed in subsequent chapters. From a poem's choice of a literary genre or mode of discourse it is often possible to infer the assumptions it is making about the nature of the aesthetic medium. Yet the status of these assumptions in Romantic texts is frequently put in doubt by the inclusion of a secondary discourse that splits the work into conflicting strata of awareness. Keats's late romances, which couple realistic and grotesque elements with romance, and in which romance functions as a metonymy for the idealizing power of aesthetic illusion in general, typify a tendency to reflect upon the conventions of a naive art by attaching them to conventions that make radically opposite assumptions. While the ambivalence of Romantic poems is sometimes reflected in a stylistic heteronomy within the poem, at other times it is expressed less obviously through an ambiguity in the illocutionary force attributed to the argument of the text. Both *Prometheus Unbound* and Coleridge's conversation poems uneasily hypostatize mental representation, by using modes of discourse that claim the status of affirmative statement for a vision that is elsewhere conceded to exist only in the subjunctive mood of desire.

My own feeling that we need to return behind existing readings of Romantic poetry to the theoretical nexus in which both idealistic and deconstructive theories have their genesis[15] arises from this sense of a doubleness or ambivalence in Romantic texts for which modern critical schools have so far been unable to invent a terminology. Romantic poetry is certainly not what Schiller calls a naive poetry, a poetry free of doubt and irony. Long before Derrida and de Man, D. G. James complained that Shelley's poetry is neither on this side nor on that, but inhabits a split in its own interpretation of existence: "Thus we complain chiefly, not that he does not show us what he thinks, but that what he shows and what he thinks cannot be reconciled."[16] Such a comment lays the groundwork for a deconstructive reading of Romanticism. Indeed, the characteristic of the Romantic text seems to be that it exists on two levels of awareness, often to the point of self-contradiction. But what the critic is to make of this self-contradiction is the crucial problem, and the guidance provided by the poetry itself is less clear than the main schools of criticism suppose. Because Romantic poetry itself conceives of its function (not simply its status) as both mimetic and idealistic, the fundamentally idealistic reading followed by organicist criticism is difficult to sustain. But on the other hand, the relationship between the mimetic and idealistic levels as surface and depth seems to vary from one text to another, and the idealistic level is not always the less "fundamental" and less "inward." It thus becomes a simplification to dismiss Romantic idealism as a willful blindness to an awareness concealed in the subtexts of poems—the view tacitly taken by proto-deconstructionists like Bostetter. Equally, it becomes a simplification to see all doubt as a deliberate strategy— the view taken by recent deconstructionists who attempt to re-

[15]The link between deconstructive criticism and the philosophy of Schopenhauer and Nietzsche is discussed in the next chapter. Organicist criticism derives even more clearly from Romantic philosophy: particularly that of Coleridge and Schelling.
[16]D. G. James, *The Romantic Comedy* (London: Oxford University Press, 1948), p. 96.

habilitate Romantic writers by suggesting that they were really more modern than their skeptical critics.

Romantic literature is better seen as a literature involved in the restless process of self-examination, and in search of a model of discourse which accommodates rather than simplifies its ambivalence toward the inherited equation of art with idealization. The first chapter of this book attempts to trace the working out of such a model dialectically, through a series of critical texts beginning with Schiller's *On Naive and Sentimental Poetry* and culminating in Nietzsche's *Birth of Tragedy*. These texts, in turn, provide a vocabulary to describe and relate the contradictory aesthetic postures assumed by Romantic poetry in its parallel attempt to reassess its own status. In focusing on some of the major work of three writers—Shelley, Keats, and Coleridge—I have attempted to be illustrative and not exhaustive. The inclusion of works so heterogeneous as conversation poems, romances, and mythological narratives suggests something of the range of the texts that, despite surface dissimilarities, can be seen as reflecting on the status of their own discourse. But since this is intended to be a theoretical and not a historical study of Romanticism, I have avoided including a number of works, such as *The Rime of the Ancient Mariner* and *Childe Harold's Pilgrimage,* discussion of which would only have resulted in the repetition of conclusions already reached with regard to works of Keats and Shelley. For similar reasons, and because of the work already done on him by Geoffrey Hartman, David Ferry, and Frances Ferguson, I have limited myself to brief discussions of Wordsworth in the course of a chapter on Coleridge. In discussing three authors (one early Romantic and two late Romantic poets) I try to provide a biography of the oeuvre, as it were, and to see individual poems as related moments in the journey of each aesthetic consciousness. But in excluding three other major poets, I assume that they too would yield to the same kind of approach, and I try to indicate at the end of the book the lines that such study might follow.

Finally, a word should be said about the theoretical vocabulary employed here. The use of words such as "naive" and "sentimental" or "Apollonian" and "Dionysiac" does not simply involve exchanging one set of terms for another, putting a Romantic vocabulary derived from German idealism in place of the more traditional Blakean terms "innocence" and "experience," or the orthodox Christian antithesis of Edenic and fallen man. On the contrary, it is a way of indicating an important shift in the Romantic conception of the structure of human experience. The traditional vocabulary of Romantic criticism, which provides secular equivalents for the stages of providential history, tacitly hypostatizes the state of innocence by identifying it with Eden, and thus legitimizes the notion of art as a corrective illusion, designed to repair the ruins of our first parents. The vocabulary of Schiller and (to a greater extent) Schopenhauer and Nietzsche not only secularizes, but also *internalizes* innocence as a psychic defence, and thus recognizes it as partly a fictive projection of the sentimental consciousness. The far-reaching consequences of this recognition for the way the mind conceives of aesthetic discourse will be the subject of the following chapters.

CHAPTER 1

Schiller, Schopenhauer, and Nietzsche:

The Theoretical Background

It might seem logical to preface a discussion of English Romantic poetry with an examination of English rather than German imaginative theory. The poetics of Coleridge, Shelley, and Keats are, however, too well known to benefit from yet another rehearsal. Such an examination, moreover, would lead me to concentrate on critical texts that themselves invite deconstruction, rather than on ones that provide frames through which to view Romantic poetry. What is striking about English theory is an insecurity in its logocentric rhetoric which makes it the prelude to rather than the antithesis of its German contemporary. Leslie Brisman has already examined the manner in which Coleridge undermines his idealistic discussion of the imagination in *Biographia Literaria* by interrupting it,[1] thus imprisoning the sublimity of its claims in the language of anti-climax. Furthermore, Coleridge defensively anticipates criticism by allowing the reader to approach the theory through the ambivalent commentary of a friend who functions as neophyte and ironist, rather in the manner of the editor of Professor Teufelsdröckh's obscure fragments of idealist philosophy. Keats is openly tentative. His neoplatonized revision of Addisonian aesthetics[2] is put forward in his letters—in a form of discourse whose authority is private rather than public, and whose

---

[1] Leslie Brisman, *Romantic Origins* (Ithaca: Cornell University Press, 1978), pp. 33–37; cf. also the discussion of "Kubla Khan," pp. 30–33.

[2] I refer in particular to Keats's description of poetry as a "pleasure thermometer," and to his famous characterization of the imagination as a repetition in finer tone of earthly happiness. In both statements, Keats seems to have been influenced by Addison's concept of the pleasures of imagination. But unlike Addison, he gives to imagination a transcendent rather than a purely recreational status.

27

mode of argument is more episodic, inconclusive, and provisional than that of the formal treatise.

Ambiguities about the transforming power of art are apparent even in so prophetic and affirmative a work as Shelley's "Defence of Poetry," regarded by Wasserman as the climax of his idealism.[3] Like Jean-Paul's *School for Aesthetics,* Shelley's essay is written from a hortatory and defensive position, in the absence of that very power to transform poetic intention into legislation that it celebrates. Thus there are uncertainties both about the epistemological status of the image, which is defined in empirical and real terms as well as in idealistic and imaginary terms, and about the historical location of a myth of poetic power, which seems to exist in the past or the future but not in the present. These lacunae in the logic of Shelley's faith will be discussed in later chapters. But for the present it is perhaps worth noting the constant and troubling vacillation of aesthetic representation between surface and depth which takes place within the essay's imagery. Thus poetry is, on the one hand, the withdrawal of "life's dark veil" from an inner beauty that abides at the core of things despite the surface corruptions imposed by history.[4] But on the other hand, it is itself a "figured curtain," a "perfect and consummate surface" which is "as the form and the splendour of unfaded beauty to the secrets of anatomy and corruption."[5] The purpose of poetry is never in doubt. But whether aesthetic theory is entitled to its idealism, whether the appearance of beauty is a literal fact or a purely figurative construction that points behind itself to the dark ground of the figure, seems less certain than Shelley will allow.

On the surface, however, English theory remains stubbornly idealistic in its assumptions. For Hazlitt, who quotes Bacon, poetry "has something divine in it, because it raises the mind and hurries it into sublimity, by conforming the shows of things to the desires of the soul."[6] The doubts which emerge from "A Defence of

---

[3]Earl Wasserman, *Shelley: A Critical Reading* (Baltimore: The Johns Hopkins University Press, 1971), pp. 204–220.

[4]Shelley, "A Defence of Poetry," in *Shelley's Prose or the Trumpet of a Prophecy,* ed. David Lee Clark (1954; corrected ed. Albuquerque: University of New Mexico Press, 1966), p. 295.

[5]Ibid., pp. 295, 293.

[6]William Hazlitt, "On Poetry in General," in *Complete Works of William Hazlitt,* ed. P. P. Howe (London: J. M. Dent, 1930–1934), v, 3.

Poetry" exist only in the subtext of the essay: as a subversive but sedated knowledge which is never potentiated by being made explicit on the level of argument. It is thus to German theory that one turns for a vocabulary which can name the specters that haunt an ideal art. Concepts such as irony, sentimentality, Schopenhauer's will and Nietzsche's Dionysos are all in some sense designed to explore the discontinuity between the ideal and the real. The purpose of considering English Romantic poetry from such a vantage point is to suggest that it reveals a far greater uneasiness about the limits of poetic idealism than might appear from the theoretical statements of the poets themselves.

In delineating the theoretical movement from a simplified to a consciously ambivalent model of aesthetic discourse, we can speak of three distinct moments. In addition, it is possible to use the tensions characteristic of the three different kinds of *critical* texts as a way of establishing a dialectical psychic chronology within which *poetic* texts can be placed as moments in the Romantic mind's dialogue with its own assumptions. The chronology is not, of course, a literal one, since its "moments" are advances in maturity rather than dates on a calendar. The reexamination thus undertaken by the Romantic mind is dialectical in form, in that it uses a process of constant self-negation to generate a momentum toward synthesis. Schiller, the first to move beyond an unquestionably idealistic view of art, nevertheless remains sentimentally committed to a vision of the far goal of literature which his own critical terminology undermines. In the case of Schopenhauer, the problem is almost the reverse. A conscious commitment to the pessimistic rhetoric of desublimation proves impossible to sustain, and he reverts to a sublimated image of art which he wishes to reject as fictitious. The sentimental and ironic views of aesthetic discourse prove harder to distinguish within individual works than a schematic classification might suggest. But broadly speaking, such works as *Alastor* and the conversation poems exemplify the former, and *Lamia* and *Isabella* (and perhaps Byron's *Childe Harold*) the latter. Idealism and irony exist in both, but are related in opposite ways as dominant and recessive characteristics. Nietzsche's aesthetic theory, finally, presents a third, resolving moment in this dialogue between illusion and reality, and finds its equivalent in such poems as *The Fall of Hyperion* and *The Triumph of Life.* Hayden White, applying to historical texts the modal classifications developed by Frye, has pointed out that discursive prose is actually a form of fiction and that its "emplotment" or narrative shaping can be discussed in literary categories such as romance and irony.[7] Romantic critical texts are simply explicit "fictions" about the nature of discourse, which is a less obvious concern of Romantic poems. A consideration of their contradictory emplotment is, therefore, one way of understanding similar ambivalences in the emplotment of the poetry of the period.

Schiller, in his distinction of sentimental from naive poetry, is one of the first theorists to concede that there may exist, alongside the art which creates a golden world, a second, non-ideal art in which the distance between human consciousness and plenitude is the structuring principle. We can therefore see him as inaugurating a process of revision that will question the derivation of art "from a single vital principle,"[8] and will attempt to confront the dichotomy we have already observed in Romantic texts. While the naive poet (typified by the poets of Greece) "*is* nature," the sentimental and Romantic poet merely "*seek(s)*" the nature which represents to him "our highest fulfilment in the ideal."[9] He imagines nature as "*idea* and *object*," an *ideal* rather than sensuous presence, precisely because she is absent from "human life as *experience.*"[10] Schiller, in revealing the compensatory structure of idealization, and indeed of symbolization itself, discloses the dividedness of Romantic vision, which involves an insight into the very emptiness it seeks to negate. Bipolar schemas (such as Coleridge's distinctions of fancy from imagination, and of talent from genius) exist in English theory, but they are distinctions of good from bad poetry and do not specifically identify Romanticism as a problematical movement. In Schiller's theory we have for the first time a questioning of the naive aesthetics on which modern or organicist interpretations of Romantic poetry as the union of con-

[7]Hayden White, *Metahistory: The Historical Imagination in Nineteenth-Century Europe* (Baltimore: The Johns Hopkins University Press, 1973), pp. 7–11.
[8]Friedrich Nietzsche, *The Birth of Tragedy* (1872), in *The Birth of Tragedy and the Genealogy of Morals,* trans. Francis Golffing (New York: Doubleday, 1956), p. 97.
[9]Friedrich Schiller, *Naive and Sentimental Poetry* (1800), in *Naive and Sentimental Poetry and On the Sublime,* trans. Julius Elias (New York: Ungar, 1966), pp. 110, 85.
[10]Ibid., p. 105.

sciousness and nature base themselves.[11] The sentimental sign is an intentional sign: it recognizes the separateness of imagination from actuality, and acknowledges that the sign, instead of "disappear(ing) completely in the thing signified" remains "forever heterogeneous and alien to the thing signified."[12] The very word "sentimental" admits to a certain bad faith in the quest for the naive. Yet it would be wrong to see in Schiller's theory a complete break with the tradition that gives language direct access to the ideal. Though the literature of his age is defined as sentimental, it is naive poetry which continues to be the source of aesthetic norms that legitimize bad faith by linking it to the necessity for hope. The sentimental poet acknowledges the real world of which the naive poet is unaware, but he is governed above all by the desire to idealize, to reapproximate to the naive. Since this desire is an attempt to cancel out a reality that is still admitted to be there, the concept of a sentimental art reveals itself as both a progressive and a regressive step in the history of Romantic aesthetics. De Man speaks of a "conflict between a concept of the self seen in its authentically temporal predicament and a defensive strategy that tries to hide from this negative self-knowledge."[13] Schiller may see through his own desire for innocence, but he is still committed to an art defined in terms of illusion or "Schein": an art that is appearance without reality.

This oscillating movement is also evident in the letters *On the Aesthetic Education of Man,* where Schiller defines the work of art as the product of two different impulses, the *Formtrieb* and the *Stofftrieb:* a pairing of idealizing and mimetic impulses which illuminates Nietzsche's distinction between Apollo and Dionysos.[14] On the one hand, Schiller defines the conjunction of form and content in terms of a skeptical Kantian dualism of mental and existential worlds, which allows the forms imposed by the mind no more than a regulative, illusory status.[15] But on the other hand he

[11] For a critique of this school of thought see de Man, "The Rhetoric of Temporality," pp. 173–209.
[12] Schiller, *Naive and Sentimental Poetry,* p. 98.
[13] De Man, "The Rhetoric of Temporality," p. 191.
[14] Schiller, *On the Aesthetic Education of Man, in a Series of Letters* (1801), trans. Reginald Snell (New York: Ungar, 1965), pp. 64–67, 76.
[15] Ibid., pp. 120–121.

holds out a naive vision of an art in which the ideal forms of desire will have become embodied in the stuff of experience.[16] We have already encountered this blurring of epistemologies in Jean-Paul. The Kantian terminology, like the vocabulary of the sentimental, is dualistic and undermines the monistic dream of a world in which desire and its object, the forms of the mind and the stuff of reality, are continuous. But the conflict between what the mind knows and what the heart feels, expressed in the coexistence of a language which is emotionally monistic with one that is philosophically dualistic, continually produces elements of self-mystification in Schiller's argument.

The sentimental preservation of the naive in the face of an awareness which exposes its naiveté is dependent on two fictions of innocence which will prove important in the study of Romantic poetry. In the *Aesthetic Education* letters Schiller, in effect, argues that an existentially innocent literature can be created through the insulation of form from content, or the assertion through form of a vision denied by what is actually said. He says elsewhere that Goethe, who deals with a sentimental theme in *Werther,* remains a naive artist because of the naiveté of his treatment. Particularly revealing, in this context, is Schiller's statement that in art it is possible to *"annihilat[e] the material by means of the form."*[17] The vocabulary here is dualistic and concedes, through the dichotomy between mind and matter, that life may not fit the form that the mind gives to it. Schiller does not claim that the union of fiction and actuality is achievable; what he claims is that form considered as disinterested, aesthetic play can free itself from the reality it embodies as content, that rhetoric can overcome reality. Yet he does seem to argue that between true innocence and this sublimation of experience through language there is no significant difference.

In *On Naive and Sentimental Poetry* the argument is slightly different. Whereas in the letters on aesthetic education the ideal is held apart from the actual through a distinction between form and material, here it is protected through the dialectical separation of an ideal classical past from a Romantic present. The hypos-

[16]Ibid., p. 75.
[17]Ibid., p. 106.

tasis of the naive through its identification with an earlier culture or stage of consciousness, and the ascribing of discontinuity to historical and therefore removable circumstances, are among the most tenacious forms of Romantic self-mystification. To a personal myth of man's fall from childhood innocence into self-division corresponds a cultural model of history as a decline from a primitive period in which man, as Nietzsche puts it in criticizing Schiller, "lay at the heart of nature and in this state of nature attained immediately the ideal of humanity through Edenic nobility and artistry."[18] By literalizing the imaginary in the past, Schiller makes it recoverable at the far goal of time and guarantees the potential innocence of language. Jacques Derrida, who "deconstructs" Rousseau's similar devaluation of a written and intentional language in relation to a prior, oral language, gives the name of logocentrism to the persistent nostalgia for a language that is absolute and pre-existential: a language that is not a language but truth. Yet as Derrida points out, signification, which reveals the separation between signs and things, is always already a feature of language. Naive cultures are always already sentimental.

Hegel, who also envisions a series of separate and dialectically related aesthetic periods, creates a similar system of accommodation to rationalize the lacunae in the aesthetic psyche by confining them within certain historical periods, which postpone rather than deny the existence of plenitude. At the same time, the impossibility of making the past a sanctuary for innocence is evident in the inconsistencies that trouble his *Aesthetics*. Greek culture produced tragedy as well as sculpture, and Hegel, unlike Schiller, reveals a crucial interest in tragedy. But the need to define classicism as a naive period leads him in his introduction to link a succession of historical periods (symbolism, classicism, Romanticism) to a system of art-forms which serve as modifying adjectives (architecture, sculpture, music), in such a way that Greek art is defined almost entirely in terms of sculpture. Tragedy, which is not an art of stability and harmony, is classified as a Romantic and postclassical art. The resulting presence of "Romanticism" within the historical phenomenon of classicism, as Nietzsche was later to

[18]Nietzsche, *The Birth of Tragedy*, p. 117.

recognize, is an undermining paradox: it unsettles any vision of art as progressing toward the historical recovery of naiveté, because it tacitly concedes that this naiveté has never existed. It reveals within the very myth of an ideal culture, invented to guarantee the possibility of innocence, a deconstruction of that myth which the committed idealist must somehow displace or ignore.

The displacement or repression of insights that are nevertheless acknowledged characterizes the sentimental text, of which *On Naive and Sentimental Poetry* is an example as well as a discussion. Schiller and Hegel, as Abrams has in effect pointed out, emplot their aesthetic theories in the millennial form of romance: a mode which purports to restore a pastoral language beyond tragedy and irony. But the terminology they employ calls this emplotment into question and allows the reader, if he wishes, to subvert it. Depending on the degree of its self-consciousness, the rhetoric of the sentimental text may bury or openly defy its subversive insights. *Alastor* and Shelley's "Defence" are, perhaps, instances of the former alternative; the "Ode to Psyche" and Schiller's theories are instances of the latter. In neither case is the author ignorant of the reality he dismisses. But because of a certain vision of what art should accomplish he regards it as legitimate to pretend ignorance to his public, and sometimes to himself as well. The ironic text may seem to take up an almost contrary position. The concept of "Romantic irony," as Arnold Hauser points out, "is based essentially on the insight that art is nothing but autosuggestion and illusion, and that we are always aware of the fictitiousness of our representations."[19] What distinguishes the ironic from the sentimental text, however, is not a greater degree of insight, but a different conception of the goal of knowledge which makes it desirable to seem more "honest" by absorbing subversive elements into the action of the text. But the interesting thing about Schopenhauer is that his emplotment of his argument in the form of irony similarly fails to do justice to the evidence he presents. Inasmuch as he explicitly takes up the demystification of appearance, the vacillating emotional rhythms of his argument can be used to illuminate a second, problematical moment in the career

of the Romantic imagination: the tendency of Romantic irony to become intermittent, to fall back into the language of sentimentality.

Schiller remains sentimental in his commitment to an ideal of
art which is cast in doubt by his analysis of actual works of art.
Schopenhauer, in the third book of *The World as Will and Representation*, seems to revise the very goal of art, which becomes not
the recovery of an innocence that precedes the knowledge of life,
but the disclosure of a knowledge that is always present beneath
the patina of innocence. Overtly, then, the goal of
Schopenhauer's argument is a pessimistic desublimation of
Romantic idealism. But before discussing his specifically aesthetic
theories one must discuss his metaphysics in general.
Schopenhauer defines reality in terms of two categories, will and
representation, which Nietzsche was to rename Dionysos and
Apollo respectively. The world as representation is the rational,
"knowable side of the world."[20] It is the world as the mind would
like to construct it as idea, rather than the world as the mind feels
it in its rawness. Science and art, as Nietzsche points out, are both
representations or idealizations, because they refine life by insisting either that it is worth living or that it can be understood and
controlled.[21] Both affirm what Shelley was to call the illusion of
"thought's empire over thought" (*The Triumph of Life*, l. 211). The
world as will, imaged in terms of figures such as Ixion and Tan-
talus, is an essentially blind world, the product of "lack-
... deficiency ... suffering."[22] This use of the term "will" is not
unrelated to its common meaning of volition, although it must be
understood that will is not something operating only in human
beings, and that in its human form it is not free will but passion,
enslavement to the body as distinct from the soul or mind. But the
will is better understood as a blind, self-perpetuating force operating through man and nature alike: a force akin to what Shelley,
and Yeats after him, call Power as opposed to Intellectual Beauty
or Wisdom. Crucial to Schopenhauer's system is a recognition of

---

[20]Arthur Schopenhauer, *The World as Will and Representation* (1819; 2nd ed.
1844), trans. E. F. J. Payne (1958; rpt. New York: Dover, 1969), I, 4.

[21]Nietzsche, "Homer and Classical Philology," in *The Complete Writings of Friedrich Nietzsche*, ed. Oscar Levy (London: Allen and Unwin, 1911), III, 148.

[22]Schopenhauer, *The World as Will and Representation*, I, 196, 99.

the illusoriness of the humanist-Christian dichotomy of soul and body, secularized by thinkers like Godwin as a distinction between Reason and the world of material automatism, which makes possible the assertion of human values against the world of Necessity. Although the world as will at first seems fundamentally different from the world as representation, the former is, in effect, the underside of the latter. Representation proves to be a "representation of the will" and therefore identical with the will. Apollo is, in effect, only the disguise worn by Dionysos for purposes of self-deception.

The broader consequences of Schopenhauer's recognitions for meliorist and humanist philosophies of man are evident. In the specific field of aesthetics, the view of representation as identical with will, and distinguished from the latter only by an attempt to sentimentalize or avoid the content of will, amounts to a deconstruction of Schiller's more hopeful view that art can somehow reduce reality to its idealized appearance or representation, and thus liberate man from what he is. It is, more important, a revision of Kant, whose epistemology had provided the basis for post-Kantian aesthetics. Kant had argued for the mind's capacity to order the real or phenomenal world within "ideal" or mental categories such as space and time; and Romantic idealism, elevating art into one of these categories, had argued that art could reshape matter through form, reality through rhetoric.

The point can be made differently. That Schopenhauer's image of the human psyche anticipates that of Freud (and ultimately that of Sartre and Lacan) is now a commonplace. The distinction between will and representation stands in an important revisionary relationship to the standard Romantic distinction between the ideal and the real which, in some ways, it seems to resemble. By assimilating this distinction to one between the conscious and subconscious minds, Schopenhauer robs the ideal of its legitimacy as a metaphysically independent category, by exposing its psychological substructure. Idealism becomes genetically linked to anxiety, as the conscious mind's way of covering up a latent awareness of anxiety. This awareness, in turn, is made prior to the fictions of idealism and ceases to be seen as a fall from some original innocence.

The consequences for a specifically aesthetic idealism are important. Implicit in Schopenhauer's argument is a deconstructive theory of fictions, which reveals all representation as only the mind's attempt to project a rationalized surface that will protect it from its knowledge of reality and itself. Schopenhauer's analysis of representation is a reassessment of the idealistic theory of figurative language and, in this respect, anticipates the theories of Derrida and de Man. Inasmuch as he unveils the "in-itself" or literal reality behind figurative and ameliorative constructions, he forces us to see texts as structures of dissimulation existing on two levels and including the very reality which they seek to deny through illusion. To speak of the philosophical affiliation between Schopenhauer and the deconstructionists seems logical in view of the use critics such as de Man have made of the former's immediate descendant, Nietzsche.[23] The notion of representation as only a fiction constructed by the will anticipates the Derridean denial of a "transcendental signified" whose presence guarantees the truth of what is represented in language. Similarly, the stratified picture of the work of art as a quarrel between the conscious discourse of representation and the subconscious discourse of the will anticipates Derrida's notion of the text as a covering up of an earlier text, the residues of which negate or decenter the text actually communicated to the reader.[24] In other words, the idea of a discourse which fails to become self-identical, and indeed becomes self-consuming, is already present in Schopenhauer, who sees language as existence without essence, an attempt at transcendence which ends by becoming a projection of nothingness.

Among the arts music alone is free of dissimulation, being nonvisual and therefore nonrepresentational, the flesh of life cut away from its external appearance. In giving music a central place in his system Schopenhauer seems to embrace an art that is without illusion, and thus to point toward the despair which is manifested in a work such as Wilde's *Portrait of Dorian Gray*, where the portrait designates art as the inner and concealed side of life rather than its transcendence. Indeed, the deconstruction of representation begun by Schopenhauer may lie behind an entire tra-

[23]De Man, "Genesis and Genealogy in Nietzsche's *The Birth of Tragedy*," *Diacritics*, 2, no. 4 (1972), 44–53.
[24]On this point see the translator's preface to *Of Grammatology*, p. lxxvi.

dition of fiction whose technical radicalism reveals a certain existential despair. From James Hogg's *Confessions of a Justified Sinner* to Sartre's *Nausea,* such works thematize the act of telling, in order to dismantle the logic of narrative representation and constitute the literary act within a knowledge that seems more inward than the official metaphysic of fiction.

But Schopenhauer is also different from Derrida in a way that brings out the inadequacy of a Derridean theory of language to a reading of Romanticism. It is important to remember that his aesthetics led directly to the essentialist poetics of the Symbolists, and to their almost blindly idealistic quest for an art of pure representation, liberated from existence and will. Walter Sokel comments on the "peculiar combination of idealism and nihilism" in Schopenhauer's work.[25] Inconsistently, Schopenhauer defines music in terms of the will, but associates art in general with representation and illusion. This contradiction is not accidental but pivotal. It marks Schopenhauer as a Romantic rather than a decadent writer, and goes to the heart of his importance for a period which is not nihilistic, but divided as to the goals of art. Representation, for Schopenhauer, always retains a value that it cannot have in terms of his epistemology. Although he sets out to abolish the post-Kantian notion of the priority of mental forms over the brutality of life, he regards as legitimate a definition of art in terms of idealization. But equally, although he defines art in terms of illusion, he also insists that it be an embodiment of life.

Schopenhauer is best understood as a theorist whose desire to separate art from the irrationality of existence is deliberately checked by a monistic epistemology which designates representation as only the representation of will. The philosophical terminology of will and representation makes impossible the dialectical separation of the ideal and the real possible for a dualist, by presenting the ideal as no more than a sublimated reflection of actuality. Because the text similarly reflects what it sublimates, it complicates its own claim to naiveté by objectifying what the author knows as well as what he desires. The figures through which knowledge is depicted (copy, mirror, representation) are always

[25] Walter Sokel, *The Writer in Extremis: Expressionism in Twentieth-Century German Literature* (1959; rpt. New York: McGraw-Hill, 1964), p. 25.

mimetic, even as the goal of knowledge remains that of purification and transformation. Consequently, while he follows Schiller in wanting an art that will civilize and erase the matter by means of the form, Schopenhauer also demands that aesthetic surfaces represent psychic depths which are discontinuous with the notion of a surface.

But the other side of this complicated equation is that the bleakness of desublimation generates the very desire for sublimation which it tries to renounce. It is largely as an attempt to reconstruct the psychic barriers that divide the ideal from the real that Schopenhauer develops a typology of art-forms which seems to distinguish among the arts in terms of their proximity to life. Music is seen as exceptional, in that it is not "like the other arts . . . a copy of the Ideas, but *a copy of the will itself.*"[26] But other arts such as painting, sculpture, and literature continue to represent the Platonic ideas and thus to liberate the mind from the suffering of existence. This typology, which tries to contain the impact of Schopenhauer's theory of music, is similar to the systems of accommodation developed by Hegel and Schiller, and is therefore an instance of the very sublimation and dissimulation that Schopenhauer criticizes. Because the ideas are only "the objectivity of the will"[27] and therefore the disclosure of the real, the difference between the Apollonian arts of literature and sculpture and the Dionysiac art of music is no more real than the difference between representation and will. In the end, Schopenhauer can safeguard an idealistic concept of art only by reinstating a form-content split invalidated by his own mimetic terminology. This split is similar to the one urged by Schiller, but unlike the earlier writer, Schopenhauer sees it as an act of bad faith rather than of creative faith. Representation, as he makes clear in the final paragraph of his argument, liberates us from life only by an illusory blocking out of its own content: by making us concentrate on the act of aestheticization in such a way that we forget for a moment the reality to which it refers.[28] That art cannot really cease to be referential and mimetic is evident in the fact that for

[26]Schopenhauer, *The World as Will and Representation*, I, 257.
[27]Ibid., p. 179.
[28]Ibid., pp. 266–267.

Schopenhauer aesthetic illusion is always a surface which includes a depth, a foreground which includes but conceals a background. It is thus clear that the protective dichotomy between music and the other arts is not a dichotomy at all, but a way of deferring the renunciation of art as a mode of ideal perfection. Because representation is no more than a higher gradation of the will, literature and sculpture can be no more than idealized versions of the knowledge that is openly confronted in music. The proximity of music to the other arts brings out, metaphorically, the deep kinship between works which reflect life and works that can only *claim* to have unbound themselves from existence by "representing" their content as other than what it is.

Schiller and Hegel show a liking for triadic dispositions of their arguments, which resemble the movement of a romance plot through death and rebirth to a moment of millennial synthesis— though these arguments turn out to be sentimental rather than Romantic in tendency. Schopenhauer, it will be noted, eschews such patterns in favor of a philosophical narrative that reverses itself and constantly exposes its own arguments as empty fictions, adopting a deliberate pedagogy of frustration. But the ambivalence of his attitude toward the ironic emplotment of his argument is as important as the argument itself. Crucial to the emotional structure of Romantic irony is a resistance to the deconstructive theory of discourse urged as a critical model by Schopenhauer and pursued in the poetry of a certain phase. The fact that a theory of deconstruction is present within Romantic aesthetics, and that it proves untenable, should warn us against seeing Romantic literature as wholly summed up by such a view of language. The literary modes which a period defines as imaginatively central can often tell us something about its view of discourse. Traditional critics such as Abrams and Frye assimilate Romanticism to romance and thus endorse the period's most idealistic statements about the power of art,[29] while deconstruc-

---

[29]Neither critic explicitly makes anything of the etymological connection between "Romanticism" and "romance." But by his own admission Frye derives from the secular scripture of Blake the plot-form which he sees as characteristic of romance: namely the spiralling movement from an original innocence, through a nightmare world, to an idyllic world recovered in the future (*The Secular Scripture: A Study of the Structure of Romance* [Cambridge: Harvard University Press, 1976], pp. 6, 53, 174). Frye, in other words, uses Romanticism as a way of explaining the

tionists tend to identify language in general with irony. I have chosen, instead, to examine a sequence of critical texts which reveals, on the part of Romantic critics themselves, a vacillating and complicated view of the status of language. Through the movement from the sentimental (a tacitly ironic form of romance) through the ironic to the tragic, the Romantic mind gradually revises its assumptions about art by experimentally identifying discourse with a variety of modes of literary experience. This movement is dialectical in character and culminates, as we shall see, in Nietzsche's identification of Romantic discourse with tragedy and lyric, considered not as formal genres, but as metonymies for a certain relationship of the creating self to reality.

The emotionally hybrid nature of Schopenhauer's aesthetics is apparent in the fact that it provides both a rhetoric of sublimation, which leads to the poetics of Symbolism, and a vocabulary of desublimation which proved crucial in the development of German Expressionism.[30] But the contradictions of this theory, in which the impulse toward disclosure and the desire for idealization remain unaccommodated to each other, suggest the need for some third category of art between the extremes of idealism and pessimism. One possible solution, which might permit Schopenhauer to retain the liberating power of aesthetic representation without repressing the content of the representation, emerges in his comments on the sublime, considered as an almost unconscious modification of the post-Kantian theory of sublimity and as an anticipation of Nietzsche's theory of tragedy. The aesthetics of the beautiful, like the aesthetics of naiveté, presumes a relationship of continuity between man and an external world which is completely contained within the dimensions of his mental representation. The sublime, which shatters this representation by causing the mind to face heights or depths that it cannot en-

---

philosophical underpinnings of romance, and thus implies that romance can provide us with a way of understanding Romanticism. Abrams, similarly, analyzes the plot-form characteristic of post-Kantian idealism in terms of a spiralling journey through self-consciousness to psychic reintegration—a philosophical version of the archetypal romance journey from night to day.

[30]See Sokel, *The Writer in Extremis,* pp. 24-54.

compass, raises the possibility of an essentially tragic encounter with the world as will. In designating as successive moments man's sense of nothingness before an object that exceeds his gaze and his sense of superiority to a hostile world, Kant makes the contemplation of sublime objects part of an aesthetics that acknowledges but ultimately triumphs over the world as will.[31] The spectator is able to take the brute facticity of existence into his imagination, and (in an epistemological rather than a qualitative sense) to idealize or represent it. From here it is but a short step to the view of the post-Kantian idealists that the process of idealization can also involve transformation, amelioration, prophetic rather than tragic sublimity.

On a theoretical level Schopenhauer's definition of the sublime follows that of Kant. Schopenhauer claims that there is no ultimate difference between a beauty which affirms the power of representation, and a sublimity which disrupts but ultimately restores the continuity of representation and truth.[32] But his actual analyses of sublime experiences do not claim to transcend or harmonize existence. In the contemplation of the sublime, as in Pascal's two infinities, opposite feelings coexist: "the insignificance and dependence of ourselves as individuals, as phenomena of will," and the sense that the greatness of the sublime object "resides only in our representation."[33] Paradoxically (in view of the antiexistential stoicism for which Nietzsche will criticize Schopenhauer) the sublime spectator's exaltation does not derive purely from the Kantian "free, conscious exaltation above the will"[34] which proclaims the mind's superiority to life. Rather it arises from an emotion that is at once constructive and deconstructive, because it allows the mind to transcend (but only on a mental or imaginary level) an existence of which it remains physically the victim. In *The Birth of Tragedy* Nietzsche will define the tragic experience as one in which the artist's simultaneous kinship with a chorus that is bound to the pathos of existence, and with a hero elevated above the choric collectivity, forces the act of aesthe-

[31]Immanuel Kant, *The Critique of Judgement* (1790), trans. J. H. Bernard (1892; rpt. New York: Hafner Press, 1951), pp. 100–104.
[32]Schopenhauer, *The World as Will and Representation*, I, 209.
[33]Ibid., p. 206.
[34]Ibid., p. 209.

tic representation to be at once a submission to existence and a liberating act. It is evident that Schopenhauer anticipates the radical revision introduced into Romantic aesthetics by defining art as a compound of Apollo and Dionysos, in which the mind celebrates the liberating power of aesthetic surfaces that also disclose their own nothingness before the forces of life. Such an art is neither will nor representation, but rather a dialogue between the two.

But Schopenhauer's final renunciation of art as a way of coping with existence reflects a failure to recognize the resolution he himself has provided in his analysis of the sublime, and thus to break out of the cycle of illusion and disillusion produced by his orthodox belief that a separation of will and representation is necessary to art. That the need to define art as both illusion and knowledge may reveal the mind's sense of a doubleness in the goal of art is something he never explicitly acknowledges, although it is implicit in his need to use two terms with opposite emotional connotations—will and representation—to describe the substance of life. In the end, therefore, Schopenhauer is left in the contradictory position of rejecting as valueless a medium which, in embodying rather than evading reality, fails to bring about a transcendence of existence already condemned as illegitimate. It is to the need to see through the serenity of the mind's representations, as well as to the role of illusion as a strategy for survival, that Nietzsche addresses himself. *The Birth of Tragedy* tries to legitimize the worship of Dionysos and thus the presence within art of a destructiveness that may deny the very goal of art as culture rather than anarchy. But it also tries to respect the legitimacy of sublimating fiction in the form of Apollo.

Apollo, the god of illusion, stands for the mind's capacity to create a shape all light that will close out the horror of life, whether by returning to a prereflective innocence or by canceling the cycles of experience through such attitudes as resignation, platonism or heroic transcendence. Imagery of surface, veil, and dream links him to what Schiller called naiveté or "Schein." But he is also a mythologized version of Schopenhauer's "representation," or freedom from the anguish of will. Part of Nietzsche's contribution to Romantic aesthetics lies in his recognition that the mind cannot know Apollo without also acknowledging his kinship to Dionysos, who is the very life from which Apollo claims to have liberated man. Dionysos is not, as one might suppose from reading Nietzsche's later work,[35] a jubilant figure. Rather he is a derivative of Schopenhauer's will, the deity of life as it exists before man has taken it into his mind and refined it. In him man encounters the brutal and the grotesque, "the original oneness," its pain and contradiction.[36] Schelling, who, however, sees the Dionysiac condition as a prelude to theodicy, describes the nature of Dionysiac awareness in imagery that is strikingly similar to the governing image of Shelley's *Triumph of Life:*

> Not without significance is the car of Dionysos, drawn by panthers or tigers, for it was the wild, ecstatic enthusiasm into which nature comes at the sight of the essence, which the ancient nature worship of prescient peoples celebrated in the drunken feasts of Bacchic orgies . . . that inner self-laceration of nature, the wheel of original birth, turning about itself as if mad, and the dreadful powers of rotary movement operating therein, are portrayed in other more terrible splendours of ancient cultic customs, by actions of self-lacerating rage, like self-castration . . . by carrying about the dismembered limbs of a mutilated god, by senseless, raving dances, by the overpowering procession of the Mother of all Gods on a car with brazen wheels, accompanied by the din of a harsh, partly deafening, partly shattering music.[37]

[35] It is important to note that Zarathustra (associated with sun and eagle images) is not Dionysos, but a *fusion* of Dionysos and Apollo, through which Nietzsche seeks to nullify pessimism by identifying it with joy. This fusion is essentially different from the *dialogue* between the two gods that Nietzsche envisages in *The Birth of Tragedy,* which recognizes only that idealism and the knowledge of existence are inescapably bound to each other (not that they are identical), and that their relationship will always be one of contradiction rather than synthesis. In pressing beyond contradiction and in transforming existence itself into a kind of vitalistic essence, Nietzsche violates his own earlier insights into the tragic impossibility of representing and standing above life. The very notion of an *Übermensch* goes against the deconstruction of the hero in Nietzsche's early work. That he himself has already shown the impossibility of moving beyond the tragic is suggested by the fact that the figure of Zarathustra is always haunted by an unacknowledged contradiction, being an impossible hybrid of "pessimistic nihilism and ecstatic affirmation" (Peter Heller, *Dialectics and Nihilism: Essays on Lessing, Nietzsche, Mann and Kafka* [Amherst: University of Massachusetts Press, 1966], p. 89). My own concern is only with the early Nietzsche (the aesthetician and not the social prophet), who stands in a certain relationship to the idealist aesthetic tradition.
[36] Nietzsche, *The Birth of Tragedy,* pp. 26, 33.
[37] F. W. J. Schelling, *The Ages of the World* (1854), trans. F. de Wolfe Bolman (New York: Columbia University Press, 1942), pp. 227–228.

It is of importance that Nietzsche breaks with the classical philologists of his time to see Dionysos as an earlier god than Apollo, and to characterize the displacement of Apollo by Dionysos as the reawakening of a knowledge which had always existed, before the Greek mind invented Apollo and the Olympians to hide its kinship with Dionysos and the Titans.[38] Unlike his friend Erwin Rohde, who views the worship of Dionysos as a late phenomenon,[39] Nietzsche thus avoids seeing the pessimistic current in Hellenism (and therefore in Romanticism) as a sign of decadence.[40] Recent scholarship has tended to support Nietzsche and Walter Otto over Wilamowitz, Rohde, and M. P. Nillson.[41] But Nietzsche is not concerned with historical scholarship, so much as with the use of Greek myth to develop a theogony of creative consciousness. What is of interest, therefore, is the symbolic significance of his theory for an aesthetics which had always located the plenitude of being before its corruption, the naive before the sentimental. The priority of innocence over experience had been the tacit justification for seeing art as the creation of a beautiful soul, and poetic language as privileged above other expressions of human existence. In reversing the genetic relationship between the two, and in suggesting that the naive is a projection of the sentimental consciousness rather than the latter being an enfeebled emanation of the naive, Nietzsche (in his words) opens "the magic mountain . . . before us, showing us its very

---

[38]Nietzsche, *The Birth of Tragedy*, pp. 29–30. Nietzsche is unique in placing Dionysos before Apollo. But the genesis of Greek culture from dark origins, ignored by Schiller but recognized by Schelling, was also pointed out much earlier by A. W. Schlegel, who acknowledged the importance of the Titans' priority to the Olympians in shaping the mythos of classical tragedy (*A Course of Lectures on Dramatic Art and Literature* [1809], trans. John Black [London: Henry Bohn, 1846], pp. 80, 88, 93).

[39]Erwin Rohde, *Psyche: The Cult of Souls and Belief in Immortality among the Greeks* (1893), trans. W. B. Hillis (New York: Harcourt Brace, 1925), pp. 256, 282–284. Of course I do not mean to suggest that Rohde is concerned with aesthetics, merely that if Nietzsche had been in agreement with him, Nietzsche would have been compelled to see the pessimistic element in art as a decadent rather than a strong element. It should also be pointed out that Rohde's Dionysos is more conventional than Nietzsche's, because Rohde is involved solely in research into ancient cults and not in the recasting of Schopenhauer's metaphysics.

[40]Nietzsche, *The Birth of Tragedy*, p. 8.

[41]See Robert Palmer's introduction to Walter Otto, *Dionysos: Myth and Cult* (1933), trans. Robert Palmer (Bloomington: Indiana University Press, 1965), pp. xx–xxi.

roots."[42] The priority of Dionysos to Apollo finds its aesthetic equivalent in the priority of music to language, and of the tragic chorus, whose mode of perception is that of pathos and immersion in life, to the heroic actor who seems, through soliloquy and dialogue, to have represented existence and thus triumphed over it. Unlike Schelling, who sees Dionysos-Zagreus as dialectically transcending himself and becoming the Apollonian Dionysos-Iacchos (described in almost Shelleyan terms as "a child in the bosom of Demeter"[43]), Nietzsche confronts in Dionysos an irreducible darkness that limits the power of art to provide a catharsis of existence.

A deconstruction, as de Man comments, "always has for its target to reveal the existence of hidden articulations and fragmentations within assumedly monadic totalities."[44] Inasmuch as it discloses the presence of Dionysos in a supposedly Apollonian culture, of an insight into the irrational in a supposedly rational language, *The Birth of Tragedy* can be seen as a deconstruction of some of the central fictions of Romantic idealism. Nietzsche's typology of art-forms, which is more unequivocal than Schopenhauer's in exalting music over the arts of representation, stands in a definite revisionary relationship to the typologies of art-forms developed by Hegel and others, who assume the primacy of sculpture and associate it with the consummation of desire in time.[45] Schiller's tendency to speak of Greece as though it produced only epic and sculpture, for instance, derives from a

[42]Nietzsche, *The Birth of Tragedy*, p. 29.

[43]See Paul Tillich, *The Construction of the History of Religion in Schelling's Positive Philosophy* (1910), trans. Victor Nuovo (Lewisburg: Bucknell University Press, 1974), p. 91.

[44]De Man, "Political Allegory in Rousseau," *Critical Inquiry*, 2 (1976), 652.

[45]This comment obviously needs qualification. Sculpture does not occupy a climactic position in the Hegelian evolution of *consciousness*, since this position is occupied by the Romantic arts (music, poetry) as preludes to philosophy and religion. But it does occupy the crucial position in the evolution of the *arts*, since the Romantic arts are negations of the very concept of art, modes in which art tries to break through its own limits and achieve something not given to art. Thus art reaches its fullest embodiment in sculpture and classical culture, not in music and Romantic culture. If we see the Hegelian system of the arts in its proper perspective, as a structure of sublimation, we can see that sculpture (the fusion of the ideal and the material) continues to furnish an aesthetic norm, and that the notion of the Romantic arts is a way of rationalizing the unattainability of this norm by suggesting that art is not man's final answer to existence. See also Chap. 4 below.

belief that art is illusion rather than knowledge, a surface that has elided its depths or somehow achieved a complete homogeneity of content and ideal form. Sculpture, which is restricted to its visual appearance or in which appearance is assumed to materialize completely what lies behind it, is peculiarly suited to such an aesthetics. Nietzsche, by contrast, also deals with Greece but emphasizes music: an art which is nonvisual and therefore presents reality unmediated by appearance.

Yet it would be wrong to see *The Birth of Tragedy* as a purely destructive text,[46] still less as a work that denies to art all power of

---

[46] Jean-Michel Rey (*L'enjeu des signes: lecture de Nietzsche* [Paris: Seuil, 1971]) and Paul de Man ("Genesis and Genealogy in Nietzsche's *The Birth of Tragedy*," pp. 44–53) begin by entertaining the possibility that Nietzsche has been guilty of some kind of fallacy in deconstructing the Apollonian as a locus of truth, without also going on to contest the Dionysiac or the will as the primary category of being. They depart from other writers such as Sarah Kofman ("Nietzsche et la métaphore," *Poétique*, 5 [1971], 77–98) in ascribing the radical contestation of all "meanings" to *The Birth of Tragedy* as well as to Nietzsche's later work. Thus *The Birth of Tragedy* is seen as a work which exposes the illusoriness of Apollo only to expose the illusoriness of Dionysos who lies behind him, and so on *ad infinitum*. It is viewed as a work that sees all meanings as "figural": a work that never arrives at "meaning" because it denies itself both the consolation of transcending the original oneness toward Apollo, and the other, darker consolation of confronting Dionysos. While Nietzsche's later work may develop a vision of all formulations of life as illusory (and this seems to me debatable), such is not the purpose of *The Birth of Tragedy*. The deconstructive endeavor here is a prelude to the attempt to reconstruct an image of art. And the art that Nietzsche envisages draws its power not from being *neither* Dionysiac nor Apollonian, but from being *both* Dionysiac and Apollonian. Nietzsche's concern is not to undermine all meanings, but to undermine specifically "Apollonian" meanings which give "being" (rather than "nothingness") a genetic priority. The debate in *The Birth of Tragedy* is not between an assumption that all meaning is figural, and an assumption that there are some figural and some "proper" meanings. Rather it is over the question of whether the discovery that Apollonian meanings are figural, and therefore untrue, means that they are without value. To the tacit assumption that there is some intellectual virtue in arguing that all meaning is figural, one might respond by saying that such an argument is self-contradictory, because it invites its own deconstruction: if all meaning is figural, then the statement that all meaning is figural is itself figural.

It might be argued (as de Man does) that not to perceive the "figural" nature of the "meaning" at which Nietzsche arrives is to treat the text simplistically and to subscribe to its surface argument. At issue is the question of whether one should perform an endless series of deconstructions on texts, whether or not they invite such an operation. De Man obviously assumes that *The Birth of Tragedy* does consciously invite such treatment. In this he seems to me mistaken. His argument is that the identification of Dionysiac insight as original truth is undermined by the fact that it is embodied in an argument which "represents" and therefore performs a function opposite to Dionysiac truth. The text as "representation" there-

signification. Nietzsche's sometimes overwhelming emphasis on music and destruction must be seen as part of a dialectical engagement with traditional aesthetics, through which he attempts to bring back into art the element exiled from it by Romantic aesthetic theory. But it is important to remember that it is not music but lyric and tragedy that provide Nietzsche with his aesthetic norms. Whereas music arises directly from that primal wound in being to which Schopenhauer gave the name of will and which Artaud will later designate by the term "cruauté" (rawness, cruelty),[47] tragedy and lyric are complex forms that compound music with language, the will with the capacity of imagination to represent life by taking it into itself and issuing it as its own product. The unique position of tragedy as a bridge between two orders of being derives from the fact that it acknowledges through its very form the genesis of language from music, and thus the presence within representation of a nonverbal, nonrepresentative element that challenges the claim of language to signify. Through the choric helplessness before life, which reveals the fragility of the transcendence achieved by the individual hero, the tragic text exposes its clarified surface to everything that remains unclarified in life. But at the same time, the tragic artist, who combines Schopenhauer's corrosive knowledge with Schiller's sense of the need for aesthetic illusion, recognizes that "only so much of the

---

fore invites deconstruction, because it has already exposed as hollow the notion that there is any value in representation. This argument, however, assumes that Nietzsche *has* exposed representation as valueless, and has exalted Dionysiac insight over Apollonian representation. What he has done is really somewhat different. He has shown the need for both Apollo and Dionysos: both representation and the awareness of something which cannot be represented. That he has succeeded in "representing" his own encounter with Dionysos is therefore part of the rhetoric of the text.

We should note further that *The Birth of Tragedy* belongs to Nietzsche's academic period, before the total transformation of his life-style and intellectual allegiances (to Wagner and Schopenhauer) which coincided with his decision to give up his professorship. The later Nietzsche experiences a conversion toward a philosophy of vitalistic transcendence which takes the form of a simplification of the tensions basic to his early work. The nature of this reversal is described by Peter Heller (*Dialectics and Nihilism*, pp. 19ff.). Tragedy is now scorned; logic and dialectic, previously abhorred terms, become terms of praise. Nietzsche's alleged relativism and perspectivism therefore date only from the period when he elevates self-reversal into a principle.

[47] Antonin Artaud, *Le théâtre et son double* (1938; rpt. Paris: Gallimard, 1969).

Dionysiac substratum of the universe may enter an individual consciousness as can be dealt with by . . . Apollonian transfiguration."[48] Though Nietzsche has little to say about lyric, it too may be seen as bridging the two orders of being. Nietzsche disagrees with Schopenhauer in seeing the lyrical mixture of emotion and tranquillity as the product of a psychic equilibrium and not as the expression of a self-frustrating restlessness.[49] Where lyric differs from tragedy, although he does not directly say so, is perhaps in its more muted and distanced awareness of the destructive substratum of life: in the greater tranquillity which distinguishes reflective works like the Lucy poems or the "Ode on a Grecian Urn" from dramatic narratives like *The Fall of Hyperion*. The inclusion of two such diverse genres as tragedy and lyric as models for aesthetic discourse suggests, moreover, that the compact struck between Apollo and Dionysos will not be identical in every work of art.

Typical of Nietzsche's ambivalence toward the idealist illusion is his description of Apollonian clarity as a kind of afterimage produced by the gaze into the Dionysiac abyss: a "luminous spot . . . designed to cure an eye hurt by the ghastly night," which is the converse of the dark spots the eye creates when blinded by excessive light.[50] The Apollonian appears here as implicated within the pathology of optical illusion. But on the other hand, metaphors of blindness and sight seem to favor Apollo over Dionysos, because it is the latter and not the former whose vision is blind. The dialogical, ambivalent nature of tragedy as Nietzsche conceives it is a measure of the distance which separates *The Birth of Tragedy* from a modern recasting of it such as Artaud's *Theatre and Its Double*. There are times when Nietzsche seems vulnerable to the charge of having replaced one exclusive interpretation of art by another: logocentrism by melocentrism and nihilism.[51] But the rigid separation between arts of will (music, dance, ritual) and arts of representation (the plastic arts, epic, scenic theater), on which a simple reversal of Apollonian idealism must depend,

[48]Nietzsche, *The Birth of Tragedy*, p. 145.
[49]Ibid., p. 41.
[50]Ibid., pp. 59-60.
[51]Although his view is more complex, Bernard Pautrat raises this possibility in *Versions du soleil: figures et système de Nietzsche* (Paris: Seuil, 1971), pp. 68ff.

tends to break down. Bernard Pautrat observes that "certain elements figure on both sides of the caesura [between Dionysos and Apollo]. . . . These irregularities are not insignificant; quite on the contrary, they form a systematic blurring of differences."[52] Nietzsche himself describes how in the work of art Dionysos always "speaks the language of Apollo," and "Apollo, finally, the language of Dionysos."[53] The fact that lyric and tragedy are the offspring of both Dionysos and Apollo, and that Nietzsche can even conceive of an Apollonian music,[54] suggests that he intends the separation of Apollonian and Dionysiac arts as no more than a kind of metaphor which enables him to isolate, for purposes of analysis, elements that are intimately linked in the actual work of art. Indeed, Nietzsche's argumentative technique, which polarizes Apollo and Dionysos in order to reveal the difficulties created by such polarization, can be viewed as a critique of the dichotomous generic and historical schemas used by Schiller and other aestheticians to segregate their desires for art from their knowledge of life.

We may, therefore, see *The Birth of Tragedy* as the culmination of a process of reassessment begun when the contradiction between aesthetics and existence, tacitly acknowledged by writers like Shelley and Jean-Paul, is relocated by writers such as Schiller and Schopenhauer as a dichotomy within aesthetics itself. Through their recognition that different art-forms reflect different readings of experience, these writers acknowledge a division within aesthetic theory as to the goal of art, but protect individual works (which are either ideal or existential) from involvement in this debate. Wasserman's reading of the relation between *Prometheus Unbound* and the roughly contemporaneous *Cenci* reflects just such a sense that Shelley can somehow quarantine his doubts about his own idealism in a separate demonic text.[55] Yet we know that it is precisely this immunity from self-questioning that is denied to the Romantic work, which is committed to the same process of self-revision that we find in aesthetic theory. Schiller's uneasy characterization of *Werther* as a naive treatment

[52]Ibid., p. 78. Translation mine.
[53]Nietzsche, *The Birth of Tragedy*, p. 131.
[54]Ibid., p. 118.
[55]Earl Wasserman, *Shelley: A Critical Reading*, pp. 127–128.

of a sentimental theme[56] suggests the manner in which the theoretical debate between naive and sentimental or ironic modes is usually repeated within the individual work, through an unenforceable segregation between content on the one hand, and rhetoric, form, or intention on the other.

The problem of an art that contains elements radically at odds with the very goals of art and culture is something which continued to preoccupy the post-Romantic mind. As late as Henry James the dialogue between a distanced, consciously aesthetic style and the sexually sordid secrets it must disclose (such as the affair of Chad and Mme de Vionnet or the guilt of the Bellegarde family in *The American*) repeats the encounter between representation and life characteristic of Romantic works, and marks the distance between James and writers such as Jane Austen. By internalizing Schopenhauer's recognition of "the immense discrepancy between the plastic Apollonian art and the Dionysiac art of music"[57] as a heteronomy within the individual work of art, Nietzsche relieves the so-called ideal forms of art (such as poetry) from the necessity of protecting their faith from doubts that reside within the works themselves, as subtexts within the text. What has changed between earlier Romantic aestheticians and Nietzsche is not the fact that the text exists on two levels of awareness, but the manner in which desire and life, or form and content, are allowed to encounter each other. The insights and self-mystifications of Schiller's theory reflect the tensions which characterize a certain kind of Romantic work: a work that is internally divided, yet offers itself as simple rather than complex. Because the sentimental text values unity, it protects itself from its subtext by repressing it or discarding it as irrelevant. In effect, the contradiction between the way the work interprets itself and what it actually contains may result in a deconstruction of the writer's surface assumptions. But this deconstruction occurs in the mind of the reader and not yet within the text itself. Schopenhauer goes further, in describing a text which exposes itself to an irony that it can neither evade nor endorse. But while the sentimental work tends toward a didactic simplification of meaning which the

---

[56]Schiller, *Naive and Sentimental Poetry*, pp. 137–138.
[57]Nietzsche, *The Birth of Tragedy*, p. 97.

reader may find unsatisfying, this second kind of work manifests only the infinite negativity of ambivalence, by refusing to guide the reader in his giddy transit between text and countertext. Nietzsche, who no longer derives the work of art from a "single vital principle,"[58] is the theorist of a very different, third phase in Romantic consciousness: one in which the text has moved beyond the state of contradiction in which it must exist either as a structure of sublimation or as a self-consuming artifact, and has come to terms with its own complicity in the darkness of existence.

It is obviously not my purpose to argue for any direct influence of German idealism on English poetry.[59] But despite the long time-span that separates the earliest Romantic poets from the last Romantic philosopher, Nietzsche, Romantic poetry and aesthetic and philosophical idealism converge on similar goals and problems. Later philosophical texts such as *The World as Will and Representation* and *The Birth of Tragedy* arise in response to the dilemmas of Romanticism,[60] and often clarify, with the wisdom of hindsight, problems in Romantic poetry to which we may not be paying sufficient attention if—like M. H. Abrams—we concentrate on the more positive exponents of idealism such as Schelling and Fichte. The modification of Romantic idealism that takes place between

---

[58]Ibid.

[59]Coleridge's acquaintance with the affirmative exponents of post-Kantian idealism is well known. A. C. Dunstan has argued that he knew Schiller's *Naïve and Sentimental Poetry* closely ("The German Influence on Coleridge," *Modern Language Review*, 17 [1922], 272–281; 18 [1923], 183–201). It is difficult to say to what extent Schiller's aesthetics, as opposed to his plays, were known to other Romantic writers. Nietzsche obviously started writing much later, and Schopenhauer did not become well known till the reprint of his major work around the middle of the century. Standard works on the literary relations between English and German Romantic writers (which, however, have little bearing on the argument of this book) are F. W. Stokoe, *The German Influence in the English Romantic Period, 1788–1818* (Cambridge: Cambridge University Press, 1926); Solomon Liptzin, *Shelley in Germany* (New York: Columbia University Press, 1924); Lawrence Marsden Price, *The Reception of English Literature in Germany* (1932; rpt. New York: Benjamin Blom, 1968). Abrams' *Natural Supernaturalism* and E. D. Hirsch's *Wordsworth and Schelling* (New Haven: Yale University Press, 1960) are not studies of direct influence.

[60]Schopenhauer quotes Byron on innumerable occasions. For an account of Nietzsche's reading of Byron, and of Shelley whom he views as an archetypal embodiment of "falschen Idealismus," see David Thatcher, "Nietzsche and Byron," *Nietzsche-Studien*, 3 (1974), 130–151.

Schiller and Nietzsche suggests, on a theoretical level, the nature and the difficulties of the change that also occurs between early poems like *Alastor* and *Hyperion,* and later poems such as *The Triumph of Life* and *The Fall of Hyperion.* What German theory progressively brings out, through its analysis of forms that recognize the discontinuity between poetic intention and the ideal aimed at, is a naiveté in the poetics of hope of which the Romantics are always half conscious. As early as 1807, Hegel, in discussing the nature of faith, points to an inevitable ambivalence that complicates its assertions. This ambivalence stems from the genetic link between fiction and reality that arises from the paradox that "the unreal," as Sartre puts it, "is produced outside of the world by a consciousness which *stays in the world.*"[61]

> The sphere of spirit . . . breaks up into two regions. The one is the actual world, that of self-estrangement, the other is that which spirit constructs for itself in the ether of pure consciousness, raising itself above the first. This second world, being constructed in opposition and contrast to that estrangement, is just on that account not free from it; on the contrary, it is only the other form of that very estrangement, which consists precisely in having a conscious existence in two sorts of worlds, and embraces both. Hence it is not self-consciousness of Absolute Being . . . it is Belief, Faith, insofar as faith is a flight from the actual world, and thus is not a self-complete experience. Such flight from the realm of the present is, therefore, directly in its very nature a dual state of mind.[62]

My reference to Sartre is not accidental. Romantic idealism (whether immediate or postponed) may seem "officially" essentialist in its belief that existence can be either transformed in the millenium or transcended through an imaginative apocalypse. The two characteristic Romantic solutions which Milton Wilson describes as radical and platonic,[63] though divided by the gulf that separates a naive optimism from a sentimental pessimism, agree in committing themselves to the realm of the ideal rather than to

[61]Sartre, *The Psychology of Imagination,* p. 243.
[62]Hegel, *The Phenomenology of Mind* (1807), trans. J. B. Baillie (revised ed. 1931; rpt. New York: Harper, 1967), p. 513.
[63]See note 4 of Chapter 2 in this book.

the world-as-will. But implicit in my argument has been a sense
that while Romantic aesthetics is explicitly essentialist in its assumption that art can free itself from existence, it is aware, in a
deeper sense, that language is existence without essence, existence
with only the fiction of essence. This insight emerges in the
Romantic awareness of the intentionality of imaginary structures,
discussed by de Man, and evident in Hegel's recognition that the
imaginary is a creation of consciousness and not a reflection of
some "transcendental signified." Hegel's insight into the psychology of the idealizing consciousness, and into the elements of repression and sublimation in its optimism, marks the point at which
Romanticism begins to diverge from other manifestations of
aesthetic idealism. Sidney's "Apologie for Poetrie," which breaks
with the medieval tradition to emphasize the role of the poet as
maker, is one of the earliest in a long line of idealist treatments of
the imagination. For Sidney, the golden world constructed by the
imagination is completely independent of the actual world. But
for Hegel, hope exists at the suture of the imaginary and the real:
because hope is the product of a mind which knows as well as
imagines, it inevitably discloses what it seeks to deny. Shelley's
image of flowers that "hide with thin and rainbow wings / The
shape of Death" (*Prometheus Unbound*, ii.iv.62-63) points to the
self-deconstructing duplicity in which a whole category of acts,
including hope, dream, and fiction find themselves trapped.

Romantic aesthetics can thus be said to approach recognitions
about the status of the poetic act reached by existential
phenomenology. It is also a forerunner of existentialism in a
much less technical sense of the word: in its sensitivity to the
experience of angst and doubt so well summed up in the word
"Geworfenheit." But if Romanticism anticipates existentialism, it
does so only insofar as existentialism remains a humanism, and
not insofar as it becomes the prelude to absurdity. It is revealing
that Schopenhauer should find himself affirming, at the end of
the third book[64] and in his discussion of the beautiful, the very
notion of an existentially innocent art that he has deconstructed
through the categories of will and sublimity. The discovery of the

---

[64]Art is "the most delightful, and the only innocent, side of life" (Schopenhauer,
The World as Will and Representation, I, 266).

duplicity inherent in an idealistic theory of art fails to resolve a crucial problem, and it is this problem which represents the challenge of the idealist tradition to existentialist aestheticians such as Sartre, Derrida, and de Man. The definition of art in terms of Apollonian representation, so inconsistent with the claim that it is a mimesis of existence, arises from a belief that the imagination is an essential dimension of human freedom. No matter how persuasive the deconstruction of idealist fictions, it is almost never the case that writers reach that zero degree of self-mystification envisaged by de Man, in which "the invented fiction, far from filling the void, asserts itself as pure nothingness," having consumed its own hopes.[65] De Man himself, in discussing Rousseau, points toward a continued tendency to self-mystification present in that writer:

> The *Social Contract* is clearly productive and generative as well as deconstructive. . . . To the extent that it never ceases to advocate the necessity for political legislation and elaborate the principles on which such a legislation could be based, it resorts to the principles of authority that it undermines. We know this structure to be characteristic of what we have called allegories of unreadability. Such an allegory is metafigural: it is an allegory of a figure . . . which relapses into the figure it deconstructs. . . . it persists in performing what it has shown to be impossible to do.[66]

The impossibility of disengaging the sentimental and the ironic in Romantic literature, to which de Man here points, is not just an accident of rhetoric, nor even the product of legitimate psychic defenses. It arises from a genuine skepticism about human potentiality, which warrants neither categorical idealism nor pessimism.

The period's ambivalent sense of the role of aesthetic representation, arising from its ambivalent sense of the human situation, is often reflected in the narrative indeterminacies of its poetry. In a poem such as *Christabel,* the victimization of the beautiful soul by darker forces asks to be read sentimentally as an external seduction which supervenes upon an originally and ultimately innocent creation. But it also asks to be read as an internal

[65] De Man, *Blindness and Insight,* p. 19.
[66] De Man, "Political Allegory in Rousseau," 674.

corruption in which Geraldine—herself a victim like Christabel—appears as the double of Christabel: an alter ego who reveals to the latter depths that had always already existed within herself, and who is genetically linked to her by an uncanny symbiosis which makes it seem that she has always belonged in the Baron's family. The deconstructive reading of the poem's events as happening within rather than to Christabel is complicated by the externality of evil in the form of Geraldine which sanctions a sentimental reading. But this very externality may be no more than the mind's method of rationalizing its complicity in the triumph of life, and reconstructing the impossible myth of its own innocence. From the feeling that the substance of life is originally ambiguous, and that the mind's constructions of innocence and beauty may be designed to veil a fundamental darkness, arises the sense of art as the medium of a disclosure, a mimesis of trauma. But Coleridge's equally strong belief in the soul's radical innocence produces a countervailing sense—evident in the sentimentality and pathos with which he depicts Christabel, and in his projection of a happy ending—that art should be a transcendence of actuality, and that its idealism is a rectification of distortions imposed by the actual world.

It is the sense that life may be not only will but also representation, a product of human activity, that Nietzsche's *Birth of Tragedy* tries to respect. We have seen in Romantic critical theory a dialectical confrontation between texts like Schiller's *On Naive and Sentimental Poetry* and Schopenhauer's *World as Will and Representation.* The rhetorical ambivalence which reimplicates both critical texts in the positions they are opposing recurs in poetic texts, whether they are ironic poems which fail to invalidate their own illusions, or sentimental poems which argue for an ideal against the knowledge of its impossibility. On balance, *Christabel* is probably a sentimental work. But the distance that separates it from *Isabella,* which is probably an ironic work, is sufficiently small to make clear that neither mode can provide a style answerable to the Romantic period's sense of the function of its own language. Nietzsche, who stands at the meeting point of existentialism and idealism, attempts to articulate and respond to the tensions in Romantic aesthetics, and to legitimize ambivalence by grounding it in the doubleness of existence. Shelley himself, who might have preferred one way or the other to unperplex the ideal shape and the trauma of existence, speaks in *Epipsychidion* of the double failure of poetry, which he will eventually discover as the source of its power:

> But neither prayer nor verse could dissipate
> The night which closed on her; nor uncreate
> That world within this Chaos, mine and me,
> Of which she was the veiled Divinity.

[241–244]

CHAPTER 2

Visionary and Questioner:

Idealism and Skepticism in Shelley's Poetry

> "their lore
> Taught them not this—to know themselves; their might
> Could not repress the mutiny within,
> And for the morn of truth they feigned, deep night
> Caught them ere evening."
>
> —*The Triumph of Life*

Martin Price writes of Blake that his critical remarks are a fierce attack on all doctrines that seem to undermine the authority of the imagination: "In this respect, he differs greatly from writers of more skeptical temper or tentative attitudes. Perhaps the greatest threat to the visionary is the sense of self-division and doubt. . . . Doubt, as Blake puts it, 'is Self-Contradiction,' the self divided into the visionary and the questioner."[1] While no one would claim that Shelley possessed Blake's confidence in the power of the imagination to resist inner doubt or external opposition, critics have tended to assume that given the choice he would have preferred the unmediated vision to the state of being in doubt and half-knowledge.[2] Such a view is based on the assumption that either *Prometheus Unbound* or *Adonais* is the central poem in the canon, and that *The Triumph of Life* is a postscript rather than a new plateau in Shelley's development, as T. S. Eliot long ago recognized it to be. Thus Bloom sees the pattern of Shelley's poetry as involving a moment of heightened relationship between the "I" and its universe, and a subsequent falling away into experience which does not, however, "invalidate the apotheosis" of

---

[1]Martin Price, *To the Palace of Wisdom: Studies in Order and Energy from Dryden to Blake* (New York: Doubleday, 1965), p. 438.

[2]C. E. Pulos, *The Deep Truth: A Study of Shelley's Scepticism* (Lincoln: University of Nebraska Press, 1954); Earl Wasserman, *Shelley*. While Wasserman discusses Shelley's skepticism at length, he seems to regard it as intermediate rather than terminal: a way of strengthening the idealism which is Shelley's final position.

the moment of relationship. Daniel Hughes, following Bloom, sees the poetic process in Shelley as a kindling and dwindling, and reads *The Triumph of Life* as a defeat of the myth which nevertheless leaves intact as the core of affirmation in Shelley's work "the continuous fire" achieved in *Prometheus Unbound.* Wasserman, for his part, does not even deal with *The Triumph of Life.*[3]

To a great extent Shelley himself encourages such views, because his encounter with skepticism leads him to postpone or relocate rather than revise his idealism, to respond to skepticism sentimentally rather than ironically or tragically. The seemingly pessimistic and platonic image of poetry as a fading coal preserves in the past the radical image of poetry as "pregnant with a lightning which has yet found no conductor,"[4] without giving up the idealistic view of art as vision and illumination implicit in both images. The radical, revolutionary image of poetry, which seems to claim the immanence of vision, is itself a way of rationalizing absence by converting it into hope. But the fact that Shelley's last poem, like Keats's last poem, is an interior dialogue between a visionary and the self-projected specter of his own doubt should lead us to ask whether *The Triumph of Life* does not revise Shelley's Promethean myth rather than confirm it in defeat, and whether it does not temper the nature of poetry to the imperfection of the self. Rousseau, the protagonist of Shelley's poem, himself wrote dialogues in which he split himself into judge and defender, for the purpose of defying criticism by perceiving it as misunderstanding. The different nature of the dialogue in Shelley's poem stands, among other things, as a reexamination of the Romantic tendency to use dialogue and drama in such a way that the very forms of self-doubt are converted into the forms of ex-

---

[3]Harold Bloom, *Shelley's Mythmaking,* p. 93; Daniel Hughes, "Kindling and Dwindling: The Poetic Process in Shelley," *Keats-Shelley Journal,* 13 (1964), 17. Ross Woodman, who sees *Adonais* rather than *Prometheus Unbound* as the poem which best sums up Shelley's vision, treats *The Triumph of Life* as a version of *Adonais,* which confirms rather than questions the logocentrism of Shelley's poetry hitherto (*The Apocalyptic Vision in the Poetry of Shelley* [Toronto: University of Toronto Press, 1964], pp. 180–198).

[4]Shelley, "A Defence of Poetry," p. 291. I have borrowed the terms "radical" and "platonic" from Milton Wilson, who uses them to indicate respectively the belief in immediate attainment of the millennium and the postponement of this attainment to the afterlife (*Shelley's Later Poetry: A Study of His Prophetic Imagination* [New York: Columbia University Press, 1959], pp. 176–177).

culpation, and inner division is projected away from the self. It seems possible to say that *The Triumph of Life* moves away from idealism and, moreover, that it is the culmination of a debate between Shelley's skepticism and his idealism that is present as early as *Alastor*. The unconventional disposition of this chapter, which begins at the end of Shelley's career and then moves chronologically forward through a selection of major narrative and lyric texts (*Alastor*, "Hymn to Intellectual Beauty," "Mont Blanc," and *Prometheus Unbound*), may seem to prejudge the discussion by giving Shelley's final poem an initial authority within the canon. It reflects, however, my feeling that the tension between text and subtext in the earlier work is best understood retrospectively in the light of the poem which "psychoanalyses" and finally subsumes and overcomes its predecessors. Because Shelley is, from the beginning, a sentimental and not a naive poet, the tragic understanding of the role of the visionary which becomes explicit in his final poem is latent even in his earlier work. It is first confronted as early as "Mont Blanc," but in the mode of lyric which, as an abstraction from life, lacks the existential finality conferred by the more extensive and public mode of narrative. It is finally confronted in *The Triumph of Life*, which seems at first to continue Shelley's sentimental commitment to a defeated idealism, but which proves to be a transitional poem involved in reformulating its own initial assumptions.

The very form of *The Triumph of Life*, which is dialogical and historical rather than annunciatory and mythic, points to a questioning of Shelley's earlier poetic stance not immediately apparent at the beginning of the poem. In the course of Shelley's dialogue with Rousseau a logocentric poem of the soul, which is predictable from *Adonais*, becomes a skeptical and existentialist poem of the self (to borrow a Yeatsian antithesis). This new poem is willing to put in jeopardy the fiction of a transcendental discourse to which Shelley had earlier aspired. It is only one of the many inconsistencies in *The Triumph of Life* that Rousseau, who begins by advising the poet to "forbear / To join the dance" (ll. 188–189),[5] ends by telling him,

[5] References to *The Triumph of Life* are to the edition by Donald Reiman, in his *Shelley's "Triumph of Life": A Critical Study* (Urbana: University of Illinois Press, 1965).

"But follow thou, and from spectator turn
Actor or victim in this wretchedness,

"And what thou wouldst be taught I then may learn
From thee."

[305-308]

Also of importance is the fact that Rousseau, who described himself as reluctantly and passively "swept" into the procession of Life, goes on to speak of himself as having "plunged" actively and voluntarily into a confrontation with the "cold light" of the Car (ll. 461, 467-468). Similarly the ribald crew which follows the chariot, though it is first shown as physically loathsome in the manner of the denizens of Dante's Hell, is also shown as possessed of an energy that makes it the object of sublimity rather than pathos (ll. 138ff.). The poem begins by insisting sentimentally on an idealist separation between the sacred few and the multitude, or as Bloom would have it, between imagination and the fallen nature where the myth must inevitably fail if it attempts to act itself out. But it ends by insisting on the Triumph as a vale of soul-making rather than a vale of tears, a tragic knowledge into which every human being must be initiated.

Of particular interest to the process of revision and reassessment at the heart of the poem are the lines on the bards of elder time:

"who truly quelled

"The passions which they sung, as by their strain
May well be known: their living melody
Tempers its own contagion to the vein

"Of those who are infected with it—I
Have suffered what I wrote, or viler pain!—
And so my words were seeds of misery—"

[274-280]

Syntactically the lines seem to insist on the contrast between the Arnoldian poet whose suffering is transcended in creation, and the Keatsian dreamer who vexes the world and prefigures Artaud's equation of literature with pestilence.[6] In so doing, they suggest that Rousseau's error can instruct one in how to bring about a catharsis of life. Yet even as Rousseau speaks the lines, they seem to change their meaning. The imagery of contagion and infection used of the great bards suggests that they differ from the dreamers who sow seeds of misery in degree rather than kind. Where the poem had previously praised the flight of the sacred few to the realm of the ideal, it now identifies the great bards with the suffering multitude in such a way as to prepare for the later recognition that there is something essentially creative even in "a world of agony" (l. 295). The metaphor of inoculation replaces an aesthetics of immunity by one which recognizes the purgative effect of submitting to contamination. Moreover, the bards, who must *temper* their own contagion in communicating it, are if anything depicted as suffering what they write at a higher intensity. Between the initial rejection of life and the final acceptance of it there is a complex process of revaluation. The shifting and ambiguous meaning of key images is symptomatic not only of this process, but also of the fact that the poem's central question receives no unambiguous answer: Rousseau cannot tell the poet what life is, for Rousseau is only an externalization of the poet's own self-doubt, and it is Shelley who must learn through experience the knowledge that will enable him to teach his specter, and still his doubt.

At the heart of the poem's ambiguity is the nature of the Shape all light, with its accompanying landscape, and the relation of both to the shape in the Car of Life. The extremes of interpretation include Allott's view of the Shape as the Wordsworthian visionary gleam and Bloom's view of it as fundamentally deceptive and evil.[7] That the same lines legitimately support such varying interpretations is evidence that the poem is more complex and undecided than either critic will allow. The "light diviner than the common Sun" which suffuses the landscape in which Rousseau has his vision (ll. 335ff.) seems to refer to what Allott calls "a Wordsworthian glory in infancy." Yet the setting of the experience is not infancy and innocence but rather "broad day," a set-

[6]Artaud, *Le théâtre et son double*, p. 42.

[7]Kenneth Allott, "Bloom on 'The Triumph of Life,'" *Essays in Criticism*, 10 (1960), 224; Bloom, *Shelley's Mythmaking*, pp. 265ff.

ting that seems to preserve "a gentle trace / Of light diviner than the common Sun," but to preserve it only for a moment. Thus one hesitates to say whether the light divine and the Shape all light are experiences of beauty and innocence, or whether the landscape of Rousseau's encounter with the Shape is already the landscape of "this harsh world in which I wake to weep," suffused only by a lingering light. One also hesitates to say whether the light, both fresh and fading, testifies to the Shape as true or as illusory. In a sense there is no question of choosing between interpretations, for both are equally true. One of the points about the Shelleyan as opposed to the Wordsworthian epiphany is that, both in the case of the vision in *Alastor* and in that of the Shape all light, the visionary gleam lacks the transcendental and unequivocal purity that it possesses in Wordsworth by virtue of being pushed back into infancy. It is already viewed with the skepticism that attends its being located in a state halfway to experience and yet close to innocence.

The ambiguity carries over into the Shape itself. Allott is true to convention in interpreting the light imagery that surrounds it as an indication of the natural goodness of the Shape. Bloom, following Yeats, insists that Shelley indulged in Blakean inversions of normal image values, preferring night to the unpurged images of day, and using light to signify a hostile if not malevolent force.[8] Again, the ambiguity of the imagery suggests that Shelley approached the mystery of light and life with no clear preconceptions, and the poem is above all a poem of questioning, doubting, and emergent knowledge, a poem in which imagistic ambivalences signal the poet's growing awareness of the fact that the "valley of perpetual dream" in which the Car of Life is seen and the "realm without a name" from which the Shape all light issues (ll. 396–397) are inextricably mingled, and that man must learn to take the measure of good and evil in a world in which all good things are confused with ill. It seems perverse not to accept the naturally positive connotations of the Shape's light. Yet one must also observe the perplexing way in which the Shape anticipates the Car of Life. The powerful lines, "the fierce splendour / Fell

[8]Allott, "Bloom on 'The Triumph of Life,'" p. 266; Bloom, *Shelley's Mythmaking*, p. 270.

from her as she moved under the mass / Of the deep cavern" (ll.
359–361), make the Shape's dispensation of grace curiously similar to the withering of grace brought on by the Car:

> "And the fair shape waned in the coming light
> As veil by veil the silent splendour drops
> From Lucifer, amid the chrysolite
>
> "Of sunrise . . ."

                                                    [412–415]

The Shape all light remains "a shape of golden dew" (l. 379) and
possesses a beauty we should not ignore. Yet the description of
her effect *prior* to the drinking of the Nepenthe contains many
disturbing elements:

> "As if the gazer's mind was strewn beneath
> Her feet like embers, and she, thought by thought,
>
> "Trampled its fires into the dust of death,
> As Day upon the threshold of the east
> Treads out the lamps of night . . .
>
> ". . . like day she came,
> Making the night a dream . . ."

                                                    [386–393]

It is difficult to deny some validity to Bloom's feeling that the
image values of night and day are reversed here. Furthermore,
the Shape's trampling of the sparks of the mind recalls the manner in which the Car of Life put out the sparks which heaven lit in
the sacred few (ll. 207ff.), thus suggesting that the Shape embodies something demonic. But one is also aware, on the other
side of the argument, that the trampling of the sparks may be a
reminiscence of *Adonais* (l. 464), that if the lines are read in context "day" and "light" still carry some of the positive connotations
they had in the earlier lines of the vision, and finally that the
whole passage on the sun putting out the stars which Bloom also
cites (ll. 76–79)[9] is in fact a carry-over from the uncanceled
C-opening printed by Matthews, which carries an unmistakably

---

[9]Bloom, *Shelley's Mythmaking*, p. 270.

positive connotation: "Whilst she, the fairest of the wandering seven / Laughed to behold how in their fiery mirth / The clearest stars were blotted out of heaven."[10]

In fact, Shelley is deeply ambivalent in his use of night and day imagery, because he is deeply ambivalent about whether truth resides in the ideal or in the reality that desecrates it, and whether Rousseau's career is a victory of darkness over light or of knowledge over innocence and ignorance. As one reads the various uncanceled openings of the poem printed by Matthews, it is evident that even as he was writing, Shelley's conception of the experience he was describing was undergoing changes. The value system of the B-version is relatively simple. At the beginning, the sun is described as coming out of the shade of night, as a spirit of glory and good which rouses the earth "out of the gloom / Of daily life." Presumably the poem, as Shelley here conceives it, is to consist of a contrast between the paradisal light of Wordsworthian nature and the inferno of the procession, between vital and daily life; and as the enthusiasm and length of the natural description indicate, the spirit of good is ultimately to triumph over the shade of night. "Life" may still be what it is in the essay "On Life." The first half of the C-version of the opening more or less repeats the tone of optimistic celebration, but a darker note begins to impinge on the poetry with the strange lines that describe the world rising out of the death of daily life as bearing "Its portion in the *ruin* of repose." Shelley in fact goes on to suggest the deceptiveness of beauty in such phrases as "false wind" and "flattering wave." But the note of doubt is quickly suppressed and Shelley returns to his initial image of the sun leaving behind the night, in the line "Before me rose the day, behind the night."

Yet the mingling of glory and doubt present in this version carries over into the final E-version which forms the present opening of the poem, where the line just quoted is curiously reversed: "before me fled / The night; behind me rose the day" (ll. 26–27). It is now the day and not the night which is behind the speaker, and the night and not the day which lies ahead of him. Thus it would seem, if we accept the conventional connotations of

---

[10]G. M. Matthews, "The 'Triumph of Life' Apocrypha," *Times Literary Supplement*, August 5, 1960, p. 503.

night and day, that the positive direction of the poem has been
reversed, and that the speaker is passing from the spirit of good
into the empire of evil. Yet the matter is not so simple, because
within the new line itself, there is a curious reversal of verbs. If the
day is behind and the night is ahead, it is the day which should be
described as fleeing and the night which should be rising. Yet it is
the approaching night which flees and the receding day which
rises. Thus within the new version, which has the dreamer moving
from day to night, the old version, which has him moving from
night to day, is still retained.

The verbal confusion indicates a deepening ambivalence on
Shelley's part as to the truth-value of light and dark terms. It
suggests that as he approaches his vision he is uncertain as to
whether it has the status of a revelation of the way things are or a
demonic parody of the way things should be. This ambivalence, as
I shall argue, is the core of truth that Shelley discovers in his
descent to the Hades of his career. He enters his vision as Keats
enters his purgatory blind, unable to take the measure of light
and dark. The heaven is above his head, but the deep is at his feet,
and the truth that he will learn may lead him in either direction.
Had he completed the poem, contradiction might have been
translated into an ambivalent but coherent image of what life is: a
skeptical but strong image which encompasses both the ideal and
its possible negation, and one which sees both the epiphanic falling of the mask of darkness from the awakened earth and the
stripping away of mask after mask of illusion by Life as simultaneous truths (ll. 3–4, 536–537).

Bloom's view of the poem as enacting a failure is dependent on
making Rousseau embody a position to be rejected. Yet he is a
complex figure whose self-awareness distinguishes him from
Shelley's earlier visionaries, and his interpretation of the procession is a strange mixture of self-rejection in which he sees himself
as defeated and condemned to the Inferno, and self-justification
in which he distinguishes himself from other members of the
procession and almost sees his suffering as redeemable. It is Rousseau who describes himself as corrupted and stained. But it is the
same Rousseau who separates himself from Life's other victims
when he says, "I was overcome / By my own heart alone" (ll.

240–241), implying that the heart which has the power to be weak may have the power to be strong again through the force of its own self-knowledge. Rousseau's revision of his self-image within the poem is indicative of the fact that *The Triumph of Life* is a poem in the process of understanding and assessing the experience it describes. He may begin by seeing the capacity of his writing to infect as an emblem of the defeat of all that artistic creation should be: the best and happiest thoughts of the best minds. Yet only a few lines later he says almost the opposite in the triumphant words "I / Am one of those who have created, even / If it be but a world of agony" (ll. 293–295). What Shelley seems to be doing here, in admitting a second kind of nonideal art, is to redeem Rousseau (and therefore himself) from the world of the procession to which he had earlier consigned him, and to suggest that he possesses a purgatorial wisdom. The process is analogous to that by which Keats softens Moneta's hard distinction between poets who pour out a balm upon the world and dreamers who vex it, and suggests not only that dreamers can become poets, but that all poets must first be dreamers who submit to the giant agony of the world. The poem as it stands provides no explicit way of transcending a world which describes the defeat of imagination. But it is not difficult to see in what direction Shelley was moving. The encounter between Rousseau and his former self provides an implicit paradigm for the way in which the poet's encounter with his own defeated earlier self is meant to function. Rousseau's interior dialogue leads to a reappraisal of Romantic idealism that releases him from the punishment which attends overidealization, the "deep night" that traps those who have feigned a "morn of truth" (ll. 214–215). Shelley's encounter with Rousseau is likewise meant to provide him with a way of confronting his own myth of a Promethean art and revising it in such a way that it does not fall victim to the inevitable disillusion that follows the failure to attain the ideal.

The point of Rousseau's lines about the creation of a world of agony, and the point also of the description of the car's harsh light as its "creative ray" (l. 533), is that the vision of the Inferno is a necessary initiation without which life is not complete. Unlike Irving Babbitt, who sees Rousseau as the victim of an untempered

overidealization and feels that the sacred few like himself can
escape the errors of Romanticism,[11] the author of *The Triumph of
Life* argues that the appalling process by which the ideal Shape
becomes the hideousness that it seeks to repress is an experience
that strikes Plato and Rousseau alike. The Car of Life has the
quality of a revelation, is described as "the coming light" and as
having majesty and "rushing splendour" (ll. 412,87), because it is
inevitable and necessary, like Keats's awakening from the fair
grove to the terrifying ancient sanctuary at the beginning of *The
Fall of Hyperion*. The Car is driven by a blind charioteer, not because it represents anything as facile as the blindness of institutions, but because, like blind justice, it impartially compels
everyone to submit to its revelation. It is not so much horrible as
terrible, using the distinction as Heath-Stubbs uses it, to signify by
the horrible the uncomprehending stare into a disintegrating
world, and by the terrible an intellectual comprehension of the
dark elements in experience[12] such as Shelley himself found in
Dante but not in Michelangelo.[13] Like De Quincey's terrible *Mater
Tenebrarum*, the Car is sent to man "to plague his heart" until it has
"unfolded the capacities of his spirit"[14] through an agony that is
creative.

Yet the ambivalence of the light-dark imagery does not only
confer a truth value upon the vision of darkness in the Car. It also
asserts, by dividing the light imagery equally between the
Wordsworthian sun of the opening and the Car of Life, that truth
is on both sides, in the terrible and chaotic and also in the beautiful and harmonious, in Apollo as well as Dionysos. There is finally
nothing in the poem which says that the "new vision, never seen
before" (l. 411) is truer than the old vision it replaces. If the
language used to describe the Car is already present in the language used to describe the Shape all light, then the reverse is also

[11]Irving Babbitt, *Rousseau and Romanticism* (New York: Houghton Mifflin,
1919).
[12]John Heath-Stubbs, *The Darkling Plain* (London: Eyre & Spottiswoode, 1950),
pp. 58–59. The horrible is a "spiritual cowardice" which shrinks from contemplating suffering, the distortion of the soul, and the perversion of beauty.
[13]Shelley, *The Complete Works*, ed. Roger Ingpen and W. E. Peck (London: Ernest Benn, 1926–1930), X, 32–33.
[14]De Quincey, *Suspiria de Profundis, The Collected Writings of Thomas de Quincey*,
ed. David Masson (London: A. and C. Black, 1897), XVI, 32.

true: "So knew I in that light's severe excess / The presence of that shape which on the stream / Moved, as I moved along the wilderness" (ll. 424-426; cf. ll. 97-98).

If Shelley had in any sense planned to follow the usual pattern of dream-visions, the poem could not have been intended to end with the passing of the Car, but would have returned to the purgatorial landscape of the opening, with the deep below and the possibility of heaven above. It is not Shelley's life but Rousseau's which ends in the Inferno—although even he acquires a purgatorial status that sets him above the inhabitants of the "oblivious valley" (l. 539).[15] But Rousseau's life is contained within something larger, namely Shelley's vision, and whereas Rousseau in his life awakes from the heaven of the visionary gleam to the hell of the Car of Life, Shelley, one must assume, would have awakened from the harsh world of his dream to the sweeter landscape of the very opening lines.

In other words, the infernal vision should not be seen as the final image of the poem, but rather as something with which the dreamer must come to terms: something which he must recognize as a perpetual possibility behind the Apollonian world of order and harmony governed by "the Sun their father" that the poet envisages in the opening (l. 18). Rousseau's life does indeed detail the defeat of the Promethean myth, but Shelley's poem is not about a defeat but rather about the inner process by which the dreamer inspects the image of that defeat and seeks to know why it is so. Rousseau, significantly, does not make a final judgment on the illusoriness of the good:

> "Whether my life had been before that sleep
> The Heaven which I imagine, or a Hell
> Like the harsh world in which I wake to weep,
>
> "I know not."
>
> [332-335]

---

[15]Another indication of the way in which the figure of Rousseau undergoes revision in the course of the poem itself is seen in the fact that Rousseau speaks of not knowing "Whither the conqueror hurries me" (l. 304), but in the end seems to have detached himself from the procession, which passes on without him: "The cripple cast / His eye upon the car which now had rolled / Onward, as if that look must be the last" (ll. 544-546).

The word "imagine" is not in the past tense, and Rousseau seems to draw back from complete defeatism. Or to put it differently, the infernal vision is mediated by the maturer Rousseau whose tentative and yet uncertain reinterpretation of his life precedes his actual account of it, and the mediation converts the infernal into the purgatorial, the agony into creation. Through the use of two framing visions (Shelley's and Rousseau's), which move in opposite directions between surface and depth, the poem thematizes the representation of life through art, and suggests that the function of art is the reconstruction of appearances as well as the disclosure of the Dionysiac knowledge that lies behind them.

There is, therefore, a kind of logic in the fact that Rousseau introduces the most terrible part of his vision of the waning of beauty with a reference to Dante's ascent to Paradise (ll. 472–479). But the reader also recognizes that the Dantesque pattern of a steady ascent from darkness to light is inappropriate to a poem which is characterized by a constantly shifting use of light and dark values and by a constant oscillation between the moment of vision and the waning of beauty. For Dante, whose guides know the moral geography of their universe, the vision of darkness and the vision of love are successive moments in the history of a spirit that believes in ascent and transcendence. For Shelley, led by a guide whose own self-image changes in the course of his narration, the outcome of the journey inevitably remains more in doubt. That is as it must be in a world where the knowledge one has is not received from a steady source of light above, but generated through an internal dramaturgy which has the soul confront the specter of its own self-doubt. The image of Life as a kind of Janus-faced power, deeply ambivalent and turned toward death as well as life, toward Dionysos as well as Apollo, is an ultimately skeptical one and promises no progress toward secular or sacred perfection. It demands a faith which recognizes that at any moment the Shape all light may again become the infernal Shape, and that such reversals are not merely temporary arrests in the progress toward the far goal of time but part of the shape of truth. Holistic ideals such as the love associated with Dante and Prometheus cannot redeem a world so lacking in serenity, because they require a simplification of the Janus-faced image and a purgation of that which gives it its dynamism. The agent of redemption is rather something which might be called the purgatorial imagination, an imagination that derives its power from the very manner in which it finds itself containing the reality that is to deconstruct it. Shelley's final poem does not deny the possibility of an optimism in which we are our own gods. But to be our own gods is also to submit to the lasting misery and loneliness of the world, and as Rilke said of the artist, to have the courage to walk beside our devils as in a triumph.

In his letters Rilke speaks of our tendency to convert death and darkness into external devils, so as to exclude from our search for meaning that which is "so close to us that the distance between it and the inner centre of our hearts cannot be registered." Yet we end by internalizing these elements, because we know that life has no meaning without death and light no meaning without darkness:

> Since the dawn of time man has fashioned gods in whom the deadly, the threatening, the annihilating and the terrible elements of life were contained, its power, its fury, its daemonic possessiveness—all amassed in one dense, malevolent concentration—something alien to us, if you will, yet at the same time permitting us to recognise it, to suffer it, even to acknowledge it for the sake of a certain mysterious kinship and involvement with it: [for] this also was part of us, only we did not know how to cope with this side of our experience; it was too massive, too dangerous.[16]

In *The Triumph of Life* Shelley moves toward an internalization of the destructive, Dionysiac element in experience which is very far from those beautiful idealisms of moral excellence which his idealistic aesthetic theory claims it is the function of the poet to provide. Yet Shelley's final poem is to a certain extent an emancipation of his imagination, and Bostetter is not wholly wrong in his comment that the basic Shelleyan conception, as it emerges elsewhere, is "of a flowing together. . . . All things are drawn together, whether human beings or elements of nature. . . . But only the

[16]Rilke, *Selected Letters of Rainer Maria Rilke 1902–1926*, trans. R. F. C. Hull (London: Macmillan, 1947), p. 265.

good and beautiful parts are so drawn, pulled away from the evil, ugly, painful and violent."[17] Shelley's theory of imagination in "A Defence of Poetry," like his theory of the epipsyche in the essay "On Love," is generally taken to be a naive, logocentric theory which emphasizes the unity of the poetic experience and its participation in "the eternal, the infinite, and the one."[18] Shelley's poetics, according to John Bayley, seeks to exclude those discords of the real world which damage his sense of primal unity, and thus cuts itself off from "everything that might give sense and weight to such a unity."[19] The definition of the epipsyche, linked in Shelley's mind with the activity of the poetic psyche, is of an impossibly selective mirror: "a mirror whose surface reflects only the forms of purity and brightness; a soul within our soul that describes a circle around its proper paradise which pain, and sorrow, and evil dare not overleap."[20]

More accurate, however, than this post-Victorian view of Shelley is the comment by D. G. James already cited, that Shelley's tendency to argue for the exclusion or ultimate powerlessness of evil coexists oddly with a considerable honesty about the existence of evil in the world. In the course of a few lines in *Alastor* the narrator claims that the world is "this so lovely world" (l. 686), that "Heartless things / Are done and said i' the world" (ll. 690–691), that worms inherit the earth (ll. 691–692), and that the symphony of nature "Lifts still its solemn voice" (ll. 694–695). James's point is that Shelley's poetry, which does not weave a circle around the poetic *logos* and yet acts as though it does, is constructed around a lacuna between rhetoric and content. Shelley, in other words, is never properly the naive spirit envisioned by Bayley and Bostetter. The unresolved contradiction between the theory of art and the poetry of experience leads to the presence, in the earlier poems, of repressed subtexts which challenge and interrupt the logic of the text, even as they contain in embryo the knowledge that will be made explicit in *The Triumph of Life*. *Alastor* is an appropriate poem to consider at this point because it includes the

[17]Bostetter, *The Romantic Ventriloquists,* p. 216.
[18]Shelley, "A Defence of Poetry," p. 279.
[19]John Bayley, *The Romantic Survival: A Study in Poetic Evolution* (London: Constable, 1957), p. 43.
[20]Shelley, "On Love," *Prose,* p. 170.

same narrative elements as *The Triumph of Life:* the visionary, the ambiguous female Shape, and a narrator who, as *spectator ab extra,* functions as an implied reader within the poem. It contains almost the same spectrum of imagery that is present in *The Triumph of Life.* The "bright silver dream" is mixed with visions of charnels and coffins (ll. 67,24), the calm sky with the dark ocean (ll. 340–344), and the moment of epiphany with the consciousness of a world that is ruled by a sightless and "colossal Skeleton" (ll. 610–615). The poem moves beyond the naive, almost to the threshold of the tragic. What distinguishes it from *The Triumph of Life* is the sentimental manner in which its narrator relates the light and dark elements of his universe. He leaves the image of the Poet "Gentle, and brave, and generous" (l. 58), somehow untouched by the dark and sometimes demonic uncertainties of his journey, and purports to present an exemplary life even as he deconstructs his own idealization.

James's observation goes to the heart of Shelley's view of literature, which is itself less naive than it seems, and which mirrors the problematics of the poetry prior to *The Triumph of Life* in conflating mimetic and expressive theories that tend to contradict each other. While Shelley's poetic theory is not self-conscious enough to provide us with an explicit terminology in which to discuss his poetry, its tensions and contradictions serve as a useful introduction to similar tensions which will emerge when we discuss the earlier poetry. On the one hand, poetry is described in terms of light and lightning imagery that makes it a transforming and renovating force: it is among other things "a sword of lightning" and the "light of life," an "immortal god" which descends "for the redemption of mortal passion."[21] But on the other hand, it is a mirror "in which the spectator beholds himself ... it teaches ... self-knowledge and self-respect."[22] The immediate occasion for the insistence on poetry as mimesis is Peacock's ironic attempt to demystify poetry by identifying it with a maximum of self-mystification. Shelley can make no claim for the high seriousness of poetry without grounding it in the world of truth, by defining it as an imitation of the real world. Yet he has the pro-

---

[21]Shelley, "A Defence of Poetry," pp. 285, 286; "Preface to *The Cenci,*" *Poetical Works,* ed. Thomas Hutchinson (1905; rpt. Oxford: Clarendon, 1967), p. 277.
[22]Shelley, "A Defence of Poetry," p. 285.

phetic artist's impatience with subservience to present fact, and
must also argue that poetry is an expressive outward projection of
the golden world within. The result is a view of poetry as a mirror
which is somehow also a lamp, a mirror which is not mimetic
because it eschews fact, and instead of reflecting, "makes beautiful" what is distorted:[23] "The drama, so long as it continues to
express poetry, is as a prismatic and many-sided mirror, which
collects the brightest rays of human nature." The mirror is therefore not one in which the spectator "beholds himself," but one in
which he beholds the epipsyche that he "would become": "The
tragedies of the Athenian poets are as mirrors in which the spectator beholds himself, under a thin disguise of circumstance,
stript of all but that ideal perfection and energy which every one
feels to be the internal type of all that he loves, admires, and
would become."[24]

The passive mirror, as Shelley uses it elsewhere, does not necessarily supply us with an image of "our entire self, yet deprived of
all that we condemn or despise."[25] It can become indifferently the
Tower of Famine absorbing the surrounding desolation, or the
mind of the hero of "Marenghi," which grows like the immeasur-
able heaven it contemplates (l. 135).[26] Yet what Shelley seems to
insist on in the "Defence of Poetry" is the impossible concept of a
mirror that has the power actually to transform what it reflects
into the ideal. The conflation of realistic and idealistic theories
may be a semantic accident, but it also goes to the heart of a
recurrent aesthetic dilemma. In the impossible identity of mirror
and lamp we encounter yet another attempt to submerge
Dionysos in Apollo, and to silence an inevitable dialogue between
the veil of language and the knowledge of life.

The disjunctive presence of a realistic poetics alongside a
visionary poetics marks "A Defence of Poetry" as a sentimental

[23]Ibid., p. 281.
[24]Ibid., p. 285.
[25]Shelley, "On Love," p. 170.
[26]The idea of growing like what one contemplates turns up repeatedly in Shelley. In "Prince Athanase," as in "Marenghi," it is used idealistically to mean reflection of bright creations ("Prince Athanase," ll. 139-141). But in *Prometheus Unbound* it is used in the opposite way, "Whilst I behold such execrable shapes, /
Methinks I grow like what I contemplate" (i. 449-450). Cf. also *The Cenci*,
v.iv.30-31.

text, which engages in strategies of self-avoidance to escape being consumed by its own contradictions. It suggests, in turn, that Shelley's visionary narratives *(Alastor, Adonais, Epipsychidion)*[27] also communicate disjunctively, as products of a poetic consciousness that exists on two different levels of awareness. Critics have noted a contradiction between the preface to *Alastor,* which seems to condemn the Poet, and the poem itself, which seems to put him forward as a pattern of virtue.[28] Within *Alastor* itself, there is a curious dissociation of sensibility which causes the poem to move in two contradictory directions. The facts of the narrative lead toward the hero's death, the failure of his quest, perhaps even the recognition of it as misguided. But the poetic sentiment idealizes that "surpassing Spirit" (l. 714) who is seen in death as the animating force in nature, even though his life had been an existence debarred from nature's living images. There is a troubled ambivalence in the poem which is symptomatic of the dialogue of Shelley's mind with itself. But the dialogue seems to stop well short of the sort of self-awareness that Wasserman envisages in his interpretation of the poem as a skeptical debate between an empirical narrator and an idealist poet. *Alastor* is not an ironic poem in which Shelley has two points of view disciplining each other, "like the Yeatsian self and the anti-self to prevent deception and to load either position with risks."[29] Although this characterization too is inadequate, the poem is closer to being a work in which Shelley seeks to push back the encroachments of sad reality onto his beautiful idealism of moral excellence, and perhaps recognizing the impossibility of doing so, retreats into the moral censures of the preface without being able to abandon completely his view of the Poet as an ideal being.[30]

---

[27]Though I deal only with *Alastor,* my method of analysis can be applied to the other two works, which are also sentimental poems.

[28]For instance R. D. Havens, "Shelley's 'Alastor,'" *PMLA,* 44 (1930), 1098–1115.

[29]Wasserman, *Shelley,* p. 34.

[30]Both Wasserman and Albert Gérard tend to see *Alastor* as a full-fledged debate. Wasserman finds two opposing (and clarified) points of view within the poem. Gérard finds a similar debate between German idealism and English respect for nature, the latter point of view being found (presumably) in the preface, since the poem itself is a "demonstration *a contrario* where the hero is made to follow the logic of idealism to its ultimate developments" ("Alastor, or the Spirit of Solipsism," *Philological Quarterly,* 33 [1954], 219). The preface does, it is true, reveal an incipient desire on Shelley's part to dissociate himself from his hero, a

The narrator and the Poet, far from representing contrary positions, are essentially similar beings, like Wordsworth and his younger sibling in "Tintern Abbey." The dialogical tendencies inherent in the form of frame-narration are thus diminished by the fact that dialogue is conceived on the sentimental model of kinship and affinity rather than dissent: the emotional kinship of an older survivor with his lost and defeated younger self. Just as the Poet has pursued "Nature's most secret steps / . . . like her shadow," the narrator has sought to unveil the "inmost sanctuary" of nature (ll. 81–82, 37–38). Just as the Poet is already "alienated" (l. 76) even at the period when he is alleged to be in harmony with nature, the narrator is a "desperate alchymist" (l. 31) who seems curiously ill at ease in his Wordsworthian environment. The conclusion suggests itself that the Poet is not the narrator's opposite but his epipsyche, that the relationship between the narrator and the Poet thus duplicates the relationship between the Poet and his epipsyche, and that both function as narrative paradigms for the relationship between poet and poem in the creative act. In the same way as the Poet's epipsyche fails to take him beyond himself into a higher, less ambiguous, perfected self, so the narrator's epipsyche fails to still his "obstinate questionings" (l. 26) by taking him beyond his peculiarly mixed existence of "awful talk" and "innocent love" (ll. 33–34), into the pure unmixed innocence that he seeks through the Poet and images in the two swans (ll. 275ff.). The Poet continues trying to still his obstinate questionings by pursuing his epipsyche; and the narrator too tries to mask the central failure of *his* quest by idealizing a being whose frail power is no more than a "decaying flame" (l. 247), a fading coal.

At the heart of the poem's failure is its inability to come to terms with the deeply ambivalent nature of the epipsyche and of life itself, because of a belief that poetry should avoid ambivalence

---

desire which counteracts the Shelley-narrator's concluding identification of himself with the Poet through the lyre image. But the central problem in the poem is surely not solved by saying that the Poet should have been a man speaking to men. And indeed so unsatisfactory is this way of condemning him that Shelley immediately goes on to condemn the multitude with whom the Poet should have associated himself as blind, torpid, and above all (like the Poet himself) selfish. In so doing he is compelled once again to exalt the Poet as one who was good and died young, and his impulse toward dissociation ends by reassociating him with what he nevertheless dimly perceives to be inadequate.

and depict life in a more simple and perfect form: "the image of life expressed in its eternal truth."[31] Shelley was obviously sensitive to the ambivalence of life. Yet as Milton Wilson points out, the skepticism that characterizes him as a thinker tends to be minimized in his poetry.[32] The Poet of *Alastor* is seen as impossibly perfect:

> all of great,
> Or good, or lovely, which the sacred past
> In truth or fable consecrates, he felt
> And knew.
>
> [72-75]

Yet the same Poet's vision of the epipsyche is a deeply ambiguous and troubling experience. It does not simply offer him "Knowledge and truth and virtue . . . / . . . and poesy" (ll. 158-160). It seems to couple "truth" with a terrible and convulsive experience, which points toward the abyss and toward a deep truth which the author of "A Defence of Poetry" does not contemplate:

> Does the bright arch of rainbow clouds,
> And pendent mountains seen in the calm lake,
> Lead only to a black and watery depth?
>
> [213-215]

The ideal is grasped, as in "Hymn to Intellectual Beauty," as a dark shadow and not as a bright substance ("Hymn," ll. 59-60); its effect is like that of the Shape in *The Triumph of Life,* who strews the gazer's mind "beneath / Her feet like embers" (*Triumph,* ll. 386-387). Where the vision comes from and what it is are uncertain: whether it is a product of innocence or experience, a vision that comes from the platonic realm without a name, or a projection from within that must inevitably be haunted by the possibility of its own death because it is born of a mortal source. The epipsyche, which is intended as a more perfect form of an already perfect Poet, seems instead to show the Poet an ambivalence in himself, and to point him toward his own "treacherous likeness" (*Alastor,* l. 474), his own soul and its doubts.

The peculiar and terrifying vacancy that descends on the Poet

---

[31]Shelley, "A Defence of Poetry," p. 281.
[32]Wilson, *Shelley's Later Poetry,* p. 219.

after this experience is a product of the need to blot out the content of his vision. This need is imposed by the inherited association of vision with illusion. Yet the duality of the Shelleyan epipsyche externalizes as image what is recognized intellectually by theorists such as Sartre, who see in the act of imagination something profoundly destructive and self-annihilating. Because the need to imagine an ideal arises only from the fact that this ideal is not possessed, because the imagination thereby posits its object as absent or even nonexistent, the imagination must enter its own nothingness to disclose the very reality that it seeks to transform. Although elegy is a sentimental form, the existence of *Alastor* in the mode of elegy rather than prelude and manifesto (like *Epipsychidion*) tacitly concedes the nothingness and death at the heart of vision. *The Triumph of Life,* in which Shelley has revised his concept of art to include suffering as well as joy, reveals how the doubleness of imagination can become a source of both triumph and limitation to the poet. But the Poet of *Alastor* can accept kinship only to the beautiful, and as a result the bright flowers depart from his steps (ll. 536–537), as the joy drops from the forms of the multitude in *The Triumph of Life.*

A troubling ambiguity about whether the source of vision is internal or external is of crucial importance here. The narrator seems to invoke an external source of inspiration, the "Great Parent" (l. 45), so as to convince himself that his epipsyche (the Poet) is real, and that his exaltation of the Poet is not just

> the dream
> Of dark magician in his visioned cave,
> Raking the cinders of a crucible
> For life and power.
>
> [681–684]

Yet the source of his vision seems to be a phantasm that "Has shone within me" (ll. 40–41). A similar ambiguity arises in the case of the Poet's epipsyche. It appears to be sent by "The spirit of sweet human love" (l. 203). Yet as he follows it he obeys "the light / That shone within his soul" (ll. 492–493). For the Poet as for the narrator, the external source seems reassuring, while the internal source opens up a world of doubts and ambiguities:

> Hither the Poet came. His eyes beheld
> Their own wan light through the reflected lines
> Of his thin hair, distinct in the dark depth
> Of that still fountain; as the human heart,
> Gazing in dreams over the gloomy grave,
> Sees its own treacherous likeness there.
>
> [469-474]

Because the internalization of vision does not mark a belief in the self as a source of value, so much as a doubt as to the reality of the ideal, Poet and narrator constantly mistake inner vision (or imagination) for external vision (or perception). Wordsworth sought to argue that the imagination could bestow a light on external nature and yet receive that light *from* nature, because the act of perception was a cooperation of inner and outer lights in which a value projected from within already existed outside. But Shelley's similar desire to hypostatize vision by transferring it to the external world relies on a confusion rather than a cooperation of epistemological theories. As we have seen in "A Defence of Poetry," the active process of illuminating something is mistakenly felt a passive mirroring of ideal forms, so that imagination can claim for itself the assurance that what it is illuminating is really there. Thus when Shelley actually faces the possibility that the source of vision may be within, he seems to be struck with a sense that his dreams are *pure* projection, with no corresponding form in the external world. His characteristic image for inner vision is not the light which radiates outwards (an image which he feels compelled to use in conjunction with the mirror), but the magician groping in his cave,[33] an image that Plato has loaded with skeptical implications, and the related image of a dark well, which has narcissistic overtones (*Alastor*, ll. 457-474). From the doubt that the possibility of inner vision seems to raise, there arises the basic structure of the Shelleyan quest as an idealism which evades skepticism, a search for an external ideal which evades the intentionality and ambiguity of an image projected from within. But the fact that Shelley must rely on a logical sleight-of-hand to pro-

---

[33]*Alastor*, ll. 681-684; "Mont Blanc," ll. 44-48; "Hymn to Intellectual Beauty," ll. 49-52.

tect his vision from its own solipsism invites the reader to see
through his strategy, and perhaps marks Shelley's incipient questioning of his own idealism.

Yeats, who depicted Shelley as governed by a desire for synthesis, and as seeking through the image of a visionary moving
"among yellowing corn or under overhanging grapes" a mask for
what he was not, suggests that Shelley uses "automatonism" or the
evasion of inner conflict to "hide" from himself and others the
"separation and disorder" that lie behind his representation of
the ideal poet.[34] Automatonism is perhaps a useful characterization of the psychology of the sentimental text, which is oriented
toward idealization, yet objectifies the total content of the psyche,
and which must therefore replace censorship with blindness. *Alastor* evades its own recognitions on two levels. The Poet, like Prince
Athanase, seems not to know that he is being consumed by a
strange suffering, for "there was drawn an adamantine veil / Between his heart and mind" ("Athanase," ll. 87–88). The narrator
seems to know, but not wholly to face, the mortality of his epipsyche. The veil, adamantine in resistance to its own transparency,
marks the unenforceable psychological bifurcation by which conscious representation seeks to be innocent of what it contains.

The peculiar misprision of interior projection as external vision
is one means which the poem uses to avoid the nothingness of its
own idealism. The surface conformity of the poem to the pattern
of quest narrative, which is oriented toward an external goal,
seems to confirm this misprision. Again, the fact that the narrator
must depict the Poet's boat as entering the whirlpool twice
suggests an initial reluctance to confront the destructive force of
the poem's imagery. Moreover the emphasis on the ascending
movement of the whirlpool, which is described as rising "Stair
above stair" (l. 380), reveals a desperate (if unsuccessful) attempt
to wrest from nothingness a kind of ascent toward epiphany,
which reaches its climax in the celebration of the Poet as a "surpassing Spirit" (l. 714). Similar in spirit is the ending of *Epipsychidion,* where the elision of death in a Wagnerian *liebestod* conflates
nihilism with ecstasy and reveals a view of poetry as the alchemical

[34]W. B. Yeats, *A Vision* (London: Macmillan, 1936), pp. 108–109, 141–144, 95.

conversion of existence into its opposite, the narrative of particular facts into poetry. The rhetoric of *Epipsychidion* claims to transform death into life, and therefore the real into the ideal. Because the poem is written in the first person, there is, moreover, no *external* vantage point from which to take a bearing on the self-enclosed rhetoric of a visionary discourse. But *Alastor* differs from the later poem through the inclusion of a narrator who survives the visionary, and remains to perceive immortality as death, thus becoming the reference point for the reader's deconstruction of the literal meaning behind the narrator's sentimentalized and figurative representation of the Poet's career. In *Adonais*, similarly about the death of imagination, the skeptical distancing of questioner from visionary through the separation of the mourners from Adonais himself is finally annulled when the mourner (Shelley) sentimentally transcends his own perception of temporality to merge with the Poet. But in *Alastor* the Poet's death returns the narrator (despite himself) to those disturbing charnels and coffins that he had sought to evade by turning his attention to something outside himself. It thus internalizes the darkness of the epipsyche as a darkness which haunts the very act of representation, considered as a flight from the nothingness of consciousness to substance and immortality. Unlike the two swans—the psyche and epipsyche present to each other in the physical plenitude of nature—the narrator reaches the Poet only through an act of imagination, which sets the latter in the space of the unreal. Whether the Poet has a historical existence is unclear. The poem's overt form as biography and quest masks its real existence as meditation and dream (l. 682). Poet and narrator never meet, and the Poet's death is thus only the consolidation of a vacancy which from the beginning lies concealed in the narrator's elegiac attempt to represent an absent Poet as embodying the living presence of his vision. Significantly, although the narrator tries to evade the nothingness of his "dream / Of youth" (ll. 669–670) by making a phantom of the actual world and postponing reality to some afterworld that the Poet is presumed to inhabit (ll. 696ff.), he perceives the Poet in the materialist, almost atheistic language of decomposition. This depiction of the Poet undermines the poem's concluding sentimental assertion of a higher transcendent realm with reference to which the fiction of a logocentric discourse can be preserved.

The climactic image in which the Poet's body is represented as a wind-harp (ll. 703–705) takes us to the point where the poem's idealization verges on its own deconstruction. We cannot but be aware that the "divinest lineaments" of the Poet, through which the wind plays, are in fact the remains of his decaying corpse. Because the lute is a metaphor for poetry, and because the narrator had previously compared himself to a lyre (l. 42), the image seems to sum up and expose the relationship between figure and ground that has characterized the poem from its opening. In "A Defence of Poetry" Shelley distinguishes between the narrative of actuality and poetic narrative: the one is "a mirror which obscures and distorts that which *should* be beautiful," while the other is "a mirror which makes beautiful that which *is* distorted."[35] But here the attempted sublimation of reality through image and figure is grotesque, not "poetic." By a kind of downward transformation, it draws attention to the very reality it had intended to transmute and reveals "the secrets of anatomy and corruption" behind the "surface" of poetry.[36] The image, finally, becomes a focus for the inadequacy of the poetic process, as Shelley defines it, to cope with the world, as he envisages it.

What Yeats called automatonism perhaps enables Shelley to elide the deconstruction of idealism consequent upon including, within a rhetorically single-minded text, a conflict of epistemological perspectives or an incompatibility of figure and meaning. But the term "automatonism" also suggests the failure of the dialectical separation of mask from life, of epipsyche from psyche. By its very transparency, the sentimentality of this poem verges on irony and invites the reader to assume the role later assumed by Rousseau, who makes explicit the subtext of vision which is the knowledge within imagination. Whether a final deconstruction of its idealism is intended by Shelley to be part of the hermeneutics of his text is extraordinarily difficult to say.[37] The inclusion of a

[35]Shelley, "A Defence of Poetry," p. 281. Italics mine.
[36]Ibid., p. 293.
[37]The problem here is not whether *Alastor can* be read as partly ironic, but whether its *intention* is sentimental or ironic: whether the irony is accessible to a

preface thematizes the act of reading, and may thus provoke in the reader a critical self-consciousness (similar to the alienation effect in drama) toward the poem's aesthetics and its sentimental depiction of its two central figures. But Shelley also seeks to make this critical distance impossible, through conventions of elegy which demand the reader's sympathy and assent, his emotional identification with the narrator in the communion of grief. This incipient but incomplete insight is what makes the sentimental text so problematical, and at the same time so pivotal, in the nineteenth century's reexamination of an idealist aesthetics.

It is evident that Shelley's poetry can be read as a suppressed debate between his idealism and his skepticism. It is tempting, moreover, to see his work as involved in a progressive deconstruction of its own assumptions. But the pattern assumed by Shelley's poetic career is not that of initial delusion followed by a progressive demystification of idealistic illusions. Rather it is a pattern of alternation between idealism and a skepticism that is first confronted long before *The Triumph of Life*. The coexistence of Shelley's skepticism with his idealism reveals the compensatory and sentimental nature of this idealism, and seems, therefore, to invite deconstruction. On the other hand, the alternation between skepticism and idealism is symptomatic of a certain resistance to deconstruction, which is reflected in the fact that *The Triumph of Life* is a revision rather than a reversal of *Alastor*. A similar search for a

---

formalist analysis, or whether it emerges only in a hermeneutic analysis, in which a rebellious reader supplies the irony that the text resists. In practice, though not in intention, sentimental texts usually contain ironic elements, and ironic texts retain sentimental, utopian elements. But these complicating elements are not conscious ones. I have tended to classify Shelley's poem as sentimental because its irony is not internalized within the poem, through a narrator who takes a consciously ironic attitude toward a visionary protagonist. In this it differs from a predominantly ironic poem such as Keats's *Isabella*, where the narrator attempts to see through his deluded protagonist. On the other hand, *Alastor* is somewhat more complicated than the normal sentimental text, because the inclusion of a preface raises the possibility of an author who is different from the narrator within the poem. As suggested, the preface induces in the reader a higher degree of self-consciousness about the process of interpretation, and perhaps invites us to resist the text because it does not completely complement the text. On the other hand it must be added that while the formal existence of a preface distances us from the text, the tone of the preface is probably more sentimental than ironic.

language that mediates betwen irony and idealism, this time in the mode of lyric rather than tragedy, is behind "Mont Blanc."

"Mont Blanc" stands in relation to the "Hymn to Intellectual Beauty" very much as Shelley's final poem stands in relation to *Alastor,* revising the myth of the ideal as *The Triumph of Life* revises the myth of the epipsyche. The "Hymn" and "Mont Blanc" (which was written shortly afterwards) are not so much unrelated cele-brations of beauty and power respectively, as poems that converge on the same problem: the mind's need to transcend life by posit-ing some transcendent, form-giving fiction, and the manner in which this transcendent force is specified. In both poems an es-sentially Apollonian element that gives meaning to life (In-tellectual Beauty, the mountain which might repeal fraud and woe) is inextricably linked to something called Power: a force indifferent to meaning, like the Zeus who rapes Leda in Yeats's poem. The "Hymn" and "Mont Blanc" are distinguished mainly by the manner in which they relate these elements: in the first case through the sublimatory rhetoric of hymn, and in the second through the skepticism of interior dialogue. "Mont Blanc" sub-sumes the "Hymn." It returns, through the dialectical separation of mountain and ravine in the third stanza, to the earlier poem's separation of Beauty from the triumph of life. But it then reexam-ines the process by which the imagination hypostatizes its desire to transcend life by identifying this desire with a form in the physical or spiritual world.

The "Hymn" does not actually begin with Beauty, but with an evocation of Power which distinguishes it from its unambiguously platonic source in Spenser: "The awful shadow of some unseen Power / Floats though unseen among us,—" (ll. 1–2). That Shelley capitalizes the word "Power," while leaving it in a lower case else-where in the poem (l. 78), suggests that it is more than just a synonym for an unseen "force" or "being". Although the power is later named as Beauty (l. 13), the dark implication of the first line continues to shadow it. The descriptions of Beauty in pastoral metaphors of flower, cloud, and music (ll. 8–10) are complicated by the strange image of it as "darkness to a dying flame" (l. 45)—an image which violates the expected association of Beauty with light and the human self with darkness. This Beauty, dark-ness and not flame, is alleged to be capable of illuminating the "dark reality" (l. 48) of which it seems itself to be a part. Yet throughout the poem, and not just in these lines, it is a presence that can be conceived only as absence and shadow, a being that is accessible only as nothingness. The ecstatic encounter with Beauty in the fifth stanza seems Dionysiac rather than celestial: something which is the product of "poisonous" thought (l. 53) and is destructive of the very world of nature that it is supposed to consecrate. Thus it seems clear that there is in Shelley's conception of Beauty a kind of lacuna, which reflects the frequent Romantic tendency to liberate representation from life and then question such idealism by basing the rhetoric of affirmation on an imagery that puts the validity of positive belief in doubt. Shelley imagines an ideal which must constantly consume itself because it internalizes the very reality from which it is supposed to deliver the mind. Like "Mont Blanc" and the "Ode to the West Wind," which are openly about the ambiguously creative and destructive potential in life, the "Hymn" is about Power and mutability. What distinguishes it from the other two poems is a certain resistance to its own conclusions, which is reflected in the neotheological and therefore sentimental tendency of hymn: the tendency to believe in salvation by a pure and unambiguous Meaning that is outside life and therefore immune to it.

It is with the deconstructive disclosure of the intimacy between meaning and Power, and later with the significance of that intimacy for the process of mental representation, that "Mont Blanc" is concerned. The "everlasting universe of things" (l. 1) is life itself, inescapably ambivalent: "Now dark—now glittering—now reflecting gloom— / Now lending splendour" (ll 3-4). Whatever ultimate cause subtends this universe manifests itself in human history as Power, which is here identified not with the mountain but with its agent, the river (l. 16). Yet because we do not see the mountain in the second stanza, we know the meaning of life only as a Power which resists even as it seems to subtend Meaning. This Power is not so much demonic as ambivalent: it expresses itself through waterfalls as well as glaciers, but it does not seem to shape the world of nature to any particular end. Through the description of his own mind as a "legion of wild thoughts, whose wandering wings / Now float above" the "darkness" of the ravine (ll. 41-42), Shelley suggests the mind's attempt to idealize life by rising above its obscurity, like the skylark in the poem of that name. But he also suggests the gap between representation and reality which produces the return to "the still cave of the witch Poesy" (l. 44). The characterization of poetry at this point seems significant. To borrow from Yeatsian terminology, poetry is not the "primary" vision of the soul, which seeks out reality and leaves "things that seem,"[38] but rather the skeptical descent into the variousness and complexity of life:

> Seeking among the shadows that pass by
> Ghosts of all things that are, some shade of thee,
> Some phantom, some faint image;
>
> [45-47]

It is into this state of doubt that Shelley (in the third stanza) suddenly introduces the mountain, which seems to rise toward a point of illumination beyond "The veil of life and death" (l. 54). The sudden appearance of the mountain must be read in the context of the work of other poets such as Wordsworth (in his ascent of Snowdon) or Coleridge (in his "Hymn Before Sunrise"), who use the mountain as the focus for a holistic vision of life that has transcended the vale of mutability and consecrated a region where there is "encroachment none" (*Prelude*, xiv, 50). We must ultimately see Shelley's poem as a deconstruction of the visionary idealism associated with epiphanic ascent and with modes, such as prophecy, that rhetorically simulate ascent. But the purpose of the third stanza is to repeat (though in a more tentative way) the attempt of the "Hymn" to envision an intelligent principle above the world of change. The association of Mont Blanc with "gleams of a remoter world" recovered through a kind of anamnesis (ll. 49-50) platonizes the mountain, and also recalls the voice "from some sublimer world" in the "Hymn" (l. 25). This is not to deny that some lines in the third stanza are deeply pessimistic, but these lines (ll. 63ff.) concern the vale and ravine rather than the mountain. The mountain remains an image of transcendence; the clear, if inaccessible, antithesis of the ravine. The stanza moves toward its climactic statement that the mountain, previously silent, has "a voice" and can "repeal / Large codes of fraud and woe" (ll.

---

[38]W. B. Yeats, "A Dialogue of Self and Soul," *The Collected Poems of W. B. Yeats* (London: Macmillan, 1950).

80–81). Here the mountain is confirmed as "The source of human thought" (l. 5), and is made the instrument of the poet's legislation, by an essentially unreal projection of human values into the external world. But the representation of the world as rational is not able to tame the chthonic gods of earth. The fourth stanza is concerned with a reentry into the world of the ravine, which deconstructs the momentary idealization of the mountain. This is perhaps the most pessimistic stanza in the poem, dominated by the cycles of mutability, the "city of death" (l. 105), and the loss of "life and joy" (l. 117). Power in this stanza is destructive rather than creative: it produces no rainbows, and leads only to the dark blue ocean which Byron was to celebrate in despair. Although the mountain is still remote, its distance from the ravine is now spatial rather than categorical and moral. Here for the first time the mountain too is named as "Power" (l. 96), as something alien to humanization, whereas it had previously been the source of human thought above the stream of time. The changing relationship between ravine, mountain, and river is of significance as allowing us to chart the poem's internal dialectic. Although he does not identify the mountain and the ravine, in this stanza Shelley no longer argues that one can separate the source of things from the manner in which this source descends into human time, the ideal from the real world. Such a separation, at any rate, accomplishes nothing: it does not repeal the disappearance of man's "work and dwelling" (l. 118) into the original oneness of life.

Yet this vision of an implacable power, which perpetuates things as they are, no more sums up the meaning of life than the earlier sense of the mountain as a revolutionary and transforming force. In some way "Mont Blanc yet gleams on high" (l. 127). It promises the meaning which it refuses by its silence, and therefore teaches faith in the ultimate rationality of things, but also doubt before the power of actuality. It does so because its very existence as a form which is physically present yet spiritually vacant provokes the mind into constantly constructing and deconstructing its ideals: into living with both sides of its own ambivalence. This perhaps is the sense in which the mountain, no longer the "source" of human thought, continues to "govern" thought (l. 140).

In the final lines the speaker wins an equivocal victory, in turning from the landscape to the perceiver and suddenly making
"Mont Blanc" a poem about itself, rather than a poem bound to
the mountain:

> And what were thou, and earth, and stars, and sea,
> If to the human mind's imaginings
> Silence and solitude were vacancy?

                                                        [142-144]

But the final claim for the autonomy of imagination is enigmatic,
not apocalyptic. Silence and solitude are, after all, not very different from vacancy. Although the mountain would be nothing to
the mind if imagination did not represent it and convert it from
fact into figure, to repeal the vacancy of life through an Apollonian act of imagination is to grow aware of that very vacancy,
which may be the dark ground of the figure. The imagination is a
paradoxical faculty, because it is something which sees through
itself in the moment of maximum exaltation. The vision of the
mountain as alternately intellect and power is simply a way of
externalizing this sense that the imagination is both greater and
no more than actuality, or in the imagery of the "Hymn," that it is
a source of both transfiguration and darkness. The human mind's
imaginings, which have the last word in the poem, are the totality
of the poem's images and not just the Promethean abolition of
fraud and woe. They include, though they are not summed up by,
the ironic and desublimating descent into the ravine of Life in the
fourth stanza. What is canonized in the last lines is, therefore, not
the oracular control of the poetic heart over time, but the very
process of poetry as the dialogue of the mind with its own nothingness.

Shelley does not, however, stay with the recognitions of "Mont
Blanc." The epistemological and therefore abstract mode of the
poem makes the resolution reached here a provisional one, arrived at through a withdrawal of the mind into lyrical privacy,
rather than through an engagement of the self in the narrative of
life. In *Prometheus Unbound* Shelley once again speaks as *vates*, in
the context of a communal poetry, rather than as scribe of his own
doubts. Thus, although Bostetter's charge that the fourth act of

Prometheus Unbound represents a "switching off" of the critical intelligence[39] may seem extreme, there is here too a repetition of the tendency we have been discussing to press beyond the ambiguities of skepticism to the finality of a holistic vision of the universe. Hence perhaps comes one's sense that there is a discontinuity between the Demogorgon of Act II, whose volcanic and amoral power reveals the imagelessness of truth, and the Demogorgon of Act IV, who participates in the "perpetual Orphic song" (IV. 415) of language and wrests a positive truth from the imagelessness. As Harold Bloom says, "In Act IV the imagination of Shelley breaks away from the poet's apparent intention, and visualizes a world in which the veil of phenomenal reality has been rent, a world like that of the Revelation of St. John, or Night the Ninth of *The Four Zoas.*"[40] The three acts which culminate in the writing of *The Cenci* are more tentative. If Demogorgon does not actually "negate" Shelley's "images of desire," as Yeats puts it,[41] he is, like Mont Blanc, a skeptical image of power, a symbol of the fact that the deeply indifferent energy of the historical dialectic may yield either beauty or the rough beast of anarchy. The imagelessness of his truth does not derive from the inadequacy of the means of human expression in relation to an ideal truth that is superior to language, as in the essay "On Love,"[42] but from a basic silence at the heart of things which refuses to be defined and yields no ultimate assurances. Asia in her visit to Demogorgon seeks to learn a dogmatic truth and speaks of the veil as having fallen (II.iv.2), thus comparing the discourse of her own heart to revelation. But Demogorgon refers her to the intentionality rather than the autonomy of the transforming imagination. In his equivocal and indirect answers he allows the discourse of the heart to come up against a wall of silence which allows it to hope, but only in solitude and monologue, and without the support of dialogue with a transcendental source. Shelley seems to take up again the ambiguities he had felt in *Alastor* about the source of vision and therefore the power of merely human ideals, when he has Panthea say that it is "lonely men" seeking certitudes who

[39]Bostetter, *The Romantic Ventriloquists,* p. 193.
[40]Bloom, *The Ringers in the Tower,* p. 96.
[41]W. B. Yeats, *Essays and Introductions* (London: Macmillan, 1961), p. 420.
[42]Shelley, "On Love," p. 170.

convert the oracular vapor into something positive, "and *call* truth, virtue, love, genius, or joy, / That maddening wine of life" (II.iii.4–7; italics mine).

Asia's visit to the Cave of Demogorgon may be read as an intratextual allegory of the creative process, an episode in which the text, by a process of autorepresentation, reflects on the status of its own vision. From Demogorgon's skeptical statement that the mind has no access to ultimate truth (II.iv.114–116), Asia attempts to draw the positive conclusion that the imagination, in the absence of objective verification and denial, is free to represent reality as it wishes:

> So much I asked before, and my heart gave
> The response thou hast given, and of such truths
> Each to itself must be the oracle.
> One more demand; and do thou answer me
> As mine own soul would answer.
>
> [II.iv.121–125]

What she argues for is a radical subjectivism of the imagination as a mythmaking power which guarantees itself on the basis of emotional truth. Paradoxically, she concedes that there is no transcendent authority for her vision, yet also nullifies this admission by elevating the voice of her own soul into a transphenomenal principle. But what Demogorgon has in fact said is that the mythmaking power of imagination is a self-projection which opens itself up to negation as well as to confirmation. Representation, the attempt to image the imagelessness of truth in language, must therefore involve a ceaseless dialogue between the possible being and the possible nothingness of human myths. In this passage, one of the most crucial in the play, Shelley calls into question his own, essentially Romantic, sense of language as the true voice of feeling. The view of language which emerges from Demogorgon's responses to Asia is profoundly antimystical and antilogocentric. Shelley continues to view imagination as a shaping rather than a self-consuming power. But the power is one that puts itself perpetually at risk in a world which furnishes no guarantees, internal or external.

Like the vacancy that the hero of *Alastor* must and cannot confront when he looks inside himself, Demogorgon reveals the ulti-

mate impossibility of affirming the epipsyche as objectively real
and therefore as attainable within this or another existence. Far
from promising the cancelation of the cycles in a linear and progressive movement toward the far goal of time (IV.289), the vision
of history in which he involves us can also point toward the cyclical
gyres of Yeats, in which an apocalyptic power enters history at
moments of crisis, and transforms the world for good or for evil.
The consequences of this idea for poetry are momentous. They
make it difficult to sustain a view of poetry as the language of the
epipsyche, and suggest instead that it must incorporate into itself
the specter of its own self-doubt—not as a failure which follows
the moment of vision without negating its intrinsic truth, as in
Bloom's version of Shelley's myth, but as a darkness which *actually*
lies within the moment of vision, like the Shape within the rushing
splendor of the chariot of Life.

In *Prometheus Unbound*, Shelley takes up his own earlier conten-
tion that "language is arbitrarily produced by the imagination and
has relation to thoughts alone," and describes his play (in the
preface) as using imagery "drawn from the operations of the
human mind."[43] There is a certain irony in this characterization
of the play as mental drama or metatheatre. Nothing tangible
actually happens in the play. The Love and Wisdom of the concluding act are allegorical personifications, signs rather than
things. Through a series of metaphors involving veils, images,
and reflections,[44] Shelley's text seems to turn back upon itself in
order to reflect on its own status as image and representation
rather than physical fact. The action takes place in a space outside
the space of history: a mental space that risks implication in the
ambiguities of the historical process if it seeks to embody itself in
fact and event, and accepts a certain abstraction if it does not
achieve such embodiment. Fittingly, Prometheus can work his
desires only on the phantasm of Jupiter, a fact which comments
on literature as an act that modifies or reshapes images, not
events.

It is clear in the account of the Magus Zoroaster (I.191–216)

---

[43]Shelley, "A Defence of Poetry," p. 279; "Preface to *Prometheus Unbound*," *Poetical Works*, p. 205.
[44]*Prometheus Unbound*, I.193, 661–662; II.i.112–113; III.iii.44–62, iii.160–166;
IV.58, 81–82, 206–213.

that only death permits the reunion of image and reality, and
then perhaps not through the transformation of image into reality, but through a kind of cessation of desire: an entropic reabsorption of life by the shadows of unconsciousness. Yet it is a very
much less ambiguous view of poetry as an activity that makes and
validates images of beauty and truth upon which the fourth act of
Prometheus Unbound seems to insist, with its statement that "our
singing shall build / In the void's loose field / A world for the Spirit
of Wisdom to wield" (IV.153–155). Here the affirming power that
is only conditionally given to Eternity itself (IV.565) is uncondi-
tionally claimed for song, and the result is that however cautious
the logic of the play must be about establishing the kingdom of
love, the celebration of that kingdom for almost one act, in language that thinks itself capable of hypostatizing what it describes,
leads one to wonder whether a part of Shelley does not actually
believe that the millennium has arrived. Shelley's theory of signs,
which is idealistic in using the skeptic's sense of a gap between
linguistic and real structures to liberate language from the need to
reflect life, is also genuinely skeptical and Kantian in claiming for
such representation a regulative and not a constitutive role. But
toward the end *Prometheus Unbound* becomes profoundly post-
Kantian and idealistic, in its tendency to image the act of representation paradoxically as the veil which represents its own unveiling. Moreover, the sense that the relation of image to reality is
prefigurative rather than intentional, that the image we see in the
water is the image of a temple already "built above" (III.iii.161),[45]
cancels the very gap it admits between the phenomenal and the
noumenal. It also displaces, into a comforting and eschatological
hierarchy of image and substance, the Magus Zoroaster's agnostic
recognition that the images of desire may be the phantoms of
further phantoms, that the "mask" of life (to use a Yeatsian term)
may be death rather than resurrection.

That Shelley was aware of the potential for further horror in
history is apparent in the shapelessness that links Demogorgon's
darkness (II.iv.2) with the imageless horror that Beatrice cannot
voice (*The Cenci*, III.i.107–111). It is also apparent in the careful
pattern of alternatives set up within *Prometheus Unbound*, in

[45]Cf. also III.iii.49–58.

Panthea's two dreams, in the two chariots that Asia sees, and in the chastening words that the Furies set against the idealism of Prometheus. For much of its duration Shelley's play is a dialogue between a hero and choric figures such as Earth, and is therefore conscious of an aesthetic model in which poetry must internalize in its very form a submission before life which may reveal the illusoriness of its claim to have transcended life. Shelley's refusal to imitate Aeschylus (like Blake's refusal to follow Milton) is part of an attempt to rewrite a body of myth which Schlegel had described as "Tragedy herself."[46] Equally, however, the generic ancestry of *Prometheus Unbound* involves its author in the deconstructive debate between Romantic prophecy and Greek tragedy that we will later see in Keats's Hyperion poems.

But somehow the fourth act seems to press beyond the skepticism of drama into the singleness of lyric: to abolish the uncertainties of dialogue where no one point of view can be said to be absolute, and to create instead a polyphonic hymn in which different voices are part of a single harmony. It is difficult to read the fourth act and not to feel that its faith in the capacity of language to transform fact repeats the fallacies of the idealizing mirror. At issue here is an evasiveness in the way the poem specifies its own illocutionary status, or the kind of speech act that it is. The uncertain combination of drama and extended ode is only one of the ways in which the discourse of innocence is *first* recognized as having a merely positional status as a claim made within a certain psychological context, and *then* reaffirmed through celebration as possessing a transcendent status independent of the dramatic situation that has called it into being. The text's hesitation between the mode of mythological prophecy and that of allegory[47] reflects a similar doubt on Shelley's part about the status of his discourse. Personified characters such as the Hours make their appearance in the play, and capitalized abstractions such as "Youth," "Hope" and "Love" are frequent. Allegory, as a form of language in which signs can only indicate abstractly,

---

[46]A. W. Schlegel, *A Course of Lectures on Dramatic Art and Literature* (1809–1811), trans. John Black (rev. ed., London: Henry Bohn, 1846), p. 93.

[47]For a discussion of Romantic concepts of allegory, particularly Coleridge's distinction between allegory and symbol, see de Man, "The Rhetoric of Temporality," pp. 174ff.

recognizes the impossibility of an incarnational and unmediated language. Similarly prophecy, though Blake may not have realized it, is purely hypothetical and therefore intentional. "The prophetic individual," as Kierkegaard notes, "does not possess the future, he merely intimates it. He cannot assert it."[48] On the other hand, *mythological* prophecy, the form extensively used by Blake, claims for aesthetic vision the status of revelation, and for the literary sign the capacity to embody this vision concretely and immanently rather than to indicate it allegorically and transcendentally. Prometheus and Asia are mythological rather than allegorical characters. That naming, instead of abstract personification, is used to identify the characters of myth is crucial for its claim to the privileged status of unmediated vision. That Blake invents his own gods rather than borrowing them from Christian tradition is, moreover, an egotistically sublime assertion of the power of mental representation over reality. Friedrich Schlegel, in his "Talk on Mythology," emphasizes the invented rather than received quality of the new Romantic mythology as a way of stressing the authority of human creativity, and insists also on mythology as a form of language which hypostatizes aesthetic idealism by uniting it with realism and giving a body to the otherwise abstract spirit.[49]

In combining inconsistent modes of discourse, Shelley is more complicated than Blake. The relation between text and subtext in terms of authorial intention is therefore difficult to characterize. Between his early use of a sentimental rhetoric in *Alastor* and his later use of it here, he has confronted the limits of idealism in "Mont Blanc." Hence, whereas *Alastor* seems to repress its own ironies, *Prometheus Unbound* seems rather to defy them in the belief that the reader, too, will discover a commitment to the sacred necessity for hope. But the image of Demogorgon stands as evidence of how much that is characteristic of Shelley such idealism leaves out. As there are two levels of discourse, so also are there, in effect, two Demogorgons: one who has existed since all

[48]Søren Kierkegaard, *The Concept of Irony* (1841), trans. Lee M. Capel (1965; rpt. Bloomington: Indiana University Press, 1971), p. 277.

[49]Friedrich Schlegel, *Dialogue on Poetry and Literary Aphorisms* (1797–1800), trans. Ernst Behler and Roman Struc (University Park: Pennsylvania State University Press, 1968), pp. 81–83.

eternity, and another (without mythological precedent) who is suddenly born for the purpose of destroying Jupiter.[50] The inclusion of the first Demogorgon, the original oneness that precedes the invention of innocence, discloses a hesitation about the power of poetry to reconstitute reality by creating a second Demogorgon, who "represents" Power as Intellectual Beauty.

Beyond Panthea's lines on the desire of lonely men to give a positive meaning to the "maddening wine of life" lies the recognition that the lifting of the painted veil may lead us to the triumph of life as well as the reign of love. That possibility is not worked out in *Prometheus Unbound*, but Shelley's final poem finds a source of strength in the ambiguity that had destroyed *Alastor:* the poet's doubt as to whether the encounter with the epipsyche reveals to him "the spectres of his own dead thoughts, or the shadows of the living thoughts of Love."[51]

Shelley's career thus encompasses two of the moments earlier discussed: the sentimental and the tragic. In his avoidance of the ironic he is revealing, if not characteristic. Skepticism is often the precursor of irony and negation, but in Shelley skepticism, on the contrary, involves a positive awareness of the possibility of both hope and despair. Where it becomes irony and threatens to consume rather than complicate certitudes, it is sentimentally repressed, as in *Alastor*. Even after he has embraced a creative skepticism in "Mont Blanc," Shelley's fear that the imagelessness of truth might lead to an infinitely ironic view of the creative act is evident in his defiant use of the logocentric mode of myth in *Prometheus Unbound*. Shelley's final poem is not logocentric, yet it manages to triumph over its own deconstruction of a visionary poetics. Here again the mode of the poem is important as an index to Shelley's view of the status of the poetic voice. As a dream-vision in the medieval tradition, *The Triumph of Life* stands beyond irony and the desacralization of language: its gaze into the abyss is nevertheless a visionary act, and its fallen hero is privileged because he suffers.

Coleridge can also be said to have faced the dilemma of human

---

[50]See Pierre Vitoux, "Jupiter's Fatal Child in *Prometheus Unbound*," *Criticism*, 10 (1968), 115–125.
[51]Shelley, "Una Favola," *Prose*, p. 359.

creativity in his late poem "Constancy to an Ideal Object," where
the central image is that of the Brocken-specter, the shadow of
oneself that the rising or setting sun casts onto a bank of mist and
surrounds with a halo. Through this image, which he recognizes
in *Aids to Reflection* as being at once a glory and a specter,[52] a
projected form of man's own being and a negation of it that
stands against him as an utterly alien shadow, Coleridge seems to
find in the very duality of imagination a source of power. At first
there is doubt as to whether the moment of vision is authentic, an
awareness of the moment as an atmospheric illusion, the projection of a brain-sick desire. The yearning for an objective epipsyche that is known once and for all to be true is so great, that the
disillusioned mind reacts to the absence of final truth by viewing
all existence ironically as a shadow. But gradually the poem develops a sense that the image with a glory is not the less true for
being projected from within, and in fact that it is stronger than
the desperately clung-to ideal beauty, because it acknowledges
within itself a doubt as to its own power. Thus, in the last lines of
the poem Coleridge accepts the condition of being in half-
knowledge and doubt. He draws from the admission of his own
finiteness an ability to believe in his own power. In "Mont Blanc"
Shelley too had created a symbol of his own power and of something alien that stood against him. And in the double-visaged
image of human creativity at the heart of *The Triumph of Life* he
encompasses both the night which closes on vision, and the world
which endures within the mind's nothingness.

[52]Coleridge, *Aids to Reflection*, ed. Thomas Fenby (Edinburgh: John Grant,
1905), p. 220.

CHAPTER 3

On the Threshold of Tragedy:

Keats's Late Romances

Pale limbs at bottom of a crystal well.

—Isabella

Keats's poetry is concerned with two very different locales of
the mind: the fictive enclosure in which the urn and the nightingale are placed and the mortal world outside the space of illusion,
or the paradise with which *The Fall of Hyperion* seems to open and
the ancient and tragic sanctuary in which its action takes place.
The "naive" definitions of poetry which abound in his letters
make it clear that he identified the aesthetic process with the
creation of the first kind of space, that he saw the poem, in Harold
Toliver's phrase, as "its own kind of transforming locality capable
of reshaping nature in art,"[1] or in Bloom's phrase, as "a
heterocosm . . . an alternative world to that of nature."[2] But an
initial desire to absorb poetry into pastoral, dream, or prophecy
gradually yields to a sense of the need to emerge from the very
genres of imaginative enclosure that simulate a discourse innocent of or transcendent to experience. Both sentimentality and
irony are modes of excess which arise in the transition between
the two locales, and repress but also herald the birth of tragedy.
Keats's first major work, *Endymion,* is a typically sentimental
poem. It is similar to *Alastor,* but less skeptical in its use of a
narrator who subverts rather than rationalizes a story of dejection, and in its use of a preface that serves as an *apologia* for rather
than an analysis of the poetics of vision. But since *Alastor* has

[1] Harold Toliver, *Pastoral Forms and Attitudes* (Berkeley and Los Angeles: University of California Press, 1971), pp. 11–12.
[2] Harold Bloom, "Yeats and the Romantics," in *Modern Poetry: Essays in Criticism,*
ed. John Hollander (New York: Galaxy, 1968), p. 501.

already received some attention, the following two chapters will concentrate on the narrative poetry of Keats's final years: his later romances and his Grecian poems.[3] These romances are products of the second major moment in Romanticism: the ironic moment. That they are chronologically intertwined with *Hyperion*, which marks a reversion to the sentimental, is significant. Equally significant is the fact that Keats, like Shelley in *Prometheus Unbound*, sees through his sentimentality only to assume it as a conscious mask in poems like "Ode to Psyche" and "Ode to Autumn." The linear movement of his career from the sentimental, through the ironic, to the tragic, is not without interruptions that help to define the nature of the resolution finally reached.

Shelley's career reveals an oscillating movement from quest-romance, which imprisons the seeker in the world of temporality but endorses his struggle for transcendence, to the prophetic style of *Prometheus Unbound*, which elevates the creative self above time, and finally to the dream-vision, which once again presents the creative self as journeying within rather than above a landscape of events. The quest-narrative undertaken in *The Revolt of Islam, Alastor,* and *Epipsychidion* shares with the mode of dream-vision an acknowledgment of temporality. But the two differ significantly in that the former seeks to eliminate the obstacles to desire, whereas the goal of the latter is insight. Keats's career reveals a

[3]I assume that Keats's major lyrics rehearse on a smaller scale the positions assumed in his narrative poetry. I do not treat the odes in detail partly for reasons of space, and partly because the problem of parallel explorations undertaken in the genres of lyric and narrative has already been discussed with reference to Shelley. The "Ode to a Nightingale" can be seen as a sentimental poem, while the "Ode to Autumn" and the "Ode to Psyche" (cf. Chapter 4) belong to a psychologically later category: that of the defiantly sentimental poem which wears the mask of idealism, having already crossed the threshold from blindness into insight. "Psyche," for example, admits that the divinity of the human imagination is a mental construct, but it names this construct as myth and not as fiction, to borrow a distinction from Paul de Man (*Blindness and Insight*, p. 18). The "Ode on Melancholy" and the "Ode on a Grecian Urn" approach a tragic understanding, though the former perhaps goes too far in the direction of the Dionysiac and the latter (cf. pp. 133–136 below) goes too far in the direction of the Apollonian. Where the odes differ from the narrative poetry, however, is in the authority of the recognitions reached. They experiment with, rather than commit themselves to, different positions. By using a brief and occasional form, Keats avoids giving any one of these positions priority over the others, and leaves the poems deliberately indecisive as a group.

similar movement from the sentimentalism of quest-narrative in *Endymion*, to the more defiant sentimentalism of prophecy in the third book of *Hyperion*, and finally in *The Fall of Hyperion* to the mode of dream-vision, which preserves the visionary power of the self, but in a world where sublimity is attained by confronting the suffering gods of the subconscious. It differs in that Keats's detour into irony makes his embrace of tragedy more somber and unequivocal than that of Shelley.

As in the case of Shelley, Keats's choice of a particular literary mode functions as a metonymy for his assumptions about literary discourse in general. His modification or abandonment of certain modes thus indicates crucial shifts in those assumptions. Central to his later poetry are his ironic revision of the romance mode and his tragic adaptation of a Hellenic mode which, in earlier German Romanticism, is one of the prime expressions of the sentimental imagination. One of the genres most central to the Keatsian canon is that of romance, which from the late eighteenth century onward assumes an increasing importance. Romance, an antimimetic mode, is initially distrusted by writers like Richard Hurd,[4] but then favorably contrasted with the realistic novel by writers such as Clara Reeve, who elevates it to the status formerly enjoyed by the epic.[5] A work such as *The Progress of Romance*, while not of great theoretical importance, lays the scholarly groundwork for the metaphysical legitimizing of an aesthetics based on the ideal and imaginary rather than the actual. The large number of Romantic works concerned with the quest for an ideal or with the union of two lovers, psyche and epipsyche, needs no comment. Four of Keats's six major narratives fall within the genre; all deal with the search for a love beyond mortality and with the desire for escape from the present into a mythic or imaginary space. As we observed before, romance is perhaps the form most central to Romanticism itself, considered as an aesthetics of corrective illusion. Its rehabilitation as a significant literary genre, when taken in conjunction with other trends such as the increasing acceptance

[4]Richard Hurd, *Letters on Chivalry and Romance* (1762; rpt. New York: Garland Publishing Company, 1971), pp. 93–104.
[5]Clara Reeve, *The Progress of Romance Through Times, Countries and Manners* (1785; rpt. New York: Garland Publishing Company, 1970), pp. 86–88, 4–16.

of a poetics of genius over a poetics of imitation, marks a major
shift in pre-Romantic aesthetics toward the affirmation of poetic
discourse as something that transcends temporality.
Endymion is described by Keats as a poetic romance. In contrast,
his decision to seek in tragedy rather than "golden-tongued Romance" the appropriate model for aesthetic discourse—evident in
his praise of Shakespeare, "a miserable and mighty Poet of the
human Heart," over Boiardo, "a noble Poet of Romance"[6]—
testifies to a growing belief on his part that he must give up the
protection afforded by an art based on what Nietzsche calls "the
commonly accepted categories . . . [of] illusion and beauty."[7]·This
belief culminates in Keats's final poem, where he diverges from
Wordsworth, Shelley, and Blake (and his own earlier *Hyperion*),
and casts his prelude to poetic autogenesis in the mode of Greek
tragedy rather than of pastoral, romance, or mythological
prophecy. It is, therefore, a matter of some significance that three
of Keats's late narrative poems are not tragedies, but poems which
explore a buried, tragic core in the mode of romance. The peculiar choice of a mode associated with illusion to represent the
mind's encounter with the grotesque, the ironic, and the melodramatic is not only of significance for Keats's career. It also
stands as an instance of a larger phenomenon already noted with
reference to Shelley's *Alastor:* the indecisiveness which attends the
Romantic deconstruction of innocence.

Keats's late romances are, of course, romances of an unusual
kind. The reader's assessment of where Keats stands in relation to
an aesthetics of illusion will depend on his answer to the question
raised by Stillinger—whether these poems are to be classified as
romances or antiromances.[8] The question is not a simple one, for
the romances are at variance with one another, and even with
themselves. For purposes of analysis, it may be useful to point out
that the problem arises at the level of rhetoric rather than narrative. The late romances share an underlying concern with the

[6]Keats, *The Letters of John Keats 1814-1821,* ed. Hyder E. Rollins (Cambridge:
Harvard University Press, 1958), II, 115.

[7]Nietzsche, *The Birth of Tragedy,* p. 101.

[8]Jack Stillinger, *The Hoodwinking of Madeline and Other Essays on Keats' Poems*
(Urbana: University of Illinois Press, 1971). My disagreements with Stillinger
should not obscure the importance of a book which, in many ways, makes possible
a new reading of Keats's poems.

status of an aesthetic discourse that sublimates reality, and they construct narratives which concur in revealing the limits of such a discourse. Their ambivalence, therefore, arises from their attitude toward their own conclusions: from the rhetoric they explicitly choose as a way of representing what *should* be (and not what is) the function of poetic language. In this choice they are experimental and finally indecisive, and they explicitly raise the problem of hermeneutics by including a narrator who, in effect, serves as a means of authorial abdication, by handing over to the reader the problem of selecting a rhetoric.

Lamia, Isabella and *The Eve of St. Agnes* are all concerned with the relationship between illusion and the actual world. The protagonists of these poems hold to illusions which were once those of Keats himself and which are, to some extent, shown up in the course of the narratives. But if realism forces the narrator of *Lamia* to see through Lamia, it is less than clear whether he wishes to do so. In both *Isabella* and *The Eve of St. Agnes* the distance of the modern narrator from the old romance he is retelling raises the possibility that the rhetoric of illusion—often sentimental and cloying—is not his own, and is being placed before us ironically. But we cannot entirely dissociate this language from a narrator who does, after all, transmit it to us with some sympathy. What is puzzling about these poems is their emotional indeterminacy, their lack of a clear rhetoric of fiction which will enable us to classify them as either sentimental or ironic in tone, as either romantic or antiromantic. Instead they seem to be ironic and sentimental at the same time, to deconstruct and yet to cling to illusion.

The problem lies in the nature of the reality that replaces illusion. Numerous critics have pointed to a shift of emphasis in Keats's later career. Chief among them is Stillinger, who breaks with the idealistic view of Keats supplied by such critics as Wasserman, and emphasizes the ironic treatment of figures such as Isabella and Madeline who shut out the demands of the real world through neurosis or dream. Stillinger correctly identifies the irony that distinguishes these poems from an earlier romance such as *Endymion*, which remains sentimental in its quest for an absent visionary ideal. But in assuming that the movement from illusion to reality is a constructive and therefore willing one, he fundamentally mistakes the emotional structure of Romantic irony as distinct from comic irony, the irony of a Hoffmann as distinct from that of a Shakespeare.[9] The reality of these poems is not a mellow, autumnal world of human and natural process. It is rather a reality in which the mind is exposed to the "eternal fierce destruction" underlying the Apollonian surface of things. If the protagonists of these poems are shown as ineffectual in holding to illusions which were once those of Keats himself, the nature of the reality that awaits them—the dead world at the end of *The Eve,* the disinterred head in *Isabella*—makes the exposure of their illusion more ambiguous and less satisfying than Stillinger suggests.

These poems are concerned not simply with the deconstruction of illusion, but also with the radical homelessness of a poetic voice that is unable to make habitable the empty space that follows the expulsion of illusions. From this homelessness arises the tendency of Keats's romances to become rhetorically indeterminate, to accept and yet to expose both the language of romance itself and those figures who exist in a state of illusion. *Isabella* is a case in point. The poem is the product of a complex consciousness, deeply ambivalent toward "simple Isabel" (l. 1), who is at once neurotic and wronged, and toward the "simple plaining" (l. 388) of a poetic tradition which celebrates her refusal to face reality. When he first wrote the poem, Keats himself was evidently unaware of the extent to which he had linked the illusions of idealism to those of neurosis, because in writing to a friend he telescoped together stanzas from different parts of the poem, in such a way as to eliminate the intervening ironies which undercut their idealism.[10] When he came to explain his reasons for not

[9]The limitations of the view of Keats put forward by the so-called Harvard Keatsians are excellently summed up by Morris Dickstein: "in presenting Keats . . . as a tragic humanist, they have also tended to reduce him to a realist and a naturalist. . . . The true schism in romantic poetry is not between the real and the ideal but between self-consciousness and vision, between nakedness (in Yeats' sense) and myth, between existential anguish and imaginative self-transcendence. The true poetry of actuality for the Romantics is not a poetry of naturalism and 'process' but a poetry of personal quest or crisis, a poetry of self-confrontation" (*Keats and His Poetry* [Chicago: University of Chicago Press, 1971], p. xiv).

[10]Thus Keats telescopes stanzas xii–xiii with xxx, omitting the realistic account of the economic infrastructure of Isabella's world in stanza xiv, and the ironic comments on Boccaccio in stanzas xix–xx. Both of these might cause us to question the romanticizing of the lovers (*Letters,* I, 274–275).

publishing the poem, he had apparently grown blind to the genuineness of his sympathy for Isabella, and suggested that he had intended an ironic reading, but had not adequately guided the reader toward it: "There is too much inexperience of live [sic], and simplicity of knowledge in it.... There are very few would look to the reality.... If I may so say, in my dramatic capacity I enter fully into the feeling: but in Propria Persona I should be apt to quiz it myself."[11] That he did publish the poem suggests that he later changed his mind, and found it possible to read it in such a way that it met the criterion of ironic realism.

The fact is that the poem cannot easily be reduced to a homogeneous reading and is, in this respect, characteristic of the ironic text. Although Keats repeatedly dissociates himself from the sentimental diction of Boccaccian romance[12] and emphasizes his concern with "wormy circumstance" (ll. 385–392; cf. ll. 145–156), he also begins with a long account of the lovers' early felicity which is not in Boccaccio, and shares in the nineteenth-century idealization of a love that earlier writers had censured as illicit.[13] A sense of impatience with Isabella, which demands that the poem leave the enclosure of neurotic fixation for the real world, is complicated by a sense of pity for her, which conscripts reader and

[11]Keats, *Letters*, II, 174. Richard Woodhouse also writes to John Taylor in 1819 that Keats thought of *Isabella* as "mawkish" (Hyder Rollins, ed., *The Keats Circle: Letters and Papers and More Letters and Poems of the Keats Circle* [Cambridge: Harvard University Press, 1965], I, 90).

[12]Boccaccio's own narrative is written in a bare, almost unadorned manner. There is nothing elaborate in his account of the meeting of Isabella and Lorenzo, which occupies about three lines of matter-of-fact prose. But what is in question here is the nineteenth-century interpretation of Boccaccio, which was by and large an idealistic one. One might refer to Coleridge's poem "The Garden of Boccaccio," and to Hunt's statement that "Boccaccio shall build a bower for us out of his books . . . and we will have daisies and fresh meadows besides" (*Autobiography*, [London: Smith, Elder, 1850], III, 21). Both implicitly credit him with the kind of lush imagery found in *Endymion*. Hazlitt and Hunt are involved in an idealistic rehabilitation of Boccaccio, and insist that he is not a writer of lascivious tales, but a high-minded writer of tales of sentiment (Hazlitt, "Review of Sismondi's *Literature of the South of Europe*," *Complete Works*, XVI, 47–48; Hunt, notes to *Bacchus in Tuscany*, quoted by Herbert Wright, *Boccaccio in England, Chaucer to Tennyson* [London: Athlone Press, 1957], p. 335). Further discussion of nineteenth-century views of Boccaccio can be found in Wright, *Boccaccio in England*, pp. 331–478.

[13]For instance Boccaccio himself and George Turberville (*Tragic Tales*). Unlike Keats, these writers are not without sympathy for Isabella's brothers, who are seen as having some justification for resenting their sister's involvement with someone of lower station.

narrator alike into keeping faith with her fruitless idealism. This ambivalence is reflected in the poem's bifurcation into two styles: a romance style replete with the sentimentality of Leigh Hunt and B. W. Proctor, and a harshly realistic style that questions the rhetorical excess and disinters the subterfuges of romance convention. The uneasy and vacillating dialogue between the two styles is never so simple as to amount to a debate between romance and reality. Because of the shadow that one style casts on the other, passages of seemingly blind idealism are constantly complicated by the possibility of self-irony; and conversely, in emphasising the realistic elements in the poem we can never be sure that we are not modernizing Keats more than he himself wished to modernize Boccaccio.

Because *Isabella* is a poem which moves toward excavation and disinterment, it is in the end the realistic element that predominates: the refusal to make "old prose in modern rhyme more sweet" (l. 156). What the reader must ask, however, is not why or whether Keats chose to present Isabella ironically, but why it is that he could not present her as ironically as he himself (and some of his critics) would later have wished. While the elements that block the poem's movement toward antiromance arise from a desire to shield the mind from a psychically destructive abandonment of illusion rather from a commitment to romance, those elements are, nevertheless, present in the poem. They are not inadvertent.[14] The poem represents its own discourse as alternately romantic and antiromantic, because it is uncertain whether to value or devalue illusion. The fact that the choice is not between simple idealism and simple realism, but between an idealism recognized from the outset as spurious and compensatory and a realism that remains unpalatable makes the poem's choice of discourse even more indecisive. In this and the other two poems, by self-consciously thematizing the fictions and conventions of what might be considered a naive mode, Keats circles round the question of whether poetic rhetoric should be a mirror that blinds us to reality or a disclosure of existence. But the complex network of hesitations and qualifications within the ro-

---

[14]I would disagree here with the view of Stillinger (*The Hoodwinking of Madeline*, pp. 31-45).

mances leaves this question unresolved. Images of art as fictionalization, enclosure, appearance, coexist uncertainly with a sense that art involves disclosure, excavation, an entry into the impure.

Romantic aesthetic theory too is concerned with the two different mental locales discussed at the beginning of this chapter, and with the radical revision in its sense of the aesthetic sign that movement from one to the other necessitates. The very concept of a Romantic art or sentimental art that is separate from the ideal constitutes an emergence into the real world and an incipient deconstruction of the naive. That it is such a half-hearted emergence, and seeks to reverse itself by recovering what it has left, perhaps reflects the impossibility of an unmediated transition from a "naive" art to one that gazes directly into the core of an eternal fierce destruction. Works such as Senancour's *Oberman* or Shelley's *Alastor* see their own mode of being as characterized by the wasting of illusion, and turn in compensation to the various modes of the naive whose fictitiousness their own existence has already exposed. But the ironic text, though explicitly antiromantic, is as half-hearted in its embrace of reality as is a sentimental work like *Alastor*. The problem facing these works that alternately confront and evade the possibility of a dark core at the heart of illusion is one that Nietzsche points to when he observes both that "art is not an imitation of nature but its metaphysical supplement, raised up beside it in order to overcome it," and that such art nevertheless cannot be a transcendence of reality.[15] Words such as "fiction" and "illusion" give expression to a certain psychic need to hold the contemplating self apart from the destruction of the real world, but by the same token they are unable to conceive of a separation which is not also evasion. A redefinition of aesthetic illusion—its structure and its effect—is thus the task that faces nineteenth-century aesthetic theory. Keats's poetry prior to *The Fall of Hyperion* includes examples of both the ironic and sentimental modes, and his work as a whole therefore provides an opportunity to study, within a single career, the larger dialectical development of Romantic poetry toward a new model of discourse.

[15]Nietzsche, *The Birth of Tragedy*, p. 142.

The Eve of St. Agnes is for most critics a central exemplification of Keats's idealist poetics. Bernard Blackstone speaks of a "vertical pattern" in the poem which is one of "growth upward through successive levels of existence" and a "horizontal pattern" which is one of "concentric circles of attainment" to a central peace "at the heart of 'Endless agitation'."[16] Wasserman sees the poem, in its concern with the relationship of dream to reality, as acting out Keats's speculation that the imagination "may be compared to Adam's dream—he awoke and found it truth."[17] In a similar vein, Frye speaks of Keats as "a poet of the *temenos,* the marked off holy place, the magic circle of *The Eve of St. Agnes,* with the lovers inside and the hostility and bitter cold outside."[18] The lovers' dream appears as another version of that perfection so insistently sought by the Romantic mind in Greece, in the pastoral world, in the dell where Blake's Lyca is found. It preserves, among the untrodden ways of the unconscious, an innocence that is sheltered from involvement in time and history, though overlaid by such oppressive institutional realities as Madeline's family, and the dead society of the opening. The double romance motifs of dream and *Eros* are significant. The discourse of eroticism reaches toward a language free of restraints, and the association of this discourse with dream rather than sexual perversion asks us to view such a language as an upsurge of the authentic self rather than as a product of decadence.

Whether the ambiguous ending of the dream[19] permits us to read it naively as an analogue for the ideal is open to debate. But one thing is clear, even if the lovers are spirited away to the Enchanted Castle in a protective storm which resembles those clouds sent by classical goddesses to hide the hero from his enemies. Keats's poem does not share in this liberation from reality. The last stanza suddenly introduces a narrator whose presence until now has not been an overt one. In thus including within itself both the thing represented and the figure who represents it,

[16]Blackstone, *The Consecrated Urn* (London: Longmans, 1959), pp. 275ff.

[17]Earl Wasserman, *The Finer Tone: Keats' Major Poems* (1953; rpt. Baltimore: The Johns Hopkins Press, 1967), pp. 101ff.

[18]Northrop Frye, *A Study of English Romanticism,* p. 160.

[19]Herbert Wright, in his article "Has Keats' 'Eve of St. Agnes' a Tragic Ending?" (*Modern Language Review,* 40 [1945], 90–94) argues, though somewhat literal-mindedly, that the lovers die in the storm.

the poem destroys what one might call the realist illusion, and sets its narrative within a framed and fictional space:

> And they are gone—aye, ages long ago
> These lovers fled away into the storm.
>
> [370–371]

The presence of the narrator prevents Keats's poem from coinciding with the lovers' dream. It compels this poem, like the two great odes, to live in the space of a discontinuity between the real and the ideal, between the empty verbal sign and the thing it evokes but does not possess.

How the narrator relates the terms of this discontinuity is difficult to assess. The ending of the poem seems simultaneously sentimental and deconstructive in its view of the role of aesthetic fictions. The lovers are made to fade away, reduced to two-dimensional phantoms (l. 361) who achieve an enviable immunity from time, yet do so by an illusory simplification of reality. Woodhouse notes that Keats wanted the poem to end with a "Change of Sentiment—it was what he aimed at," but adds significantly that he "affected the 'Don Juan' style of mingling up sentiment & sneering."[20] It seems that Keats feels that art should affirm the supreme fiction against the pressures of reality, but sees through the illusoriness of such affirmations. The lovers are at once perfect and flat, without substance. The distance which separates the narrator from his fiction is simultaneously one of yearning and one of dissociation from a naive ideal that seems irrelevant to human concerns.

So far we have spoken as though a break successfully defended against in the dream-world of the lovers erupts in Keats's poem in the differential realm of narration, which separates the human narrator (willingly or unwillingly) from his fiction. The integrity of the dream itself has appeared to remain unviolated: the internal doubts that beset Keats's poem have seemed to reflect uncertainties about the value of art in a mortal world, but not questions about the nature of art itself, which remains what Shelley calls a soul within our soul,[21] a world undivided by complexity. Yet there is evidence that the dream exists in this state only so long as

---

[20]Rollins, ed., *The Keats Circle*, I, 91.
[21]Shelley, "On Love," p. 170. This is Shelley's definition of the epipsyche.

it is confined to the insubstantial fantasies of St. Agnes' Eve and that Keats recognizes this fact. From the moment that the actual, physical Porphyro enters into it, the dream is haunted by darker possibilities, by a sense that the pure is being profaned by the impure, implicated in the alien world of storm and darkness that it seeks to exclude:

> Her eyes were open, but she still beheld,
> Now wide awake, the vision of her sleep—
> There was a painful change, that nigh expelled
> The blisses of her dream so pure and deep.
> . . . .
> "This is no dream, my bride, my Madeline!"
> 'Tis dark; the icèd gusts still rave and beat.
> "No dream, alas! alas! and woe is mine!"
>
> [298-301, 326-328]

What is in question here is the change that the dream undergoes in the process of being made real, and therefore mortal. Porphyro's eyes are no longer "spiritual and clear" (l. 310) but clouded by the possibility of his death (l. 315) or deception (ll. 328-333). Paradoxically it is the realization of the dream, seen as an aesthetic victory in Keats's letter, that contaminates and exposes it. And paradoxically, without this exposure, this encounter with both sexual deception and the storm, the lovers could not achieve that consummation of their dream which forever bars a return to the unravished innocence which is the very purpose of dream. Through metaphors of dreaming and waking Keats explores both what it is to exist in the state of pure ideality, pure illusion, and what it is to find the dream true. Before the intrusion of Porphyro, which introduces a duality, an ambivalence, into the silent unity of dream, Madeline's innocence is associated with paradise(l. 244): her condition is that of an angel "free from mortal taint" (ll. 223-225). Yet there is clearly something regressive about such innocence, "As though a rose should shut, and be a bud again" (l. 243). If she is "Blissfully havened both from joy and pain" (l. 240), she is also in a state of fixation, "Blinded alike from sunshine and from rain" (l. 242). Her dream can remain as it is only if she renounces the desire which is part of the impulse behind dreams, and (like Orpheus) does not look behind her, does not ask that her dream refer to a reality outside itself and leave the space of the fictive (l. 234). The image of the "tongueless nightingale" which dies "heart-stifled" in the purity of its dell (ll. 206–207), lacking a voice to communicate its song, suggests how unacceptable it is to leave the dream in the untrodden region of innocence. Yet to cross the barrier of fictitiousness that keeps the dreams of St. Agnes' Eve innocent is to menace their very existence. From this contradiction arise the moral questions that Porphyro's deceptive stratagem raises: questions which Stillinger sees as contributing to the ironic deconstruction of romance,[22] but which in fact reflect Keats's own enormous anxieties about the relationship of the fictive to the real. Our uneasiness about Porphyro's machinations, our suspicions about his conduct, expose the dark underside of a dream that is not content to remain in the sphere of fiction but seeks consummation in the real world. Keats's poetry of this period shows an increasing awareness that, while pleasure may attend the dreams of gods, the realizing of man's dreams inextricably mingles joy with pain. Without Porphyro's stratagem there could be no consummation of the dream, and the consummation of the dream inevitably entails a loss of innocence, metaphysical as well as sexual. That Keats himself was very concerned with the problems of consummation we know from his comments on this poem to Woodhouse.[23] An uneasiness about Porphyro's tactics which constantly complicates our identification with him reveals the difficulty that Keats himself has in embracing the loss of innocence involved in actualizing the dream. Somehow he would like to respect both Porphyro and Madeline, to realize the dream and yet keep it virginal and untainted.

Thus the problem is not really whether Porphyro's conduct in covertly entering the bedroom of a young girl is ethically excusable. Rather it is a question of what the stratagem reveals about the ambiguities at the heart of dreams that awaken into reality and seek to transform it. Such dreams must make use of the very reality they are designed to negate, if they are to have any existence at all. In the course of the poem Keats grows aware that the

---

[22]Stillinger, *The Hoodwinking of Madeline*, pp. 74–82.

[23]Woodhouse writes that Keats says "he should despise a man who would be such a eunuch in sentiment as to leave a [Girl] maid, with that Character about her, in such a situation" (Rollins, ed., *The Keats Circle*, 1, 92).

consummation of love—and also of aesthetic fictions—requires that a certain deception enter into the sphere of the pure to render it tangible. This ambiguously creative and destructive quality of love is present in erotic, mythological narratives from *Hero and Leander* onwards. But here it reflects also on the radical ambivalence of the incarnate (as opposed to the disembodied) aesthetic sign. It is not so much that the dream is deceptive and must be renounced (the conclusion of critics like Stillinger who see Porphyro as a Satanic figure), as that it contains a deceptive element. At the heart of its brightness it must acknowledge also that wasting of illusion which Rousseau knows in *The Triumph of Life* and which Lycius will prove unable to face in *Lamia*. At the heart of its utopian desire for a restoration of freedom beyond the limits of a hostile society, it must acknowledge contamination by the reality of which it thinks itself innocent.

The dream is thus because it is not a counterworld, but merely a repetition in finer tone, a clarified mimesis of this world. In Keats's letter to Benjamin Bailey (November 1817) on the imagination as Adam's dream, a curious epistemological slip, similar to Shelley's ambiguity as to whether the epipsyche is an external form or an internal projection, allows the dream to be no more than an objectification of present reality. Thus while Keats begins by describing the relationship of the real and the ideal in conventional neoplatonic terms of shadow and substance ("a Shadow of reality to come"), he ends by ascribing ontological priority to the actual, of which the ideal becomes only an emanation: "its empyreal *reflection* . . . its Spiritual *repetition*."[24] Because the actual world as Keats thinks of it in the letter happens to be an idyllic one, there is no immediate problem. But the exuberant tone of this passage belies the more disturbing implications of a monistic epistemology for an idealist poetics which requires some separation of the pure from the impure. In the "Epistle to John Hamilton Reynolds" the problem is faced more openly, and not introduced as an accident of terminology. Here Keats acknowledges that dreams are not foreshadowings of the "material sublime" which liberates us into the country of the rainbow, but are a mental repetition of anxieties present in the real world, a disclosure

[24]Keats, *Letters*, I, 185. Italics mine.

rather than a transformation of the self (ll. 67-72). This holds true not only for literal dreams, but also for waking dreams: the products of aesthetic vision (l. 67). Significantly (though perhaps unintentionally) the work of art within the poem, a pictorial equivalent of golden-tongued Romance, is not related antithetically to the distempered insight which replaces it and which seeks a cure in a return to "new romance" (l. 111). Rather the fictive surface of Claude's painting already contains, in the knife that gleams above an animal about to be sacrificed (ll. 20-21), what Keats will see when he looks behind appearances "into the core / Of an eternal fierce destruction" (ll. 96-97). In so relating the fictive to the real, Keats effectively closes off the possibility that art may offer a return to the ideal: the very possibility of which he tries (somewhat unconvincingly) to persuade himself in the concluding lines.

The Eve of St. Agnes shares with other poems by Keats a self-duplicating structure which enables the poem, through its inclusion within itself of an aesthetic object or aesthetic analogue, to represent the nature of aesthetic representation. The urn and the nightingale provide the most obvious instances of such a procedure. But other examples are the inclusion within a poem of dreams or visions, or of fictional sources (old legends, Boccaccian romances) which the actual poem claims to repeat. This phenomenon of automimesis or self-reflection has two aspects. The fictive analogue within the poem is intended to be a model of what art should be, to project within the inner space of the enclosing poem the ideal that the latter seeks to reach. But because it is a structural repetition of the enclosing poem, it proves to be a disclosure to the latter of what the enclosing poem actually is, and tends to confirm this actuality as normative for art. The dialogue between the intended and actual functions of the fictive analogue is part of a larger dialogue between old and new images of art that constantly complicates Keats's poems.

The crucial importance of the break that occurs in Madeline's dream when she awakens and confronts the real Porphyro should, therefore, be apparent. On the face of it, it has seemed that the fictive analogue of the lovers' dream is utopian in structure, that it projects a realm of pure illusion liberated from the constraints of actuality, and that the lovers take possession of this future as the narrator can not. A certain inhuman frigidity on the part of the lovers seems only the necessary consequence of their immunity from the real. Yet on closer inspection the dream, seemingly enclosed and protected within a world of illusion, turns out to repeat certain characteristics of the narrator's world, and thus to suggest the impossibility of the kind of art that Keats described in terms of the *figura* of Adam's dream. Just as the integrity of Keats's poem is breached at a crucial point by the incursion of a narrator who can not partake of the dream, so also the integrity of the dream itself is broken at the moment when Madeline awakes and recognizes that her dream abuts on the real world. Both moments are fissures in an otherwise closed structure, fissures by which the real world enters the fictional, as a third dimension that at once removes the dream from the flat ideality of romance and makes it vulnerable.

In the midst of a poem that is almost entirely decoration and artifice, it is in fact this vital crevice in the structure of illusion which for a moment humanizes the lovers, removing them from the sphere of those beings—gods and abstractions—who have eliminated the bitter furies of complexity from their veins. For a moment, but only for a moment, the poem stands on the verge of a radically new awareness of the work of art as constituted by its tragic emergence from the ideal. As Michel Leiris has said, the ideal can have meaning only if it embraces something nonideal, something "which draws the beautiful out of its glacial stagnation, as the life of the One passes into the concreteness of the Many at the price of a degradation."[25] It is by no means clear, however, that Keats sees the problem in these terms. While he is aware of the state of ideality as something unreal, and to that extent is hesitant about embracing it, the concept of an ideal that may be contaminated is something threatening and destructive. Impurity is not, as it will be in *The Fall of Hyperion,* the constitutive element in the work of art. *The Eve of St. Agnes* has its place in the process of reassessment that leads Keats toward a new typology of creative artists: one which recognizes that the gods (such as Hermes and his nymph) are immune from experience, but that those who

[25]Michel Leiris, *Miroir de la tauromachie* (1936; rpt. Paris: GLM, 1964), p. 30. Translation mine.

attempt to reproduce such innocence in the human sphere are merely fanatics who have refused to risk their dreams in the real world. But the poem seems sentimentally unwilling to commit itself to so radical a revision in its sense of what poetry is. In the crucial section which begins with Porphyro's intrusion into Madeline's dream, the poem vacillates uneasily between Madeline's desire to preserve the unravished purity of illusion, and Porphyro's desire to awake into reality, his fear of lapsing into the undifferentiated unity of sleep (ll. 278–280, 285–286). The problem of choosing between virginity and consummation, between dreaming and waking, is never resolved but seems somehow to be elided from the narrative. As the dream moves toward the perilous moment of consummation, it is as though illusion and reality are superimposed on each other without ever quite coinciding. A consummation occurs, as Keats was at some pains to point out, but it does not seem to be a real consummation. Madeline and Porphyro become one, but on two different levels, because his consummation is real and hers illusory. Keats's revised version of stanza xxxvi reemphasizes the divergence of illusion and reality within the moment of consummation, and points to something deeply problematic in his notion of the aesthetic sign:

> See, while she speaks his arms encroaching slow
> Have zoned her, heart to heart . . .
>   . . . and still the spell
> Unbroken guards her in serene repose.
> Still, still she dreams, louder the frost wind blows.[26]

The style of this passage is peculiarly ambivalent: it is at once oneiric and physically precise, and seems to combine sexual realism with romantic fantasy. Somewhat unconvincingly the poem compels the marriage of two elements whose divergence elsewhere in the text had made *The Eve of St. Agnes* a work which questioned its own literary mode. The same duplicity that charac-

---

[26] *The Poems of John Keats,* ed. Miriam Allott (London: Longmans, 1970), p. 474n. Keats allegedly introduced the lines quoted above to make the consummation more explicit (Rollins, ed., *The Keats Circle,* 1, 90–92). But they only serve to emphasize an element already present in the lines they replace. I refer to the divergence between two experiences of consummation: that of Porphyro, described in urgently physical language, and that of Madeline, seen through the illusory glaze of dream and enchantment.

terizes the consummation also characterizes the communication of text to reader. The lovers move toward what is supposed to be a happy ending, but their exit is by "a darkling way" (l. 355). In the final stanzas they are ambiguously made to emerge into the reality of the storm and recede into the fictitiousness of old romance. The narrator at once realizes and dematerializes his dream, makes it true, but only on an illusory level.

The peculiar, inconclusive ecstasy toward which the lovers proceed must be seen as a kind of optical illusion, designed to realize the dream while preserving its fictionality and immunity from time. In this manner Keats, by a kind of automatonism characteristic of the sentimental poem, avoids confronting a crucial lacuna in his sense of what happens to the dream when it is incarnated in reality and made to disclose its potentialities. One critic comments that the lovers "demonstrate, by the combination of highly practical actions necessary to escape from their worldly prison and the language of romance with which that escape is described, that they have found the border between the waking and dreaming worlds."[27] Keats might perhaps have wished that he could create a naive poem: a poem in which romance could become real without also awakening into tragedy. But the lacuna whose menace is covered up in the relationship of the lovers to their dream reappears outside their world in the analogous relationship of the narrator to his fiction. Even if we can go against all the canons of logic and believe that the lovers can realize their dream without awaking into reality, we cannot believe that the narrator can keep his dream fictive, pure, and untainted by mortality, while at the same time bringing it to life in the real world. In his world, at least, Adam's dream cannot be simultaneously true and a dream. The failure and sense of anticlimax that intrude into the final stanzas of the poem tacitly acknowledge this problem. The mutually irreconcilable alternatives which confront the narrator raise again the impossible choice between fiction and mimesis that divides Keats's poems considered as works that are concerned with their own epistemological status. Insofar as the dream remains a fiction it also remains something phantasmal,

[27]Clifford Adelman, "The Dangers of Enthrallment," in *Twentieth Century Interpretations of The Eve of St. Agnes,* ed. Allan Danzig (Englewood Cliffs: Prentice-Hall, 1971), p. 115.

unconsummated, a mere intent of consciousness from which the sense of concreteness has evaporated. Its protagonists, in the end, seem unreal. A decorative, antinaturalistic diction and a sense of the tale as existing in a naive genre, whose flatness and resistance to complexity make it alien to the structure of our own consciousness, prevent the narrator from making his dream credible either to his readers or to himself. But equally, and perhaps more persuasively, the storm and the bleak moors stand just outside the circle which the story describes around itself, as evidence that to make this fiction real might be to destroy altogether the fragile foundation of illusion on which it rests.

In a poem such as *Endymion* the desired movement was from the actual world into a fictive space. The intention behind *The Eve* is more difficult to sum up: the movement from reality to dream and from present to past suggests a sentimental attitude, but the final anticlimactic shift of perspective from a sublimated narrative to a mortal narrator seems more deliberately ironic than the similar shift in *Alastor*. The irony, however, seems a postscript which should not be read back into the body of the poem, but should rather be read forward into Keats's next poem. *Lamia,* at first, seems emotionally clearer. Here the movement is from the essentially fictive and simplified existence of Hermes and his nymph to the greater complexities of Lycius' love for Lamia, and from the fairy palace into the real world which exposes it as pretense. The exposure of Lamia as a phantasm, like the digging up of the putrified head beneath the pot of basil and, to a lesser extent, the emphasis on the less than honorable means that Porphyro uses to realize his dream, reveals something tenuous and self-deceptive in romantic illusion, which in turn reflects on the nature of aesthetic illusion. But the deconstructive movement of *Lamia,* seemingly canonized by the bitter concluding quotation from Burton, in no way sums up the emotional ambiguities of the poem. Keats thought that *Lamia* was immune from the complicity in the rhetoric of illusion that marred *Isabella;* and through his allegorical, fabular style[28] and the ironic distance that he maintains from his principal characters, the narrator does indeed try to place

[28]Cf. *Lamia*, II.7-9, 12-15.

himself beyond illusions. But the poem does not quite fit into the mask of irony, inasmuch as the reader accords to Lamia, as well as to Apollonius, the right to represent some portion of the truth. At times Lamia seems deliberately deceptive, as when she claims to have lived for a long time in Corinth or diminishes three leagues to a few paces (1.310–312, 345–346). But at other points the narrator is less certain, and speculates that she may be "the demon's self" or merely "some penanced lady elf" (I.55–56). Significantly, Lamia does not so much die as disappear, perhaps to be reunited with Lycius in some higher realm. She can never simply be seen through like Peacock's Rhododaphne, Thomas Hood's Lamia, or Auranthe in the roughly contemporaneous *Otho the Great*. Thus there is, here too, an imbalance between text and subtext. That Lamia is projected from two radically inconsistent points of view, alternately humanized and demonized, reflects Keats's continuing uncertainty about the value of illusion in life.[29] Ironic and idealistic interpretations are, alike, simplifications, and suggest that in *Lamia* Keats approached some kind of crisis of aesthetic vision: a crisis which both the old image of art as the construction of a fictive ideal and the newer sense of art as disclosure and emergence into the real were inadequate to resolve.

It is possible to see *Lamia*, as Geoffrey Hartman sees the Hyperion poems, in terms of an attempt to develop a "psychotheology of art" and hence an image of poetic vocation more viable than the idealized one characteristic of Romantic theory. In an essay on the problems of poetic autogenesis, Hartman speaks of the rituals that societies have for "the passage out of latency and into the public light," and of the parallel between such rites of passage and the effort of poetic consciousness to emerge from itself or "appear" in the world through a process of individuation.[30] More overtly than *The Eve of St. Agnes*, *Lamia* is about the struggle of

[29]Most critics take a realistic and ironic view of this poem as concerned to expose the demonism of imagination. See C. I. Patterson, *The Daemonic in the Poetry of Keats* (Urbana: University of Illinois Press, 1970), p. 211; Walter Evert, *Aesthetic and Myth in the Poetry of Keats* (Princeton: Princeton University Press, 1965), pp. 275ff.; Stillinger, *The Hoodwinking of Madeline*, pp. 54–55; Blackstone, *The Consecrated Urn*, p. 299. For views more sympathetic to Lamia, see Bloom, *The Visionary Company*, p. 381, and Wasserman, *The Finer Tone*, pp. 166–168.

[30]Hartman, "Toward Literary History," *Beyond Formalism* (New Haven: Yale University Press, 1970), pp. 368–369.

Keats's poetic consciousness to emerge from the enclosed bower of an ideal and innocent art. Two attempts at emergence, both of them abortive, are made in the poem. One involves Lamia's metamorphosis from elfin to human existence; the other involves Lycius' decision to take his love out of the realm of the private and into the public light. In both cases there is an inability to come to terms with the consequences of the encounter with the real world, except through further illusion or death, and a consequent inability to make of the process of emergence a constructive act.

The problem arises from the absence of a vocabulary adequate to respect the conflicting psychological claims involved in poetic emergence. Keats, involved as he is in reexamining the role of art, knows only two images of art: that which he has embraced in the poetry up to and including *Endymion,* and another which reverses his previous assumptions. But the uncertainties of these poems derive precisely from the inadequacy of competing conventional solutions. As Hartman observes of *Hyperion,* the poems's exploration of its own vocation is rendered more painful and complicated by the fact that it takes place because of the failure of existing models for literary or personal growth: "The artist must always find his own way to 'appear.' . . . The conventions at his disposal do not lessen the agony of self-election."[31] The terms of reference in Keats's romances are obviously different from those in the Hyperion poems. But a similarly indecisive movement between illusion and demystification makes known the need for a mode of vision that will respect both claims, and arises directly from the failure to find that third mode of vision.

The Eve of St. Agnes circles around, but does not face directly, the problem of emerging from illusion and latency into the real world. *Lamia,* by contrast, seems committed to the process of emergence, though unable to cope with its destructive consequences. The poem begins with an odd, fantastic account of Hermes' pursuit of a nymph, similar in the playfulness of its style to Shelley's *Witch of Atlas.* The structural separateness of this episode from the main narrative underlines the irrelevance of its assumptions to Keats's poem.[32] Hermes' world stands as an allu-

---

[31] Ibid.
[32] Two useful discussions of the Hermes episode exist. E. T. Norris ("Hermes and the Nymph in *Lamia,*" *ELH,* 2 [1935], 322–325) notes that Hermes resembles

sion to the kind of art Keats had sometimes held up as an ideal: an art of pure illusion and dream, or as Herder said of Greece, an art of "god-like and youthful forms, full of truth in illusion, and of illusion filled with sweet truth."[33] Such an art acknowledges no discrepancy between dream and reality because it is pure fiction, liberated from the claim to reality that gives depth, but also ambiguity to aesthetic appearances. Its gods can experience consummation and take no harm from the loss of their innocence because they are imaginary beings, who play with the semblances of things rather than with their realities. But Keats's poem is defined by its distance from the beautiful mythology of Greece, and by a commitment to enter a world where art can no longer be "unaffronted, unassailed" (l. 101).

In Hermes' world visibility and invisibility, or reality and freedom from actuality, do not seem to be incompatible. The episode of the nymph's ravishment may refer back to problems of realization and fictionalization at the end of *The Eve of St. Agnes*. But in making the nymph visible to Hermes, Lamia does not really violate the invisibility which had kept her protected from the eyes of the profane, as old Angela had done in revealing Madeline to Porphyro, or as Lamia herself must do in revealing herself to all of Corinth. Significantly, the materialization of the nymph is followed by the disappearance of both Hermes and the nymph into the woods where they once again become invisible, removed from the real.

Before her metamorphosis Lamia too enjoys some of the benefits of fictiousness and invisibility. Keats describes how

> she could muse
> And dream, when in the serpent prison-house,
> Of all she list, strange or magnificent:
> How, ever, where she willed, her spirit went;
> . . .

---

the poet and Lycius the dreamer. Wasserman comments that the "legend of Hermes and the nymph and the legend of Lamia and Lycius are explorations of the same system of symbols as it functions under two different conditions" (*The Finer Tone*, p. 164). I would agree with both of these distinctions, although not with the implication that Keats favors the poet over the dreamer or the immortal over the mortal.

[33] Quoted in E. M. Butler, *The Tyranny of Greece Over Germany*, p. 77.

> And sometimes into cities she would send
> Her dream, with feast and rioting to blend.
>
> [1.202-205, 213-214]

Her invisibility is the equivalent to a purely imaginary existence, in which she is able to play with the semblances of things, enjoying them without being involved, unbound by the responsibilities of being visible and human. Yet because she is (or has been at one time) a human being, fictitiousness and reality diverge: the freedom from reality is felt as an imprisonment. There comes a point when she is no longer satisfied with the insubstantiality of being a god, and yearns to possess Lycius in the real world as well as in the abstract realm of ideality.

Yet to live in the real world is also to be compromised by it. The consequences of Lamia's emergence from an imaginary into a human existence are too difficult to face immediately, and the invisible palace into which she retreats with Lycius is an attempt to perpetuate the realm of Hermes within a radically different world. Lamia's serpentine condition suggests what is also suggested by Hermes' dual role as god of dreams and thievery: namely the dishonesty of a state of pure, unbound imagination within human terms. It is not simply Lamia, however, but also Lycius who seeks to enjoy an imaginary existence within the real world. Indeed the poem's complicated movement between emergence and retreat, disclosure and invisibility, may reflect Keats's own ambivalence about what must be given up in the renunciation of illusion.

Illusion, and an increasing insight into the complications of an illusion that exists in the real world, are the central concerns of Lycius' relationship with Lamia. Lycius appears to seek in her some kind of epipsyche that will liberate him from the difficulties of living in a flawed world and "unperplex bliss from its neighbour pain" (1.192). He expects, impossibly, a love that is innocent and yet possessed of the flesh and substance of the real world: "A virgin purest lipped, yet in the lore / Of love deep learnèd to the red heart's core" (1.189-190). Although Lamia herself entices him "To unperplexed delight and pleasure known" (1.327), it is clear that she is never the miraculous being that she seems, and that their love is both more real and more flawed than that of Hermes and the nymph. The narrator insists, for the sake of convention, that the lovers' bliss was "too short . . . / To breed distrust and hate" (II.9-10). But distrust, deception, even cruelty, beset it from its inception. Plenitude and emptiness seem to coexist in the first encounter:

> And soon his eyes had drunk her beauty up,
> Leaving no drop in the bewildering cup,
> And still the cup was full—while he, afraid
> Lest she should vanish. . . .

> [1.251-254]

It is at once an experience which gives new life (1.294-295) and an experience of death (1.322): similar in its doubleness to so many other Romantic encounters with beings whose beauty "pierce[s] like honey-dew / Into the core of [the] green heart" (*Epipsychidion*, ll. 262-263).

Lycius nevertheless persists in seeing Lamia in terms of unalloyed beauty, and is therefore rightly described as "blinded" (1.347). He is blind not because he refuses to see Lamia as demonic (which is only the construction put on her by an unsympathetic philosopher), but because he refuses to recognize her fundamental ambivalence. Human phenomena are inherently incapable of separating the "ambiguous atoms" of life (1.196). The "life" Lamia gives is ambiguous and deceptive. Yet it is, after all, life; and when it is withdrawn Lycius' arms are "empty of delight, / As were his limbs of life" (II.307-308). To imagine a Lamia more beautiful and pure than she really is is to be guilty of self-deception. But to see through her and reduce her to nothingness is equally unsatisfactory. A significant change that Keats makes from the fair copy of *Lamia* reveals his judgment of Apollonius. The latter's climactic statement "From every ill / That youth might suffer have I shielded thee" is changed to "From every ill / Of life have I preserved thee to this day" (II.296-297). Though Keats begins ironically, by feeling that captivation by Lamia is the product of immaturity, he ends tragically by equating it with life itself. Like Rousseau who must experience the Shape all light and her deconstruction by the car, Lycius can no more refuse Lamia's beauty and the subsequent wasting of that beauty than he can refuse to live. And as in *The Triumph of Life*, where the Shape all light proves simultaneously true and deceptive, Lamia's beauty remains real even when it is shown to be illusory. The demonic distortion of the illusory figure that occurs as a result of "seeing through her" in disillusionment does not represent the complexity of life any better than the illusion which it replaces.

At the heart of this poem's complicated oscillation between idealization and deconstruction of Lamia are Lycius' inability to accept that deception and failure are a part of the human enterprise, and Keats's own lack of a vocabulary that will enable him to recognize and accept ambivalence. Lycius is confronted with a love that is radically ambivalent, but he seeks to know only its purer elements: the "full-born beauty new and exquisite" (1.172) without the "pain and ugliness" that underlie it (1.164). Ironically (as Keats perhaps recognizes) it is this very evaporation of disagreeables that makes Lycius' illusion vulnerable to the insight of Apollonius and traps him in the cycle of illusion and reality. The ambiguity of her nature is what gives Lamia a substance and humanness denied to the nymph, without which she becomes an illusion without reality.

But the state of self-mystification that keeps her alive as pure appearance cannot continue, because Lycius is not Hermes. Inevitably he hears the sound of trumpets, and his spirit passes "beyond its golden bourn / Into the noisy world" (11.32-33). If there is something willful and perverse in the movement out of the palace that culminates in Lamia's destruction, this movement is also part of a necessary process of looking too far out to sea and probing beneath illusions. The love of Lycius and Lamia, protected from the contagion of the "busy world" (1.397), is introverted and claustrophobic. The image of an unbudded rose (11.54) aptly conveys its essential quality as a frustration of natural process. Vanity and self-display mar Lycius' decision to publicize his love, but the option of remaining in this artificial paradise is not a real one. To put it differently, his love can have neither value nor solidity unless it is made public and taken into the real world: recognized in marriage rather than kept in the illicit realm of illusion where it exists only for "those two alone, / And a few Persian mutes" (1.389-390).

Through the exposure of Lamia's fairy palace Keats seems to criticize a perfection that avoids the responsibilities of the human, by refusing to suffer and learn. The guests who enter it are freed "from human trammels" and permitted to do as they please (II.210, 219–220). The palace itself appears magically in a street where it is not literally possible for it to exist (II.150–155). We can no more accept this divorce of the imaginary from the laws of the real than Lamia herself could accept her existence in the world of Hermes. For all the palace's elaborate and careful opulence— "The fretted splendour of each nook and niche" (II.137)—there is something frustrating in the artifice of illusion. Lamia, shut up in the intricacies of a palace which endlessly appears and disappears, seems to know the essential impoverishment of her world. It is perhaps for this reason that she consents to her own disclosure. Keats is at some pains to emphasize that she is no serpent, that "She burnt, she loved the tyranny" (II.80–83). She too seems to recognize that only through this destructive entry into the real can her love be truly consummated. But pathetically she knows of no way to cope with the new reality except by retreating into further artifice. Lycius too is unable to cope with the process he has inaugurated, and condemns as demonic the very insight he had invited in publicizing his love (II.289).

The narrative of Lamia has affinities with a group of myths in which the gods sanction human enjoyment of the ideal but deny it real status. Psyche is loved by an immortal, but can experience her love only in the obscurity of the night, where she must imagine what she cannot see. Orpheus, because he is a poet, is granted the unique power of transcending mortality and recovering the dead past. But he recovers it only on a fictitious level, by not seeking to behold Eurydice directly. The illusory, self-canceling nature of poetic fiction is also a concern of Keats's poem, which explores, through the fairy palace and the narrative of Hermes, the sufficiency of illusion as a basis for art. Like Hegel's "beautiful soul," the human desire for an ideal finds itself caught "in the contradiction between its pure self and the necessity felt by this self to externalise itself and turn into something actual."[34] To take the illusion into the real world is to negate it. But to hold it apart from reality, in a realm that separates the ambiguous atoms of bliss and

[34]Hegel, *The Phenomenology of Mind*, p. 676.

pain, is to reduce it to an abstraction. Thus Hegel describes how the beautiful soul

> lives in dread of staining the radiance of its inner being by action and existence. And to preserve the purity of its heart, it flees from contact with actuality, and steadfastly perseveres in a state of self-willed impotence . . . to transform its thought into being. . . . The hollow object, which it produces, now fills it, therefore, with the feeling of emptiness. Its activity consists in yearning, which merely loses itself in becoming an unsubstantial shadowy object. . . . its light dims and dies within it, and it vanishes as a shapeless vapour dissolving into thin air.[35]

It is because Keats is intensely, self-critically aware of the dangers of idealism that the hero of his poem finds himself driven to divulge his ideal to the profane world of action and existence, "the populous streets and temples lewd" (1.352). Yet this proves as self-defeating as the beautiful soul's refusal of reality. If Lycius reduces Lamia to nothingness, so does Apollonius: the former because the blindness of his illusion will not allow a radiance stained by existence, the latter because his awareness of illusion blinds him to its radiance.

Because the ending of the poem does no more than reverse the assumption on which Lycius' faith in Lamia had been based, it does little to solve the underlying problem of how to define illusion so that it can enter meaningfully into the real world. Indeed it may repeat, from the opposite direction, the terminology of perception whose inadequacy the poem exposes. Apollonius' dissipation of Lamia recalls Addison's comments on the imagination:

> We are every where entertained with pleasing Shows and Apparitions, we discover imaginary Glories in the Heavens, and in the Earth, and see some of this Visionary Beauty poured out upon the whole Creation. . . . our Souls are at present delightfully lost and bewildered in a pleasing Delusion, and we walk about like the Enchanted Hero of a Romance, who sees beautiful Castles, Woods and Meadows; . . . but upon the finishing of some secret Spell, the fan-

[35] Ibid., pp. 666-667.

tastick Scene breaks up, and the disconsolate Knight finds himself on a barren Heath.[36]

Addison had confined art to a realm of fictive recreation without bearing on reality. Romantic idealism had preserved intact the Enlightenment opposition of magic and logic and had simply reversed the value assigned to the two terms. Because *Lamia* simply reverses the reversal, and because Keats criticizes his earlier self[37] by way of a rationalist mirror-image of Romantic idealism, this poem remains as unable to break out of the cycle of illusion and deconstruction as *Endymion* was unable to find a point of equilibrium between epiphany and dejection.

In the end the narrator seems to recognize this fact, in distributing wreaths among his principal characters and offering the reader a choice between allegiances that represent equally destructive and inadequate readings of the poem:

> What wreath for Lamia? What for Lycius?
> What for the sage, old Apollonius?
> Upon her aching forehead be there hung
> The leaves of willow and of adder's tongue;
> And for the youth, quick, let us strip for him
> The thyrsus, that his watching eyes may swim
> Into forgetfulness; and, for the sage,
> Let spear-grass and the spiteful thistle wage
> War on his temples.
>
> [II.221–229]

The reader may view the poem in terms of the betrayal of imagination or in terms of the unmasking of error, following either of the two thematic conventions (idealist and realist) with which Keats works in *Lamia*. If we see Lamia sentimentally as a sensitive plant, a pure being withered by contact with a hostile world, we ignore her obvious deceptiveness. If we read the poem ironically as an account of a dreamer's temptation by a delusory and demonic imagination, we ignore the absence of an alternative female figure to draw sympathy away from Lamia and clarify her de-

---

[36]Joseph Addison, *The Spectator* (1753), ed. Donald F. Bond (Oxford: Clarendon, 1965), III, No. 413.

[37]Cf. Newell Ford's comment that *Lamia* is an inverted *Endymion* (*The Prefigurative Imagination of Keats* [Stanford: Stanford University Publications, 1951], p. 142).

monic status: a "pure" figure such as Calliroe in *Rhododaphne,* Erminia in *Otho the Great* or Scylla in the narrative of Glaucus and Circe. It seems that Lamia is neither wholly pure nor impure, and that in her the poem encounters the radical ambivalence of life: its dreams and deceptions. In the essay already cited, Hartman speaks of the Romantic poet's need to find his own ritual for "appearing" in the world, in the absence of adequate literary precedents. By offering us conventional readings of the poem that are so obviously limited, the narrator of *Lamia* simultaneously reemphasizes the need for a way of coping with this ambivalence and confesses his own failure to find it.

It is almost axiomatic that the figure of Lamia is built around the discrepancy of appearance and reality. Appearance, however, can have meanings beyond simple epistemological untruth. Works of art are illusions which "appear" to be something they are not, or represent something which (in a physical sense) is not there. Schiller thus uses the word "Schein" to indicate the phenomena of aesthetic appearance, combining in the German word the senses of radiance and illusion. Indeed it is possible to speak of an extensive Romantic tradition which constellates aesthetic experience in the form of a surface—a rainbow or a shape all light—which is magically liberated from fact and depth. *Lamia* takes its place as part of this tradition, but also as part of a very different attempt to repatriate, through aesthetic typologies that are concerned with depth and implication as well as surface, elements exiled from works of art by an idealist aesthetics. Nietzsche, the prime critical exponent of such revisionary typologies, describes the replacement of a naive art by a more disturbing mode of perception, in which "the intense clarity of the image fail[s] to satisfy us, for it seem[s] to hide as much as it reveal[s]." In such a moment the eye finds itself simultaneously invited "to pierce the veil and examine the mystery behind it," and held back from probing deeper by the "luminous concreteness" of its own illusions.[38]

Questions of sight and insight trouble *Lamia,* and indeed are present as early as "The Epistle to John Hamilton Reynolds," which explores, through its description of a painted canvas, the

[38]Nietzsche, *The Birth of Tragedy,* p. 141.

link between questions of surface and depth and problems of fiction and reality. Nietzsche recognizes, in the writer's need to "look and at the same time to go beyond that look," the necessity of an art that can compound illusion and knowledge, making them transparent to each other. He describes the tragic artist as one who shares with "the Apollonian the strong delight in illusion and contemplation" and yet "denies that delight, finding an even higher satisfaction in the annihilation of concrete semblances."[39] Keats's *Lamia*, however, is committed to the complete deconstruction of illusion. Lamia at first appears as a "lady bright," associated with song and stars and the phenomena of romantic epiphany (1.171, 249, 265). But in the end she is revealed as a serpent, seen through by a knowledge that penetrates behind her appearance to the pain and ugliness that underlie the semblance she tries to create. The fact that Lycius (unlike his predecessor in Burton) dies of his knowledge is evidence that the poem cannot integrate into the epistemology of aesthetic vision the power of Apollonius to see beyond the shape all light to its illusoriness, without making of this skepticism something that corrodes the very shape of art.

At the same time, however, the figure of Lamia—a denizen of two different orders like the Titans in *Hyperion*—belongs to a family of images through which the Romantic mind confronts the doubleness of existence, and explores the possible conversion of contradiction into ambivalence. Among these images we may include the Shelleyan epipsyche and such psychological hybrids as Coleridge's Geraldine. The Romantic encounter with beauty is seldom unambiguous. Even before he has been forced to confront the fierce destruction within shapes of light, Rousseau in Shelley's poem can see the sun only as an "image radiantly intense" reflected in the depths of a well (ll. 345–348). The perception of light is deliberately made phenomenal, reduced to a surface that invites further probing. In *Alastor* the image of a "bright arch of rainbow clouds" that leads to the "black and watery depths" of the reflecting lake (ll. 213–215) similarly couples contradictory elements within the process of aesthetic mirroring, and perhaps alludes ironically to the more naive images of reflection sometimes

[39]Ibid., p. 142.

used by Wordsworth, in which the surface is reduplicated rather than questioned by the depth.[40] Nietzsche's very similar image of aesthetic appearance as a "luminous cloud shape reflected upon the dark surface of a lake"[41] suggests an eventual acceptance of art as a knowledge of both surface and depth. It is toward just such a concept of aesthetic mimesis that we have seen Shelley move in *The Triumph of Life*. The epipsyche in that poem is initially associated with the purer phenomena of aesthetic appearance: such things, intense and evanescent, as rainbow and dream, music and light. But she makes us know at the same time the shattering of this veil of appearance, in the moment when the gazer's mind is strewn beneath her feet like embers and "All that was, seemed as if it had been not" (ll. 385–388). Because both senses of her are true, she becomes the deity of a new kind of art: an art that recognizes itself as simultaneously the projection of a realm of appearance and beauty, and (in Nietzsche's words) the "annihilation of concrete semblances"[42] through the disclosure of what lies behind them.

Keats does not embrace this new image of art in *Lamia*, but remains trapped in a sense of art as pure illusion, either liberated from or lacking in reality. Yet we can see in the figure through whom he explores the contradictions and complexities of aesthetic appearance the beginnings of a new understanding. Lamia is at once light and dark, innocent and contaminated, real but always haunted by the possibility of her own vanishing. She constellates something of the ambiguous semantics of aesthetic illusion. At the beginning of the poem we seem to receive an insight into her true nature:

> in moments few, she was undressed
> Of all her sapphires, greens and amethyst,
> And rubious-argent; of all these bereft,
> Nothing but pain and ugliness were left.
> Still shone her crown; that vanished, also she
> Melted and disappeared as suddenly.
>
> [1.161–166]

---

[40]Cf. *The Prelude*, v.384–388; *The Excursion*, IX. 439–451.
[41]Nietzsche, *The Birth of Tragedy*, p. 63.
[42]Ibid., p. 142.

In these lines she undergoes a kind of dis-carnation, and is reduced to what Nietzsche calls "the original oneness," the pain and contradiction which precede and underlie all fictitious constructions of beauty. Yet we can never be sure whether this anguished and naked creature, or the mythical shape who sings "Happy in beauty, life, and love" (1.298) is the truer representation of what Lamia really is. Lemprière defines lamias as "monsters of Africa, who had the face and breast of a woman, and the rest of their body like that of a serpent." They devoured men and were not endowed with the power of speech.[43] But this lamia is neither grotesque nor primitive. If Keats could be as certain as Burton that she is a serpent who has assumed the guise of a woman, we would be content to see through illusion and fiction, as phenomena that do no more than conceal primary ugliness. But because Lamia's existence as a woman precedes her existence as a serpent (1.117), we wonder if she is not, after all, the beautiful shape that she appears to be. And yet, because she only claims to have been a woman "once" (not originally), the possibility of a previous serpentine existence behind her first human incarnation is never entirely closed.

Similar ambiguities surround Lamia's moral nature. Though deceptive, she is herself the victim of Lycius and Apollonius, and originally of the being who may have changed her into a serpent (1.55). In Christabel, Coleridge had found himself exploring a similarly ambiguous figure: "devoid of guile and sin" (l. 599), and yet capable of being reduced, by some obscure, inner deterioration, to an undifferentiated, animal muteness. The horror of both texts arises from an irrational bifurcation in the very substance of life. But more clearly than Coleridge, Keats seems to recognize that our contradictory need to sympathize with figures such as Lamia and to perceive their falsity derives from a sense that life itself respects the radical innocence of beauty and yet sees through it. Keats is not quite able to put these two senses together, and neither Lamia nor Lycius ever becomes the tragic figure that each might be. But *Lamia* must be seen as one of the crucial moments in the process of Romantic self-revision, inasmuch as it thematizes and raises to a higher level of self-consciousness the

---

[43]J. Lemprière, *Classical Dictionary* (1788; rpt. New York: A. T. Goodrich, 1816).

dilemma of those many other works which find it necessary to contradict themselves, by simultaneously projecting a surface and going behind it.

Like *Lamia, Isabella* too is a poem which is unable to mediate between illusion and reality. Keats's statement that in his own person he might have been apt to quiz the feelings expressed in the poem suggests that this is not an ordinary romance, but one that is engaged in questioning its own mode of language and perhaps the function of poetic language in general. *Isabella* is not the kind of naive romance, "agrest-rural" and "fountain-voic'd,"[44] that Keats was hoping to write. But on the surface it remains committed to the rhetoric of idealism by its affinity with a tradition of sad romances, that are sentimental in their desire to preserve a love that may be "cold, dead indeed, but not dethroned" (l. 400). Though separated from a condition of wholeness which they posit as having existed somewhere in the past, such poems protect, through mementoes of what is lost and through a language that is itself elegiac and commemorative, what Shelley called "the cold, the buried image of the past."[45]

Keats's poem, however, deliberately distinguishes itself from the tradition in which it exists. His attitude toward romance conventions is evident in his treatment of the poem's central symbol, that of a head buried beneath a plant. The pot of basil is quite literally a fiction, a "very nothing" (l. 462). It functions as a metaphor for aesthetic fictions and comments on the legitimacy of imagination. We may interpret it like the lute-corpse at the end of *Alastor,* as an emblem of the power of illusion to make beautiful what is ugly, to keep alive the ideal in a hostile world. Alternatively, we may regard it as the object of a fixation, the delusion of a neurotic mind which does not so much transmute as conceal decay and putrefaction. For Hazlitt and others, the sensitive plant growing from a severed head expressed both the ironic incommensurability of the real and the ideal, and the continued, legitimate impulse of the human mind to repossess the ideal.[46] That

---

[44]Keats, *Letters,* II, 174.
[45]Shelley, "A Defence of Poetry, p. 294.
[46]Thus Hazlitt, writing about the fact that Kellerman had left his heart to be buried on the battlefield of Valmy during the French Revolution, alludes to Boc-

there is something rather forced in this interpretation of Boccaccio's bizarre symbol was perhaps evident to Proctor, when he replaced the head buried in a pot by a crazed girl with a less incon-
gruous heart buried under a tree at the injunction of the dead
man himself.[47] But Keats exaggerates rather than sentimentalizes
the grotesque element. He even suggests at one point that the
plant is prospering because the head underneath it is decompos-
ing and providing it with fertilizer (ll. 429-430).[48] Such details
lead the reader to suspect a poet who is clearly aware of the
neurotic, compulsive element in idealism, and who is involved in
laying bare the archaeology of his own poetic endeavor. The fictive recovery of beauty in an ugly world, Keats seems to say, is no
different from Isabella's recovery and preservation of the head
which represents her love: it is, quite literally, a recovering of a
darkness already known, an attempt to enclose and bury the
knowledge of "Pale limbs at bottom of a crystal well" (l. 364)
somewhere where it does not immediately intrude itself upon
consciousness.

The purpose of the poem is thus to deconstruct its own fictions,
to search beneath the illusory, fictive transmutation of reality
achieved by the pot of basil in order to disclose the nothingness
that illusion seeks to hide. The deconstructive intention is directed not only against the physical emblem of the mind's fic-
tionalizing activity—the plant—but also against the poem's sentimental language. The one dream in the poem comes "like a fierce
potion, drunk by chance" (l. 267) to awaken Isabella to "Pale limbs
at bottom of a crystal well." So too Keats's poem, although with
hesitation and sometimes with compassion, seems designed to
deny us shelter in the "gentleness of old romance" (l. 387), and to

---

caccio's story: "Oh! might that heart prove the root from which the tree of Liberty
may spring up and flourish once more, as the basil-tree grew and grew from the
cherished head of Isabella's lover" (*Table Talk, Complete Works,* VIII, 121). He attributes a similarly idealistic interpretation to Coleridge ("On Consistency of Opin-
ion," *Complete Works,* XVII, 30).

[47]B. W. Proctor, *A Sicilian Story* (1820), X, XIV-XV. Proctor's use of the symbol
removes from it the outrageousness that it possesses in both Keats and Boccaccio.
The idea of someone who has received improper burial being laid under a tree
which is part of a sentient and sympathetic nature and the idea that the spirit of
this person continues to haunt the place of his burial are both conventional motifs
in folklore and in classical writers such as Virgil.

[48]When Leone, the brother of Isabella in Proctor's version, digs up the head, it is
still "unperished" (XVII).

force us to confront that horror which underlies and generates, almost in compensation, the palliating rhetoric of romance.

Although Keats claims to honor Boccaccio (and indeed would like to do so if realism permitted), he speaks almost mockingly of his source, reducing Boccaccio's *alleged* imagery to the flatness of cliché. Whether Keats's irony is directed toward Boccaccio himself, or toward a nineteenth-century sentimentalization which makes "old prose in modern rhyme more sweet" (l. 156), is not of importance.

> O eloquent and famed Boccaccio!
> Of thee we now should ask forgiving boon,
> And of thy spicy myrtles as they blow,
> And of thy roses amorous of the moon,
> And of thy lilies, that do paler grow
>
>   . . .
>
> Grant thou a pardon here, and then the tale
> Shall move on soberly, as it is meet.
>
> [145–149, 153–154]

Inevitably this tone of mockery, directed at the language-world which precedes Lorenzo's death, also exposes the conventions through which the poem preserves this world: the silken scarf, the cypress glooms, the ancient harps (ll. 409, 439, 396). We are made aware of the Romance world, even in its defeat, as a kind of painted veil. And we are made aware that this fictive covering hides something beyond the mitigation of linguistic conventions. It is not so much that the pathos and sentiment focused in these images are unwarranted, as that pathos and sentiment are inappropriate responses to the harsh and brutal circumstances actually depicted in this poem. They form a surface which seeks to protect itself from a hideous reality: to regress, to idealize or somehow preserve the beautiful through images that transmute the ugliness of an alien world. They represent an evasive attempt to interpose between the mind and the poem's events a layer of words that will shelter us from darkness and cover the nakedness of the narrative.

In *Isabella* features of conventional romance combine with elements from what Wordsworth called the "short, bare narrative of unrelieved distress." Throughout the poem there is a discontinuity between the rhetorical surface and the narrative core, which splits the poem into irreconcilable strata of expression. The language of pathos and idealism is played against the harsher realities of the tale, surface against depth, in order to generate in the mind of the reader a reassessment of the relationship between the horror of life and the words in which the mind covers it. This reassessment could be, but is not, part of a constructive dialogue leading to the liberation of areas of knowledge hitherto suppressed. In his analysis of *Hamlet*, Nietzsche points to a similar divergence between the spoken or written word and underlying events so destructive that they are beyond the power of any verbal representation to convey. He goes on to speak of tragedy as an instance of the kind of art which is able to generate significance from the ensuing dialogue between its different strata of awareness.[49] But the encounter of surface and depth in *Isabella* can only be a destructive one, even though it may be necessary to the more tempered sense of the power of aesthetic surfaces that Keats eventually reaches. Because the structure of illusion is analyzed in terms of neurosis, illusion (whether fictive or pathological) is inevitably perceived as a barrier to knowledge. The poem thus leaves itself no alternative but to see through its illusions, by becoming an act of excavation which deconstructs its own fictive rhetoric imaged in the pot of basil. This self-deconstruction is never made explicit in the poem, but we recognize it as the logical terminus of the narrative process. At the end, the Boccaccian surface with its echoes and music is still seemingly intact, allowing the naive minstrel who provides Isabella with emotional accompaniment to turn his eyes away from the hideous reality (l. 481). But the crucial difference is that the surface has now become transparent, and prevents the narrator and his modern readers from taking refuge in the mental fixation of old romance. We have been forced to behold directly the Gorgon's head in which Rossetti was to recognize "the death we live by" (cf. *Isabella*, ll. 393–394). That a certain sentimental sympathy for Isabella stays with us even at the end suggests that the mind may need the palliation of aesthetic surfaces, even when they are seen to be deceptive.

Isabella is a stark poem which removes all saving fictions in

[49]Nietzsche, *The Birth of Tragedy*, pp. 103-104.

order to make us confront a darkness more primary than illusion. As such, it reveals the potential destructiveness of Keats's abandonment of idealism, and marks an extreme against which we can measure both the accommodation reached in *The Fall of Hyperion* and the artifice of evasion built into such poems as *The Eve of St. Agnes* and the "Ode on a Grecian Urn." Seemingly poles apart from *Isabella*, the ode nevertheless has something in common with it. The exterior of the urn displays a leaf-fringed pastoral, but its interior contains the ashes of the dead, of a civilization that is past. This poem too is concerned with problems of surface and depth, with the figured curtain of art and with what lies behind it. It too is concerned with the relationship between fiction and reality, and with the problem of whether a convergence of beauty and truth is possible within the aesthetic sign. If the poem finally avoids some of its deeper recognitions and shelters its vision of the urn in a fictitiousness that excludes the urn's real function, it is partly because the alternatives, in poems such as *Isabella* and *Lamia,* have emerged so bleakly.

As there are two aesthetic objects in the poem (the poem itself and the urn), so also there are two very different images of art to be discovered in the "Ode on a Grecian Urn." The vision of the aesthetic medium that Keats's poem, in its concluding lines, seeks to project on the urn is constantly challenged and disrupted by the vision of art that emerges from the urn itself—in all probability a funeral urn.[50] It seems that Keats seeks in the urn a closed, Apollonian form: one that will, to borrow Leiris's words, "banish death or mask it behind the architecture of a nontemporal perfection."[51] Certain elements in the initial description of the urn appear to correspond to this desire. There is the pastoral surface which, as one critic points out, actually "embowers" its legend.[52]

[50] Ian Jack notes that Keats is probably thinking "of one of the large neo-Attic urns made in Rome between c. 50 B.C. and c. A.D. 50. These urns ... were intended either as funerary caskets or as purely decorative objects" (*Keats and the Mirror of Art* [Oxford: Clarendon, 1967], p. 217). The conclusion that Keats has in mind the funeral associations of the urn is supported by Blackstone, who notes that the urn in Book III of *Endymion* was originally described as "silent as a corpse upon a pyre" (*The Consecrated Urn,* p. 332).

[51] Leiris, *Miroir de la tauromachie,* p. 57. Translation mine.

[52] Mario L. D'Avanzo, *Keats' Metaphors for the Poetic Imagination* (Durham: Duke University Press, 1967), p. 166.

There are the perpetually green trees (l. 16), and the constant references to music and melody which point to an immediacy that cancels out the distance intervening between the spectator and this relic of a dead and silent culture. But if we go beyond the surface and shape of the urn, as we are encouraged to do by the probing questions directed at it in the fourth stanza, we encounter something very different. We encounter an awareness of frustration as well as perfection (l. 17), and finally a recognition of the other side of silence which takes us almost into the core of destruction:

> What little town by river or sea shore,
> Or mountain-built with peaceful citadel,
> Is emptied of this folk, this pious morn?
> And, little town, thy streets for evermore
> Will silent be; and not a soul to tell
> Why thou art desolate can e'er return.

[35-40]

The pastoral scene is slowly replaced by a scene of sacrifice and emptiness, and a sense of desolation even at the heart of a perfect culture. The urn no longer appears as a closed and completed form, but as one which discovers within itself a vital crevice, which is the knowledge of death. It no longer appears as a second version of the nightingale, but as the emblem of an art which has become contaminated by the entry into time and history that makes it a human, not a natural, artifact. Whatever strange epiphany it achieves is achieved not by blocking out this awareness, but by celebrating it and, literally (because it contains the ashes of the dead), by containing or representing it.

At first sight the urn, set apart from the human world in a separate space and time, had seemed to stand for the power of aesthetic fiction to achieve an illusory suspension of the laws of reality. It had seemed to depict the entire range of human emotions, and yet to be miraculously untouched by their consequences. The lover was stopped short of fulfillment and yet, because this was a fictitious world, his frustration was not real but meant only that his love would not be tarnished in being realized (ll. 17-20). But a deeper reading of the urn suggests that its creator recognized what Leiris conveys in using for art the metaphor of a bullfight rather than an ordinary game. The bullfighter cannot claim that imperviousness to tragedy characteristic of players in other games, because the possibility of his death is more than a fiction.[53] So too the urn does not merely simulate the possibility of its death in the arabesques and curves of its surface, but because it is a funerary casket, touches directly upon the reality of death.

A reading of the poem generates a dialogue in the mind of the reader between what appears on the outside of the urn and what is within it, between the innocent surface and the depth. Two very different concepts of the aesthetic medium lie side by side for much of this poem: one which separates the visual appearance of art from its deeper reality, and another which is aware that surfaces exist in relation to a depth. In the penultimate stanza Keats's poem is brought almost to the verge of redefining the semantics of aesthetic illusion. But such a redefinition, which would recognize that the aesthetic surface is related to the knowledge it encloses as a transparency rather than as a barrier, that aesthetic signs can represent but cannot banish the "world as will," does not occur except perhaps in the mind of the reader. Irrespective of who speaks them, the last lines of Keats's poem reaffirm the rhetoric of the surface and reduce questions to the flatness of statement and the urn itself to its merely decorative appearance.

Thus in the end the urn (or Keats's "representation" of the urn) is returned to a fictive space like that of Hermes and his nymph, a world in which beauty and truth do not diverge because there is no reality to give depth and ambiguity to the fictive appearance. To search beneath the surface, by seeking the historical Greece underlying the Arcadian fiction, would be to ask what becomes of the abstractions of idealism when they are incarnated in the real world and made the property of real men and lovers. In the fourth stanza Keats almost does this. But at the crucial moment he draws back from excavating too deeply in the archeology of the idealizing consciousness, fearing a complete dissolution of the surface. An emphasis on the aesthetic qualities of the surface, on "marble men and maidens overwrought" (l. 42), fictionalizes the urn and absorbs the menace of its truth into the innocence of its

[53]Leiris, *Miroir de la tauromachie*, p. 57.

beauty. Thus it is able to accomplish what "art" should ideally accomplish, but what the real urn, a historical and time-bound object, cannot do. It is able to liberate itself from the force of reality, to play with possibilities and suffer no harm from its relish of the dark side of things.

By the same token, however, the urn becomes more remote from us: a "Cold pastoral" (l.45). Problems of realization and fictionalization also beset *The Eve of St. Agnes,* where at the end there is a similar attempt to stop the aesthetic camera and remove the lovers from a world which continues without them on its journey toward death and destruction. As we have seen, a sense of the poem as enclosed within itself is reinforced by its existence in an antimimetic genre, and by its artifical, highly decorative language which, as Todorov's notion of poetic discourse as "discours opaque"[54] suggests, prevents us from passing through the language to the reality it signifies. References to the sculptural quality of the lovers (l. 297), and our constant sense of dream as the medium in which the action takes place, further contribute to this fictionality which retards movement through the text to the world, and makes us treat the poem as an autonomous verbal object, liberated or turned away from the real world. This reduction of the aspirations of art to fiction or illusion is perhaps the final, defensive manifestation of the Romantic refusal to consent to incompleteness. It relocates the ideal without having to question it: on this occasion not at the far goal of time, but in some untrodden region of the mind. Paradoxically, the ideal is preserved only by denying it existence.

The *locus classicus* for a fictive theory of art comes toward the end of Schiller's letters *On the Aesthetic Education of Man,* where he renounces the hypostasis of the ideal through its identification with a naive culture, and instead insists on it as play and fiction, arguing for the validity of human metaphors as long as they are recognized to be metaphorical. In so doing, he restates in more sophisticated epistemological terms a view of art already articulated by Addison, Duff, and Young among others. Addison, in particular, by describing imaginative ornamentation in terms of

[54]Tzvetan Todorov, *Littérature et signification* (Paris: Larousse, 1967), pp. 102–103.

Locke's secondary rather than primary qualities, dissociates the aesthetic sign from any claim to reality and from any limitation by reality, setting it in a separate, naive and purely fictive space: the space of pure appearance.[55] In the same vein Schiller writes:

> with unrestrained freedom [Man] can join together what Nature sundered. . . . But he possesses this sovereign right positively only in the *world of appearance,* in the unsubstantial kingdom of the imagination, and only so long as he conscientiously abstains, in theory, from affirming existence of it, and renounces all attempts, in practice, to bestow existence by means of it. . . . The poet similarly steps outside his boundaries when he attributes existence to his ideal, and when he aims at some definite existence through it.[56]

One senses in this statement a renunciation of the more grandiose claims made by the Romantic imagination, and a countervailing sense that the artist is now justified in reasserting his idealism. But unlike Wallace Stevens, who has built his poetry around such a theory of art as play, the Romantics are given to this insulation of aesthetic fiction from reality only in moments of defensive self-irony such as Shelley's *Witch of Atlas* or Byron's *Don Juan.* Few Romantic poems are content to respect the boundary which divides mental representation from what Schiller calls "the existence of things or Nature."[57] More often they are driven to take the dream into reality so as to make of the poetic fiction something that legislates to the world. "This Lime-Tree Bower, My Prison" moves beyond the hypothesis of a state in which the speaker will no longer be separate from nature, to the actual enjoyment of that state through the "naive" figure of Lamb. *Prometheus Unbound* likewise blurs the line between present and future and ends by hypostatizing its fictions.

[55] Addison, *The Spectator,* III, No. 413. Cf. also William Duff, *Essay on Original Genius* (1767; rpt. Gainesville: Scholars' Facsimiles and Reprints, 1964), p. 143; Edward Young, *Conjectures on Original Composition* (1759; rpt. Leeds: Scolar Press, 1966); Kant, *Critique of Judgment,* pp. 37–81; Wallace Stevens, *The Necessary Angel* (1942; rpt. New York: Vintage, 1965); W. H. Auden, *The Dyer's Hand and Other Essays* (London: Faber, 1963), pp. 70–71.
[56] Schiller, *On the Aesthetic Education of Man,* pp. 127–128. Cf. also Nietzsche, *The Birth of Tragedy,* p. 21.
[57] Schiller, *On the Aesthetic Education of Man,* p. 127.

But as Schiller recognized, it is only by a virginal encasement in its own privacy that poetry can retain its own purity. With the drive to realize the ideal comes the recognition that realization radically alters our sense of what the ideal discloses. Modern theorists such as Derrida agree with Schiller in pointing to the dangers of confusing the representation of the thing with its actual presence, of imagining that the literary sign can merge with the object it projects.[58] But it is one thing to insist that sign and thing cannot be identical, that the process of making the ideal real will not make the real ideal. It is another thing to renounce all involvement in the cycle of desire that knows both the search to make the sign real and the inevitable corruption of the ideal in the process of incarnation. This is what the Witch of Atlas does in choosing as her companion a hermaphrodite who exempts her from the tarnishing knowledge of consummation. It is what the poet in *Alastor,* seeking to embrace the epipsyche who comes to him veiled and in a dream, does not do. Because he wants consummation, the aesthetic act becomes for him an act of disclosure, a movement behind that fictive veil which allows art to appear as a shape all light.

We are faced with a choice between a mode of representation that is purely playful and one which seeks a marriage with reality even at the cost of forfeiting innocence and security. A curiously double-edged image at the beginning of *The Witch of Atlas,* comparing the poem to a young kitten, comments on the poem's own existence in the mode of fiction rather than mimesis:

> What, though no mice are caught by a young kitten,
> May it not leap and play as grown cats do,
> Till its claws come? Prithee, for this one time,
> Content thee with a visionary rhyme.
>
> [5–8]

The image recognizes both the innocence and the ineffectuality of a language that is play and simulation. It recognizes that a poetry which seeks to legislate to the world will discover that words themselves do violence to their own illusions. But in the last analysis, because the kitten must become a cat, the image also

[58]Derrida, *Of Grammatology,* p. 144.

recognizes that the construction of a fictive cosmos apart from reality can be no more than a detour from that inevitable process of psychic and biological maturation to which Keats referred as soul-making. More than his previous poems, the dark romances of Keats's final years show awareness of the consequences for aesthetic discourse of taking Adam's dream into the real world. Metaphors of virginity and consummation, or neurosis and insight, force Keats to explore the problems inherent in the protective separation of fiction from reality. Schiller notes that only "insofar as it is *candid* (expressly renouncing all claim to reality), and only insofar as it is *self-dependent* (dispensing with all assistance from reality), is appearance aesthetic. As soon as it is deceitful and simulates reality, as soon as it is impure and requires reality for its operation, it . . . can prove nothing for the freedom of the spirit."[59] But ironically Porphyro's dream cannot exist without this assistance from reality that puts in question its purity as dream, and causes the language of illusion to depend on the language of mimesis. In practice, if not in theory, the idea of a purely figurative language denying itself referential or denominative status proves untenable.

The attitude toward problems of realization and idealization remains unsettled in *The Eve of St. Agnes*. But the metaphor of consummation involves a tacit recognition that the literary sign cannot remain innocent. The same awareness haunts the "Ode on a Grecian Urn," where the urn is described as a "still unravished bride" and not a virgin, as the "foster-child" and not the natural child of silence (ll. 1-2). As is suggested by the use of biological metaphors to describe the relationship between innocence and reality (metaphors such as Shelley's kitten and Keats's unbudded rose), fiction and idealization are not seen as a transcendence of reality. They are at most an arrest of process, an abstention from reality which avoids potentiating tendencies that exist already, though undisclosed.

The hesitation in Keats's romances between an art which constructs a separate existence and one which emerges from the sanctuary of fiction into the real world will be restated in different

[59]Schiller, *On the Aesthetic Education of Man*, p. 128.

terms in the Hyperion poems, as a debate over the relative valuation of classical and Romantic art. But the anxiety that here attends Keats's renunciation of idealism suggests that there is something unsatisfactory in simply replacing the language of enclosure with the language of disclosure. Through its existence within the contradictory generic traditions of romance and naturalistic narrative, *Isabella* explores the question of whether poetic rhetoric should transmute or reflect the events it describes. In *The Eve of St. Agnes* and *Lamia* the coexistence of the language of dream or idealism with the deconstructive language of psychological realism or irony likewise exposes Keats's vacillations on the relationship between poetry and illusion. Indeed a self-conscious concern with the act of telling, an awareness of the tale as a fiction which can be followed, deconstructed, or otherwise amended, justifies us in seeing all three poems as sharing a certain anxiety about the nature and function of the aesthetic medium. The narrator of *Lamia*, for instance, though clearly biased in a particular direction, suggests that there is actually a choice to be made between preserving the illusory palace of an ideal art and replacing it with "truth."

> And but the flitter-wingèd verse must tell,
> For truth's sake, what woe afterwards befell,
> 'Twould humour many a heart to leave them thus.
>
> [1.394–396]

In dissociating fictional convention from actuality, he puts into relief a troubling discontinuity between the idealizing and mimetic aspects of the process by which experience is converted into art.

Hazlitt was to return to essentially the same problem in his scathing criticism of Crabbe, whom he attacks for showing the "naked object" without the "tinsel of words" and "the illusions of sentiment."[60] His very phraseology, however, in its epistemological dissociation of object from affect, suggests that the problem is not so simple as he might imagine. A fear that the "foliage" of poetry, in Coleridge's phrase ("Dejection," ll. 80–81), may be extrinsic to the naked object haunts the Romantic mind and compels all attempts to robe the world in a fictive veil to exist in the mode

---

[60]Hazlitt, "Mr. Campbell and Mr. Crabbe," *Complete Works*, xi, 166, 164.

of bad faith. Neither in fictionality nor in deconstruction does Keats seem to reach any kind of poetic equilibrium. Rather, the poems of this period all converge on that ambiguous moment described by Nietzsche, when the luminous imagery of the aesthetic surface becomes transparent to darker possibilities within itself, but without any means of mediating its entry into these possibilities.

Whether we speak of surface and depth, of fiction and mimesis, or even of brightness and darkness, we are simply seeking terms to define the problematical space that the aesthetic sign must inhabit between an illusory ideal and a destructive reality. Like the urn, the poems which precede *The Fall of Hyperion* live simultaneously in two very different kinds of psychic space: the painted exterior which represents an existence disengaged from the world, and the interior which contains a knowledge of reality capable of dissolving this appearance. The Romantic discovery that illusion and reality are related not as past and present but as surface and depth requires a radically new optics of the imagination. But this new optics cannot be the fusion of beauty and truth or of dream and reality sought by so many Romantic writers who describe the aesthetic act in the vocabulary of marriage or communion, the language of interpenetration and liberation. The radical heteronomy in the self and its enterprises disclosed by the movement beyond the sphere of illusion cannot be covered up or healed, but only mediated.

It may be that the urn itself embodies such a mediation and thus transcends the oppositions that divide Keats's poetry. In it surface and depth do not fuse, but nevertheless converge toward the impossibility of their own convergence. The beauty and truth that Keats's poem seeks to reduce to an identity do not become identical, but somehow they coexist, as layers of consciousness between which there is a perpetual dialogue. On the one hand, the urn is only apparently a serene and unravished form, because "at the point that matters most the Apollonian illusion" of the surface "has been broken through and destroyed"[61] by the death which it encloses. Yet, in another sense, the illusion holds: the break is contained, represented, encountered across "an inter-

---

[61]Nietzsche, *The Birth of Tragedy*, p. 130.

posed Apollonian medium"[62] whose beauty prevents the eye from being blinded by reality. The duality of the urn points toward an art in which knowledge of the depth does not overwhelm the surface, but in which the surface is no longer a barrier to such knowledge. Such a possibility, which is worked out more fully in *The Fall of Hyperion*, becomes all the more important in view of the divisions that unsettle the poems we have been examining.

[62]Ibid., p. 141.

CHAPTER 4

Keats's Hyperion Poems:

The Dialogue of Apollo and Dionysos

A vast shade / In midst of his own brightness.

—*Hyperion*

In his rather harsh way, Yeats characterizes Keats as a school-boy "with face and nose pressed to a sweet-shop window," con-structing through art a deliberate happiness which nevertheless leaves his "senses and his heart unsatisfied" in the realm of real-ity.[1] In effect, he points to the possibly compensatory nature of poetic idealism earlier recognized by Schiller.[2] Keats's own aesthe-tic statements, summed up in the famous description of the imagi-nation as Adam's dream,[3] would seem to characterize him as a kind of naive artist.[4] Yeats, on the other hand, was one of the first writers to recognize that such statements are only half "of a doubtful dialectic," to borrow Bostetter's phrase, and that they remain "haunted by the spectres of their contraries."[5] What Yeats perhaps did not understand is the extent to which Romantic poetry, far from constructing an antithetical simplification of real-ity, internalizes the very recognitions of which he speaks. On the one hand, it betrays a nostalgia for naive modes of discourse. On the other hand, it also probes beyond the protective limits it has

[1]Yeats, "Ego Dominus Tuus," ll. 52–59.
[2]Schiller, *Naive and Sentimental Poetry*, pp. 105, 110.
[3]Keats, *Letters*, I, 185.
[4]Thus according to Reynolds, Keats "comes fresh from nature,—and the origi-nals of his images are to be found in her keeping ... we find in his poems the glorious effect of summer days" and unlike Byron, when Keats paints nature "You do not see him, when you see her" (*Selected Prose of John Hamilton Reynolds*, ed. Leonidas M. Jones [Cambridge: Harvard University Press, 1966], pp. 100, 226–227).
[5]Bostetter, *The Romantic Ventriloquists*, p. 5.

chosen by imposing on itself a certain set of generic or formal
expectations, and links the discourse of innocence sentimentally
or ironically to styles which undermine it.

Keats's aesthetic theory, insofar as it emerges from the letters, is
a naive theory. He sees poetry as a medium which evaporates
"disagreeables," and as "Pleasure Thermometre" leading through
successive gradations of happiness.[6] His desire for a poetry of
sensations rather than thoughts[7] recalls Schiller's definition of the
naive as an immediate sensuous harmony undisturbed by reflection, in valuing a sense of simplicity and inner unity over complexity and ambivalence. Of equal significance is Keats's characterization of the negatively capable poet. As a theory which allows the
poet to play with light and shade without being affected by them,
the notion of negative capability has affinities with Nietzsche's
description of the naive Apollonian poet who "lives in [his] images, and only in them, with joyful complacence . . . while even the
image of angry Achilles is no more for him than an *image*" which
he "enjoys with a dreamer's delight in appearance."[8] As a theory
of poetic objectivity, it can be linked to Schiller's praise for a
poetry that is possessed entirely by objects so that only they exist,[9]
while "we ourselves" are reabsorbed into "the tacitly creative life"
and "serene spontaneity" of nature.[10] Keats (in his letters and in
poems such as *Endymion* and the "Ode to Psyche"[11]) is fond of
analogies between the poetic fiction and the natural object, conceived in accordance with Romantic canons of naiveté and spontaneity. Such analogies see poetry as blissfully ignorant of its
inherent temporality, even as the decision to cast a poem like *Endymion* in the form of a visionary quest concedes the absence of an

[6]Keats, *Letters*, I, 192, 218, 232.
[7]Ibid., p. 185.
[8]Nietzsche, *The Birth of Tragedy*, p. 39. Nietzsche is here contrasting the Apollonian narrative poet, who plays on the surface, with the lyric poet who also becomes
his images, but for the purpose of self-knowledge. Compare Keats's statement that
the poetical self "enjoys light and shade. . . . It does no harm from its relish of the
dark side of things any more than from its taste for the bright one; because they
both end in speculation" (*Letters*, I, 387).
[9]Schiller, *Naive and Sentimental Poetry*, pp. 102, 106; cf. also Schopenhauer, *The
World as Will and Representation*, I, 199. With this compare Keats: the poetical self
"has no self" and is continually "filling some other Body" (*Letters*, I, 387).
[10]Schiller, *Naive and Sentimental Poetry*, p. 85.
[11]Keats, *Letters*, I, 238–239; *Endymion*, 1.7.

ideal which exists only in the sentimental mode of hope, dream, or fiction.

Yet in the previous chapter we saw how Keats questions his own theoretical presuppositions and reveals the inseparability of idealistic and mimetic discourses, both through his use of genre and through the kind of narratives he constructs. The Hyperion poems continue this questioning, on a narrative level through the undermining relationship between the Olympians and the fallen Titans, and generically through the encounter between mythological prophecy (a naive mode) and tragedy. More significantly— because they are Hellenic or classical poems—the Hyperion poems explore the relationship between innocence and experience in terms of the contrast between past and present. Initially, they are actuated by a belief that there are literary choices which will lead to the recovery of an ideal art through a return to past, naive forms of awareness. Their discovery that the past already contains the problems of the present is, therefore, crucial to the larger Romantic recognition that innocence and experience are related not antithetically but as surface and depth. *Hyperion* copes with this recognition sentimentally, by transmitting itself first as elegy, then as prophecy, and finally as a fragment whose broken logic merits sympathetic reconstruction by the reader. The relationship between text and subtext in this poem, therefore, remains a repressive one. *The Fall of Hyperion,* however, deals with it tragically, bringing the illusions of the modern dreamer into constructive dialogue with a past that challenges the sentimental myth of antiquity.

This chapter will deal only with the Hyperion poems and their relationship to the Hellenic mode which, because of its centrality to the Romantic period, merits some discussion even at the risk of digression. But the movement from the sentimental through the ironic to the tragic, which is evident in Keats's work as a whole, is also present in his attitude to the past. *Endymion,* which refers to itself in terms of "the stretched metre of an antique song," is one of the earlier instances of a thematic and generic choice that seeks to exclude the problematical from the poetic universe, by enclosing the poem in a past which is an antithetical simplification of reality. Its narrative seems to offer a union of human and divine, and its use of romance promises a return to the green-recessed woods. But the thing of beauty also discloses, through the terrible knowledge of Glaucus (III.338ff.), the dark passages in the Romantic psyche from which a return to Greek mythology was supposed to save it. Toward the end of the poem, as he confronts Endymion's death, the narrator sadly concedes that the classical tale has become modern and has internalized the very complications it was designed to exclude (IV.770–779). That the narrator has thus frustrated the dialectical separation of past from present serves to comment on the aesthetic process itself, conceived as the making of a shape all light in opposition to a world which negates it. The undermining modernization is, moreover, described as "truth" in relation to the older version which is, presumably, illusion (IV.774). But, characteristically, the narrator sees his failure to create a naive discourse as a personal one, a betrayal of the happy ending that still exists in the "old tale" (IV.779). In ending the poem with the deification of the visionary, he finds it legitimate to bury once and for all the subtext he has briefly acknowledged.

The "Ode to Psyche," though a less self-mystified poem, is equally sentimental. The projection into the past of a myth of imaginative divinity is openly recognized as fiction, through the fact that the goddess celebrated is the human soul, and lacks the theological sanction of belonging to the Olympian hierarchy. Psyche is enshrined only "in some untrodden region of [the] mind" (l. 51), in an imaginary temple. But the poem defies its own metaphorical status by conceiving this temple on the analogy of a natural bower rather than a human artifact such as the Grecian urn: there is an attempt here to naturalize the imaginary in order to give the poetic fiction the reality of the objective world. It is important, in this context, that Keats chooses the ode, a form which emotionally hypostatizes through celebration what can be no more than faith. The fiction of a transcendental discourse existing in the past is exposed, yet defiantly sustained.

In Keats's late romances, too, the relationship of present and past is used to focus an exploration of the conflict between illusion and reality. But this relationship is now radically different from the one which obtained in *Endymion,* and the poems therefore mark the beginning of a process of self-revision that culminates in *The Fall of Hyperion.* In *Isabella* the meeting of "old prose" and "modern rhyme" (l. 156) tempts the mind toward a repressive sentimentalization of life, but also becomes the occasion for a breaking down of the temporal barriers between what the modern mind knows and what it has imagined through fictive convention. Though the narrator at first makes his irony seem a modern problem, by putting it to us that his recasting of Boccaccio is a departure from the naiveté of the old tale (ll. 145-152), he goes on to suggest that it is a return, behind the modern rhymers who have tried to sweeten Boccaccio, to the authentic recognitions of the latter's "old prose." The shift within the poem, from the location of an innocent discourse in the past to the recognition that the past is itself the subconscious of the modern literary mind, anticipates the larger shift that Keats will make between *Hyperion* and his final poem, where the knowledge of the present is explicitly disclosed as the subtext within the language of the past.

Endymion may be seen as a first draft of the Keatsian encounter between formal intention and the content of life—an encounter already discussed on a theoretical level with reference to Schiller. But the deflection of naive romance into sentimental quest, which says something about the impossibility of disengaging an ideal past from the knowledge of reality, is seen only as a personal or formal—at most a historical—failure. In ascribing his disappointment with *Endymion* to the poem's inability to be sufficiently classical, Keats keeps alive the fiction of a recoverable innocence: the idea that there exists a state of simplicity available to a more complex consciousness through the recovery of a past culture or the mimesis of an older art-form. The programmatic announcement of *Hyperion* in a letter to Benjamin Haydon divides poetry implicitly into classical and Romantic, objective and subjective modes, and continues to favor the Greek over the modern as the repository of perfection:

> —in Endymion [sic] I think you may have many bits of the deep and sentimental cast—the nature of *Hyperion* will lead me to treat it in a more naked and grecian Manner—and the march of passion and endeavour will be undeviating—and one great contrast between them will be—that the Hero of the written tale being mortal is led

on, like Buonaparte, by circumstance; whereas Apollo in *Hyperion* being a fore-seeing God will shape his actions like one.[12]

Standard distinctions between classicism and Romanticism, in which the former is austere, universal, and detached, and the latter overwrought, personal, and emotional, lie behind the characterization of Greek poetry as "naked" and the descriptions of *Endymion* in terms which (coincidentally) echo those of Schiller.[13] The use of classical myth in *Hyperion* is thus a gesture of self-mystification, undertaken despite the recognition (in the comments on *Endymion*) that aesthetic naiveté may be impossible.

In an interesting passage in the letters *On the Aesthetic Education of Man*, Schiller takes up the question of a possible marriage between knowledge and innocence with reference to the relationship of present and past. The artist, according to him, is to live beyond and within the actual, to grow up in Greece and then to return to his own country as an alien but redeeming figure: "He will indeed take his subject matter from the present age, but his form he will borrow from a nobler time—nay, from beyond all time.... As noble Art has survived noble nature, so too she marches ahead of it, fashioning and awakening by her inspiration."[14] Implicit in Schiller's injunction is a view shared by Keats. Schiller argues that although the work of art embraces both past and present (in his terms both the ideal and the real), it achieves through the emulation of earlier forms a triumph of aesthetic soul

---

[12]Keats, *Letters*, I, 207.

[13]Greek art is typically associated with noble simplicity. Thus Johann Winckelmann, who inaugurates an imitative mode for the classical, contrasts Greek art with the ornamentation of baroque art, to the disadvantage of the latter (*Reflections on the Painting and Sculpture of the Greeks*, trans. Henry Fuseli [1765; rpt. Menston, England: Scolar Press, 1972]). Goethe distinguishes classicism from Romanticism in terms of a "predominance of sentiment" in the latter (J. P. Eckermann, *Conversations with Goethe* [1836–1848], trans. Gisela C. O'Brien [New York: Ungar, 1964], p. 192). Cf. also A. W. Schlegel's description of Romantic poetry as "interessante Poesie," whereas classical poetry is universal in its appeal. To go from German to English criticism, the various distinctions of negative capability from the egotistical sublime in Hazlitt, Keats, and Coleridge (who distinguishes between Shakespeare and Milton) are simply different versions of this basic contrast between objective and subjective genius, the simple and the complex. For other distinctions between Romanticism and classicism cf. A. W. Schlegel, *Lectures on Dramatic Art and Literature*, pp. 24–26; Jean-Paul, *Horn of Oberon*, p. 52.

[14]Schiller, *On the Aesthetic Education of Man*, pp. 51–52.

over historical matter. He leaves unexplained the more troubling question of whether a work of art whose form is a refusal of its own content does not become vulnerable to the deconstruction of the aesthetic surface by the knowledge that the form contains. Keats's letter ascribes to classical antiquity the almost canonical status with which it was generally credited in the nineteenth century. That *Hyperion* itself is remote from the optimism of the letter is obvious. However, the pages which follow will be concerned not only with the poem as it stands, but also with the complex of intentions behind it, with the aesthetic gesture involved in the choice of a Grecian subject as an allusion to a certain set of cultural and artistic expectations. From the disjunction between content and formal intention, between actuality and desire, arises a dialogue between the surface and depth of the aesthetic psyche that proves crucial in Keats's career.

From Winckelmann, who idolized Greece, to Spengler, who did not, there was a tendency (particularly in Germany) to simplify Greek culture to the point where it became almost a second Eden. Spengler's "Apollonian" culture exists in a pure present which is the negation of time, in a world that "is not continuous but complete." It does not know the incompleteness of desire and, even in so neutral an area as mathematics, represses the concept of irrational numbers introduced by Pythagoras.[15] Pater, who wrote "A Study of Dionysus" at about the same time that Nietzsche wrote *The Birth of Tragedy*, continued to describe the Greek spirit as a "unifying or identifying power, bringing together things naturally asunder."[16] Even in a much later essay on Winckelmann, he described Greek art as having no "backgrounds," no tendency toward self-analysis, and as communicating "not what is accidental in man, but the tranquil godship in him."[17] Arnold acknowledged the presence (in later Greek culture) of the dialogue of the mind with itself, but rejected this tendency as foreign to the sweetness and light characteristic of true Hellenic culture.[18]

[15]Oswald Spengler, *The Decline of the West* (1918–1922), trans. Charles F. Atkinson (London: George Allen and Unwin, 1926–1928), pp. 9, 64ff.

[16]Walter Pater, "A Study of Dionysus," *Greek Studies* (London: Macmillan, 1895), p. 23.

[17]Pater, *The Renaissance* (London: Macmillan, 1893), pp. 224–225.

[18]Matthew Arnold, "Preface to First Edition of Poems (1853)," *The Complete*

Romantic Hellenism is of crucial importance to the study of Romantic idealism, and therefore to the ongoing exploration of the limits of an idealistic poetics in which the Hyperion poems play an important role. By admitting the Dionysiac into a culture which until then had been considered purely Apollonian and serene, Nietzsche was radically to revise the Romantic myth of Hellenism and therefore the Romantic period's image of its own art. Far earlier in the history of Romanticism, by introducing the Titans into a poem that was intended to be a celebration of the Apollonian moment, Keats too found himself drawn into reassessments of a similar magnitude.

It was not necessary for Keats to have read particularly widely in order to have been aware of a view of classicism that was very much in the air. Homer and the Elgin Marbles represent summits of the spirit at which the modern self can only gaze like a sick eagle. The Grecian urn as represented by Keats seems the very embodiment of an Apollonian art that is pure space, having no knowledge of history and duration. Something of the aura which attached itself to Greece is evident in Keats's reference to "the beautiful mythology of Greece" in the preface to *Endymion,* and in his depiction of the Latmians: a people who live in a golden age, in harmony with nature and removed from time "in old marbles ever beautiful" (II.896, 1.319).[19] The reality of *Hyperion* stands in dialectical opposition to its intended recovery of the ideal, and

Prose Works of Matthew Arnold, ed. R. H. Super (Ann Arbor: University of Michigan Press, 1960), I, 1-2.

[19]Bernard Blackstone also points out that Keats conceives of the era of Greek myth as one of "holiness or wholeness when man [was] integrated to his environment" (*The Consecrated Urn,* p. 172). There is a discussion of Keats and classicism in M. A. Goldberg, *The Poetics of Romanticism* (Yellow Springs, Ohio: Antioch Press, 1969), which looks at the problem in terms of the relationship between rationality and emotion, not the main concern of this chapter. Perhaps most worth mentioning is R. W. Stallman's "Keats the Apollinian: The Time-and-Space Logic of his Poems as Paintings," (*University of Toronto Quarterly,* 16 [1946–1947], 143–156), which is influenced by Joseph Frank's discussion of time and space in modern literature, and which makes a very interesting use of Spengler's distinction between Apollonian and Faustian world-forms. Stallman recognizes the tension in Keats between the Apollinian self and the Faustian self, the latter a historical consciousness, aware of duration and time. But he argues that at its best Keats's poetry "is a poetry of the moment and the near and the still," a poetry which arrests action and suspends the intellect in Apollonian calm (pp. 144, 147–150). My own conclusion, that Keats radically revised an early Apollonian ideal, will be rather different.

provokes a reassessment of inherited aesthetic canons which is only completed in *The Fall of Hyperion*. Part of the significance of Keats's two poems in the idealist debate is perhaps suggested by Pater who, very late in his essay on Winckelmann, begins to question the validity of the reigning view of Greek culture and seems to associate the origins of his doubts with Keats's Hyperion poems. Pater points to the limits of a view that is oblivious to Greek tragedy and suggests that the association of classicism with a godship denied to Romanticism may be more a matter of desire than of historical fact:

> A sort of preparation for the romantic temper is noticeable even within the limits of the Greek ideal itself, which for his part Winckelmann failed to see. For Greek religion has not merely its mournful mysteries of Adonis, of Hyacinthus, of Demeter, [perhaps a reference to Pater's own "A Study of Dionysus"], but it is conscious also of the fall of earlier divine dynasties. Hyperion gives way to Apollo, Oceanus to Poseidon. . . . The placid minds even of Olympian gods are troubled with thoughts of a limit to duration, of inevitable decay, of dispossession.[20]

The presence of decay and death in an allegedly perfect civilization means in effect that no historical period can be peculiarly privileged in its immunity from time. More important, and inasmuch as Greek culture provided a norm for art in general, it suggests that art itself can no longer claim to be a thing of beauty untarnished by the darker knowledge that attends other modes of existence.

Allusions to Greek culture are frequent, if unremarkable, in English literature of the pre-Romantic and Romantic periods. Thus Wordsworth, in the famous lines on "the lively Grecian, in a land of hills" (*The Excursion*, IV.718ff), depicts a race of beings who live in a pristine harmony with nature, born after the fall but possessing a radical innocence which guarantees their immunity

---

[20]Pater, *The Renaissance*, p. 237. Pater does not mention Keats. But his reference to Hyperion, a god so little known that, according to E. B. Hungerford (*Shores of Darkness* [New York: Columbia University Press, 1941], p. 153), Keats had to borrow for him the attributes of Helios, suggests that the Hyperion poems were at the back of his mind. He could, of course, have been thinking of Swinburne's poem on Hyperion as well.

from "the doom / Of destitution" (IV.649–650). Greek life is characterized by the proximity of the natural and temporal world to the divine, by a natural plenitude which is penetrated by spirit and finds "commodious place for every God" (IV.721). Though Greece can hardly be said to occupy a central place in Wordsworth's scheme of things, the description of the Greek ethos reveals the ease with which the myth of Greece could become linked to the Romantic dream of a marriage between nature and spirit in the affirmation of "Life continuous, Being unimpaired;... existence unexposed / To the blind walk of mortal accident" (*The Excursion*, IV.755–758). Addison claims that the ancients "lived and conversed, as it were, in an enchanted region, where everything they looked on ... gave a thousand pleasing hints to their imagination."[21] Edward Baldwin in his *Pantheon* describes how "the Grecian mythology replenished all nature with invisible beings, so that whether these ancients walked in fields or gardens... they felt on all occasions surrounded with divine nature."[22] Addison, Baldwin, and others think of Greece as a utopia where the dreams of gods and men alike are real. Tacitly they associate it with the pleasures of imagination,[23] with the ability to keep a bower quiet for the mind by recreating a naive condition. Thus Greek culture as a historical recreation of prelapsarian perfection provides a model for the idealizing role of art itself among the forms of human expression.

[21]Addison, *The Spectator*, III, No. 284.

[22]Quoted in J. R. Caldwell, *John Keats' Fancy: The Effect on Keats of the Psychology of His Day* (Ithaca: Cornell University Press, 1945), p. 17. In a similar vein R. M. Milnes speaks of Greek poetry as "a brighter region ... / Haunted by gods and sylvane nymphs and lovers, / Where forms of grace thro' sunny landscapes bounded / By music and enchantment all surrounded" (Quoted in Stephen Larrabee, *English Bards and Grecian Marbles* [New York: Columbia University Press, 1942], p. 276). For accounts of the vogue for Hellenism in the nineteenth century see Larrabee; Bernard H. Stern, *The Rise of Romantic Hellenism in English Poetry, 1732–1786* (London: Oxford University Press, 1940); Marshall Montgomery, *Friedrich Hölderlin and the German Neo-Hellenic Movement* (Oxford: Clarendon, 1923); E. M. Butler, *The Tyranny of Greece over Germany*.

[23]Note the similarity of the descriptions of Greek poetry and mythology cited to William Duff's description of the "proper sphere of Fancy" as an "ideal region ... in which she may range with a loose rein, without suffering restraint from the severe checks of Judgment" (*An Essay on Original Genius*, p. 143), or Keats's own definition of poetry as "a little Region to wander in" where one can "pick and choose, and in which the images are so numerous that many are forgotten and found new in a second Reading" (*Letters*, I, 170).

These rather random references to classical antiquity, couched in the language of eighteenth-century primitivism, sometimes betray a condescension toward their subject that reflects the ambiguous valuation of imagination itself in rationalist Addisonian aesthetics. They are important, however, for what they point toward. Beyond such references one sees the contours of a Romantic myth of Greece which tries to recover for man what was formerly ascribed to the gods, and thus to affirm the possibility of a natural supernaturalism. Associations of Greece with liberty and the arts, commonplace in the eighteenth century, lay the goundwork for a more organized vision of Greece as an estate of the spirit in which total human freedom has been achieved and Prometheus has been unbound from his temporal destiny. The temporary enslavement of Greece to the Ottoman Empire does not reduce the country's exemplary value for the Romantic mind. Shelley, writing of the "twofold perfection of the arts and society" in Periclean Athens insists that "never was blind strength and stubborn form so disciplined and rendered subject to the will of man, or that will less repugnant to the dictates of the beautiful and the true. . . . Of no other epoch in the history of our species have we records and fragments stamped so visibly with the image of the divinity in man."[24] In the preface to *Hellas* he describes the ancient Greeks as "glorious beings whom the imagination almost refuses to figure to itself as belonging to our kind."[25] Elsewhere he absorbs Greek civilization into the Romantic dialectic of hope, as a means of insisting on the actuality of the possible: "What the Greeks were was a reality, not a promise. And what we are and hope to be is derived, as it were, from the influence and inspiration of these glorious generations."[26]

But it is to German aesthetic theory that one turns for a systematic view of the place of Greek civilization in a mythology of cultures that details the changing relations between spirit and reality. Winckelmann inaugurates a nostalgia for the classical era which sees it as privileged above all others in unity, harmony, and the immediate possession of a beauty for which modern man must struggle. He claims, incredibly, that "diseases which are destruc-

---

[24]Shelley, "A Defence of Poetry," p. 283.
[25]Shelley, "Preface to *Hellas*," *Poetical Works,* p. 447.
[26]Shelley, "A Discourse on the Manners of the Ancient Greeks," *Prose,* p. 219.

tive of beauty were, moreover, unknown to the Greeks."²⁷ Winckelmann's ideas contain the germ of what is developed with greater philosophical depth by Schiller, when he distinguishes between classical (naive) art and Romantic (sentimental) art as forms of consciousness involving different relationships of inner to outer reality. Thus sentimental art is crippled by a disjunction between human inwardness and its external conditions, between desire and its projected ideal, that is unknown in the naive art to which the modern self aspires.²⁸ Although Schiller can sometimes concede that the distinction between the two kinds of art is not a historical but an optative one, by and large Greece becomes the paradoxical embodiment of a light that never was on sea or land.²⁹ The description of the Juno Ludovici stands as an emblem of the culture which produced it: "a completely closed creation, and—as though it were beyond space—without yielding, without resistance . . . no force to contend with force, no unprotected part where temporality might break in."³⁰

Hegel, even as he dismisses classical art and art itself as mere stages in the evolution of Spirit, strengthens the allure of Greece as the home of a race "In will, in action free" (*Hyperion*, II.210). It is in Greece that art, as the expression of the divinity of the human form, reaches its zenith. Classical art is "the free and adequate embodiment of the Idea in the shape peculiarly appropriate to the Idea itself."³¹ It annuls the disjunction between inner desire and outward circumstance, between the ideal and the actual destinies of man. Classical art is the realization of the "completed Ideal," purified of "the contingent finitude of the phenomenal world."³² Perhaps Pater, who read Hegel but wrote from a literary point of view, brings out more clearly the pertinence of the myth of classicism to Romantic aspirations. Throughout the

²⁷Johann Joachim Winckelmann, "On the Imitation of the Painting and Sculpture of the Greeks," *Writings on Art*, ed. David Irwin (London: Phaidon, 1972), pp. 67, 63, 65. Henry Fuseli translated Winckelmann into English in 1765. Shelley read him in 1818 (Richard Holmes, *Shelley: The Pursuit* [New York: Dutton, 1975], p. 469).
²⁸Schiller, *Naive and Sentimental Poetry*, pp. 98ff.
²⁹Cf. Schiller, *On The Aesthetic Education of Man*, pp. 39, 43.
³⁰Ibid., p. 81.
³¹Hegel, *Aesthetics*, I, 77.
³²Ibid., I, 77–78.

history of art there is, according to him, "a struggle, a *Streben*, . . . between the palpable and limited human form, and the floating essence it is to contain."[33] Greek art alone marks the moment of peace in which the timeless becomes incarnated in the temporal. Classicism, the moment at which spirit becomes humanized and the body is lifted to the highest degree of spirituality, is essentially a myth of the human form divine, a myth which, in Pater's words, makes "for the human body a soul of waters, for the human soul a body of flowers."[34]

Although an increasing antiquarian interest in Greece may have provided the foundations for it, the Hellenic myth is most importantly a manifestation of Romantic idealism: poetic and philosophical. Greek culture furnishes a historical analogue for the myth of perfection embodied in such figures as the *schöne Seele* and the Shelleyan epipsyche, the images of a peculiarly privileged and ideal state of existence: "a soul within our soul that describes a circle around its proper paradise which pain, and sorrow, and evil dare not overleap."[35] The presiding deity of this ideal world is appropriately the god of poetry, Apollo, whom Nietzsche describes as "the 'lucent' one," "the god of light" who reigns over "the fair illusion of our inner world of fantasy" and allows us to dream and contemplate free of suffering.[36] Keats's own references to Apollo move between the pastoral and the prophetic, but he is always a god of harmony and light, associated with fruitfulness and joy[37] and not with the "misty pestilence" of *The Fall of Hyperion* (1.205). The link between Apollo and an ideal

---

[33]Pater, "A Study of Dionysus," p. 28.
[34]Ibid., p. 23.
[35]Shelley, "Essay on Love," p. 170.
[36]Nietzsche, *The Birth of Tragedy*, p. 21. Cf. also his comment, "the same drive that found its most complete representation in Apollo generated the whole Olympian world, and in this sense we may consider Apollo the father of that world" (ibid., p. 28).
[37]"Apollo to the Graces," l. 6; "In Drear-Nighted December," l. 13. Other references to Apollo are in "Ode to Apollo," "To Apollo," "Epistle to my Brother George" (ll. 9–12), "On First Looking into Chapman's Homer" (l. 4), "I Stood Tip-Toe" (ll. 47–56), "Sleep and Poetry" (ll. 58–61), *Endymion*, 1.141, iii.776. Keats's concept of Apollo is discussed at length by Walter Evert, who notes that Apollo is "the generative god of nature and art," symbolic of the imagination's power to create a "law of universal harmony, by which all existing things are held in a balanced relationship with each other, and initially discrete elements are fused" (*Aesthetic and Myth in the Poetry of Keats*, pp. 39, 31).

art that "does no harm from its relish of the dark side of things"[38]
is suggested at one point in the letters, where Apollo is close to
becoming the symbol of a purely naive and negatively capable
poetry: "let us open our leaves like a flower and be passive and
receptive—budding patiently under the eye of Apollo."[39]

The myth of revolution and fall which Keats chooses is radically
at odds with such aspirations. But vestiges of the optimistic intention behind the letter to Haydon remain in *Hyperion,* as blind
spots that point to a tenacious, but now impossible, idealism.
Among these are the almost unconscious alterations Keats makes
in the history that preceded the fall of the Titans, and in the
genesis of the children of Uranus and Gaea. Although it has often
been claimed that Keats confused the Titans and the Giants,[40] it
seems rather that he was aware of the difference between them
(*Hyperion,* ii.200), but reluctant to make separate mention of the
Giants because of what they represented in a world which, in
Shelley's words, was not supposed to know "pain or guilt" (*Hellas,*
l. 999). The Titans are "earth-born / And sky-engendered"
(i.309–310), symbolic, even in their fall, of a possible marriage
between nature and spirit, the human and the divine. The Giants,
born of the same parents,[41] point to an unacknowledgeable
awareness in the Greek mind that there were also darker possibilities in its history. They are children of what Yeats calls "the
blood-saturated ground," the ground which has known the pillag-
ing of hope by "Soldier, assassin, executioner."[42]

Of related significance is the remarkable change that Keats
makes in the Titans themselves, who become not Greek Titans but
Romantic Titans, symbolic of a ruined but recoverable perfection.
The era which precedes Saturn's fall in *Hyperion* is remarkable for

[38]Keats, *Letters,* i, 387.
[39]Ibid., p. 232.
[40]E. B. Hungerford, *Shores of Darkness,* p. 151; Pierre Vitoux, "Keats' Epic De-
sign in *Hyperion," Studies in Romanticism,* 14 (1975), 167–168.
[41]In Hesiod the Giants are the children of Gaea and Uranus, differing from the
Titans in that they have sprung from the blood of the mutilated Uranus. In
Hyginus they are the children of Gaea and Tartarus. In Lemprière's *Classical
Dictionary,* and elsewhere, they are described in such monstrous terms that they
could not possibly harmonize with Keats's idealized picture of the Titans. Cf. also
Harry Levin, *The Myth of the Golden Age in the Renaissance* (New York: Oxford
University Press, 1969), p. 17.
[42]Yeats, "Blood and the Moon," ll. 35–36.

the complete absence of the blind cycles of violence and cruelty so prominent in Hesiod's *Theogony*. Oceanus supplies a genealogy of the gods (ii.190–243), but makes no mention of Saturn devouring his children or of Uranus' castration by Saturn. Instead the Titan is a child of light distanced by his parents, the Heavens and Earth, from the darkness which is the original progenitor of his race. One thinks, by contrast, of Renaissance and medieval depictions of Saturn that concentrate on the cruel elements in the figure.[43] Keats transposes into the era which precedes the fall of the Titans the golden age of Saturn in Italy, which either follows his exile from power or forms a completely separate myth.[44] In so doing, he idealizes Saturn to make him the representative of a perfected, even if lost, moment in history. He blots out from Greek mythology the vision of son preying on father which constitutes the heart of darkness in its seemingly Arcadian world. Thus Saturn's reign is a peaceful, agrarian one, "all innocent of scathing war" (i.110, ii.336). He rules over realms of beauty and light (ii.201), over a beautiful and free humanity such as the Romantics associated with the myth of Greece.

Keats's tendency to gloss over the darker elements in the reign of the Titans is best understood as part of a desire to project onto the past his aspirations for art and culture in general. The Romantic mind, typified by such poems as *Endymion* and *Alastor*,

---

[43]Cf. Jean Seznec, *The Survival of the Pagan Gods*, trans. Barbara Sessions (New York: Harper, 1961), p. 176. Harry Levin even mentions a gruesome woodcut in Colard Mansion's *La Bible des poètes de Ovide Métamorphose* (Bruges, 1484), which depicts Saturn simultaneously eating an infant and being emasculated (*The Myth of the Golden Age in the Renaissance*, p. 195).

[44]The mythical golden age of King Saturnus in Italy became identified with Saturn because of the similarity of the names. Thus there are two myths involving Saturn: one which depicts the series of savage episodes that together make up the *Theogony*, and the other a pastoral myth of cultural and agrarian perfection. Lemprière tries to reconcile what are essentially two different myths, by describing an ideal period *after* Saturn's overthrow and banishment, in which he flees to Italy and civilizes the barbarians. But he does not depict the world before Saturn's fall as an ideal world. Ovid does depict an unfallen golden age of Saturn, which is followed by the rule of Jove, who curtails the everlasting spring and introduces the seasons (*Metamorphoses*, trans. Arthur Golding, ed. J. F. Nims [New York: Macmillan, 1965], 1.129ff.). But he does not specifically associate the loss of the golden age with the titanomachy. The uniqueness of Keats's version is that he conflates the two myths, superimposing the pastoral myth upon another myth whose vision of savagery and revolution must inevitably threaten the claims made by the myth of the golden age.

must conceive of its relationship to the ideal in dualistic and transcendent terms. But the classical world seems to hold out for it the naive possibility of an immanent beauty, "Diffused unseen throughout eternal space" (*Hyperion,* 1.318). Ironically, Keats's sentimentalization of his chosen myth simply displaces, without eliminating, the elements which block a dialectical separation of present and past. The darker elements kept out of Saturn's reign return in the world after his fall, which is beset by the rebellion of "son against his sire" and by the very emotions of fear and anxiety which Winckelmann had banished from his supreme fiction (1.333-335, 11.94-95). The occurrence of a fall raises the question of whether this fall is a contamination of perfection or the disclosure of a fault in being. It therefore undermines the notion of a lost but original innocence, necessary if the attempt to reconstruct a "fresh perfection" (11.212) is to be more than mere mythmaking. Oceanus tries to argue for a view of civilizations as progressively surmounting such lacunae in their genesis, but what he also points to is a vision of time as a series of cycles in which the potential for chaos that underlay the attempt to produce the first (Titanic) world of light is confirmed by the darkness that will lie behind the second (Apollonian) world of light.

Hyperion is important in the history of poetic idealism because, half a century before Nietzsche, it discovers the dark underside of one of the central myths of Romantic idealism. Apollo, who has hitherto always appeared in Keats's poetry as an autonomous being, is now presented in conjunction with a previous divine hierarchy to which he is linked through metaphors of genesis and psychological filiation that are only reinforced by Oceanus' attempt to see history as the *Bildungsroman* of a single consciousness. Implicit in the antecedents of Apollonian innocence is a knowledge that makes this innocence impossible. Keats shows Hyperion as the victim of the same corrosive awareness of mortality that strikes the dreamer at the foot of the stairs in *The Fall of Hyperion*:

> Am I to leave this haven of my rest,
> This cradle of my glory, this soft clime,
> This calm luxuriance of blissful light,
> These crystalline pavilions and pure fanes
> Of all my lucent empire? It is left

> Deserted, void, nor any haunt of mine.
> The blaze, the splendour and the symmetry
> I cannot see—but darkness, death and darkness.
> Even here, into my centre of repose,
> The shady visions come to domineer,
> Insult, and blind, and stifle up my pomp.
>
> [1.235–245]

The figure of Hyperion, splendid and yet carrying the knowledge of dusk within the appearance of dawn (II.357, 374–375), bursts on the poem like the terrible light of the Car in *The Triumph of Life*, which also discloses a core of fierce destruction within a Shape all light. Like the Car, the fallen Hyperion is an emblem of what happens to the attempt of the psyche to create an epipsyche, the attempt of the mind to create gods that will tame its chaos and multiply in it "a brighter ray / And more beloved existence" (*Childe Harold's Pilgrimage*, IV.v). His presence within the poem suggests how for Keats the Greek theogony becomes the disclosure of a genealogical link between the ideal and the real ignored by a tradition that seeks to segregate aesthetic appearance from the content of consciousness.

But Keats is still unwilling to build his palace of art in what Yeats calls "the crevices / Of loosening masonry."[45] The mode of *Hyperion* is more accurately that of the sentimental, which alternately recognizes and tries to minimize the gulf between the self and its projected ideal, using what Yeats called automatonism to move toward and away from tragedy. In linking his notion of an ideal culture to the very myth which explores its tenuousness, and in then blocking out the deconstructive elements in this myth, Keats reveals a desire both to demystify and to reconstruct the fiction of an ideal Greece. In this respect he is no different from the theorists of the period who also try to develop through the ironic and sentimental modes forms that will contain their uncertainties without renouncing the aspirations of idealism.

The end of *Hyperion* raises curious problems and suggests an emergent awareness of the split in the poem's strata of awareness that makes it impossible to complete. The scene with which the third book opens is initially one of pastoral plenitude, recalling

---

[45]Yeats, "Meditations in Time of Civil War," ll. 142–143.

the green world at the beginning of *Endymion* and the light of the
Chamber of Maiden-Thought. Mnemosyne, although nominally a
Titaness like Moneta, is less an admonitory than an inspirational
figure. She is the representative of a transition from "old and
sacred thrones" to prophecies of the future (III.77–79), rather
than the priestess of an enduring desolation. Although Apollo
sees her for the first time, she is familiar to him—something
which suggests a return through memory to lost sources of
plenitude within the self. She is even, in a sense, akin to the
Shelleyan epipsyche—but with the difference that she is unveiled
and reveals directly the beauty, truth, and poesy that the other
can only represent figuratively and evasively. Like the poet of
Alastor, Apollo is initially born into "the magnificence and beauty
of the external world,"[46] but then images to himself a vision that
is more than natural, a *spirit* that attends him in the grassy sol-
itudes of nature. Unlike Shelley's poet, he awakes and finds his
dream to be true:

> "Yes," said the supreme shape,
> "Thou hast dreamed of me; and awaking up
> Didst find a lyre all golden by thy side,"
>
> [III.61–63]

But almost immediately the poetry of earth is seen to contain a
darkening center. Apollo's description of himself is curiously reminiscent of the opening description of Saturn estranged from
nature and divinity (I.17–19): "a melancholy numbs my limbs; /
And then upon the grass I sit and moan, / Like one who once had
wings" (III.89–91). Although the awareness of Apollo's temporal
status is rapidly replaced by a surge of revelatory power, as his
consciousness is flooded by the knowledge of rebellions and history (III.112–119), the increasingly ecstatic tone of the book cannot blind us to the obstinate questions raised in it. Apollo's enormous knowledge, if experienced in terms of its content rather
than simply listed as a catalogue of events, ought directly to contradict the kind of art that Keats set out to create and still claims to
create in Mnemosyne's affirmation of "loveliness new born"
(III.79). From a later perspective the reader recognizes how much
these lines point foward to the power to see like a God that comes

[46]Shelley, "Preface to *Alastor*," *Poetical Works*, p. 14.

to the dreamer in *The Fall of Hyperion* (1.303–304), and to a mode of creation which does not allow the artist to transcend what he sees in Olympian apocalypse. An Apollo who has endured such an experience knows, as Yeats says, the fragility of the illusion by which the cycles of civilization are "hooped together . . . under the semblance of peace."⁴⁷ Logically he can bear little resemblance to the Apollo of the letter to Haydon or the unviolated young god of the earlier poetry, and one questions whether it is even useful to call him by the same name.

But it is clear that beyond the darkened present Keats continues to imagine some kind of restoration of the landscape he has left. Apollo at the point of rebirth is still the young god that he was before his encounter with experience, a slightly effeminate god who is described in terms of fair limbs and golden tresses that undulate round his neck (III.125, 131–132), and who is more like Adonis than Hyperion.⁴⁸ The manuscript version of the apotheosis reveals even more clearly Keats's feeling that the experience Apollo was undergoing could somehow be softened and pastoralized:

> Soon wild commotions shook him, and made flush
> All the immortal fairness of his limbs;
> Roseate and pained as any ravished nymph.
> Into a hue more roseate than sweet pain
>   ravish'd   warm
> Gives to a nymph ~~new~~ when her   tears
> Gush luscious with no sob. ~~Or know~~ Or more severe
> More like the struggle at the gate of death
> Or liker still to one who should take leave
> Of pale immortal death.⁴⁹

⁴⁷Yeats, "Meru," ll. 1–3.

⁴⁸Keats's depiction of Apollo is not inconsistent with other descriptions of Apollo, so much as the figure of Apollo is itself inconsistent with some of the tragic implications latent in the third book. Thomson describes Apollo as "a manly softened form. The Bloom of gods / Seems youthful o'er the beardless cheek to wave" (quoted in Larrabee, *English Bards and Grecian Marbles*, p. 81). Byron describes him in more masculine terms but also speaks of "his delicate form—a dream of Love, / Shaped by some solitary Nymph" (*Childe Harold's Pilgrimage*, IV.clxii). Cf. also Wordsworth, *The Excursion*, IV.859–860; Seznec, *The Survival of the Pagan Gods*, p. 178. But one might note that Joseph Spence depicts Apollo both in positive terms, and as a tormentor and inflicter of plagues (*Polymetis Abridged* [1755; rpt. London: J. Johnson, 1802], pp. 162–170, 171).

⁴⁹*Hyperion: A Facsimile of Keats' Autograph Manuscript*, ed. Ernest de Selincourt (Oxford: Clarendon, 1905).

The reference to the roseate nymph is very definitely a reversion
to the voluptuous landscape of the opening of the book (ll. 14ff.),
perhaps with the implication that the virginal earthly paradise can
be made better—more like Blake's image of Beulah as the mar-
ried land—by a consummation analogous to sexual completion.
Since he removed these lines from the poem Keats must have
recognized the absurdity of a transformation which couples a
nymph, ravished yet clinging to her adolescence, with the struggle
at the gate of death. Yet even as it stands Apollo's transformation
is "hot pastoral,"[50] as Geoffrey Hartman puts it. The poem does
not face the impossibility of conflating pastoral and nihilism, but
presses beyond it to an affirmation that Apollo is reborn. But it
seems from the manuscript version, where Keats is clearly grap-
pling with several alternative versions of the rebirth—one pastoral,
another tragic, and a third apocalyptic—that his apparent confidence masks a deep uncertainty about whether he has in fact
found an answerable style for his new climactic knowledge. Although he elects for the moment to move his poem toward
apocalypse, *The Fall of Hyperion* is evidence that he is troubled by
his failure to drain the urn of bitter prophecy to its dregs. In the
figure of Moneta "deathwards progressing / To no death"
(1.260–61), Keats ultimately chooses not to pass beyond the pale
world of death, whose immortality he already concedes in the
earlier poem even as he claims to have transcended it (III.128).

Hyperion, begun before two of the romances, is only incipiently
a deconstruction of the myth of an ideal art. For the greater part
of its two and a half books it is a committedly idealist poem,
concerned to project beyond itself the divine world which is
known only by the failure to possess it, and which is paradoxically
affirmed in terms of the shadow its absence casts upon an empty
world: an absence that, it is felt, must be the absence of something
once present. As Stuart Sperry points out, the birth of Apollo
from Hyperion was meant to bring about the purgation of the
"unstable, tormented" self and "the birth of the secure, serene,
type of creator Keats wanted to become."[51] In its inability to be-

---

[50]Geoffrey Hartman, "Toward Literary History," *Beyond Formalism,* p. 370.
[51]Stuart Sperry, *Keats the Poet* (Princeton: Princeton University Press, 1973), p.
192.

come Apollonian—to repossess the naive heaven that supposedly existed before the fall of the Titans or to project Apollo in a convincing manner beyond tragic antecedents that deny him sovereignty even in the title of the poem—Keats's poem calls into question the possibility of a naive art. But it is typical of the Romantic mind at a certain stage that even as it acknowledges the temporality of its own art, it is still haunted by the self-projected fiction of a more perfect art. Oceanus' speech tells us that the Greek theogony began in chaos and not in paradise. Yet the position of the Titans in relation to a myth of imaginative divinity which is actually later than they is paradoxically sentimental, and reveals Keats's own tendency to avoid the anxiety of imaginative nothingness by replacing it with a safer anxiety about the belatedness of Romantic in relation to "classical" culture. Rather than view his imaginative complexity constructively, Keats sees his relationship to the "beautiful mythology of Greece" which he seeks to recover as that of a later, Romantic poet in relation to a classical culture from whose simplicity he is forever excluded. Rather than depict the self-doubt of the Titans strongly, as an act of self-discovery, he views it weakly, as a decline from original perfection.[52]

[52]Of relevance here is Bloom's notion of the anxiety of influence, according to which poetic influence is "a variety of melancholy or anxiety-principle." "Weaker talents," according to him, "idealize," while stronger poets wrestle with their precursors in order to stake out for themselves a new imaginative space (*The Anxiety of Influence* [New York: Oxford University Press, 1973], p. 7). The sentimental classicism of the Romantics is, in this context, an expression of poetic weakness, in that it confers an absolute priority on the so-called precursor (or in this case, the precursor culture), and reduces the later poet to the status of failed apprentice. The extent to which Romantic sentimentalism inhibits creativity should therefore be apparent. The problem for the Romantic poet is to become a strong poet by moving beyond the sentimental and executing one of Bloom's revisionary ratios. In using the mode of irony the Romantic poet, it could be said, executes a *clinamen,* with regard not only to his precursor, but also to himself considered as his own precursor. Such a revision is, however, an incomplete movement. The revision of the precursor carried out by such texts as *The Birth of Tragedy* and *The Fall of Hyperion* might be considered an example of *apophrades,* defined by Bloom as follows: "the return of the dead; I take the word from the Athenian dismal or unlucky days upon which the dead returned to reinhabit the houses in which they had lived. The later poet, in his own final phase, already burdened by an imaginative solitude that is almost a solipsism, holds his own poem so open again to the precursor's work that at first we might believe the wheel has come full circle, and that we are back again in the later poet's flooded apprenticeship, before his strength began to assert itself in the revisionary ratios. But the poem is now *held*

The inability of Romantic art to think of itself as other than a failed idealism—evident in the use of elegy rather than tragedy in *Hyperion*—continues to impede the movement back to the real world begun in Keats's two odes, the "Ode to a Nightingale" and the "Ode on a Grecian Urn." In their separation of a mortal spectator from a timeless, ideal object, the odes seem to recognize and consent to the disjunction between the real and the ideal characteristic of Romantic consciousness. Yet they celebrate objects which are symbolic of a different kind of art: a naive art of pure song or a classical art of Apollonian and timeless space. Inevitably these emblems of an art that knows no dissonance become norms in relation to which the odes, as aesthetic objects themselves, must see the kind of art which they represent as a negation of aesthetic vision.[53] If fusion with the urn or the nightingale is sometimes seen as escapist, it is because art itself is reluctantly felt to be a simplification in a post-naive world, and not because Keats has revised his aesthetic canons to admit of an art that is not purely Apollonian.

It is essentially to this problem that Keats will return at the outset of *The Fall of Hyperion*, when Moneta distinguishes between poets and dreamers in terms that bring to mind Goethe's claim that classicism represents a norm of health in relation to which Romanticism is a sickness:[54]

> "The poet and the dreamer are distinct,
> Diverse, sheer opposite, antipodes.
> The one pours out a balm upon the world,
> The other vexes it."
>
> [1.199–202]

That the identification of poetry with the power to heal and harmonize was pervasive in the nineteenth century is evident in the

---

open to the precursor, where once it *was* open, and the uncanny effect is that the new poem's achievement makes it seem to us, not as though the precursor were writing it, but as though the later poet himself had written the precursor's characteristic work" (*The Anxiety of Influence,* pp. 15–16).

[53]A related problem arises in Coleridge's "Dejection: An Ode." Clearly the inability to create produces a poem; nevertheless the poem so produced is seen by Coleridge as contrary to the essence of poetry.

[54]Eckermann, *Conversations with Goethe,* p. 154. Cf. also Schiller, *Naive and Sentimental Poetry,* p. 105.

high status which both Arnold and Mill accorded Wordsworth for his therapeutic power. As in the early stages of *The Triumph of Life,* where Rousseau distinguishes between himself and the bards of elder time, the writer who sows seeds of misery in his readers is conceived as a failure in relation to another kind of creator who remains untarnished by the corruption of life. The Titans, like the captives in the procession of life, are deities of the tarnished imagination. In terms of the dichotomy between a serene, classical art and a restless, unsatisfied Romantic art which Keats and Shelley alike assume, the poem which depicts such deities is condemned to the status of failure. The opening of *The Fall of Hyperion* merely makes explicit what is perhaps less apparent in *Hyperion*: namely that the stuggle of the Titans and Olympians is part of Keats's own struggle to develop a hermeneutics of art.[55] Apollo stands as the fictional surrogate for the poet who contemplates life without suffering, while Hyperion is the troubled creation of a dreamer who is unable to separate the dawn from the dusk, pleasure from pain. Thus in retrospect the reader can see the significance of Keats's discovery that he could not celebrate Apollo without recognizing Hyperion, and also the protective motivation behind his abrupt shift from Hyperion to Apollo at the end of the third book.

We have already suggested that a deep uncertainty about idealistic vision led Keats to install Hyperion in the aesthetic pantheon, but that he was too committed to an idealist poetics not to see this uncertainty as something destructive. The relevance to the Hyperion poems of the debate over aesthetic naiveté between Schopenhauer and Nietzsche should therefore be evident. *The World as Will and Representation* is at least partly a questioning of the aesthetic ideals that the Romantic period projects onto the classical era. Schopenhauer's descriptions of the world as will, restless, yearning, and unsatisfied, match standard descriptions of the Romantic temperament. His idea of the world as representation (whether aesthetic or rational) conforms to norms of objectivity, detachment, and calm associated with classicism as a cure for

---

[55] In this respect Keats, as we will see, is closer to Nietzsche's treatment of the war of the Titans and Olympians as an allegory of aesthetic consciousness, than to Shelley's treatment of it as a political allegory.

the ills of Romanticism. But unlike Schiller's theories, which are motivated entirely by a desire to recover a lost innocence through a compensatory act of fiction, Schopenhauer's definition of art in terms of representation involves both the sentimental valorization of classical innocence over Romantic experience and the tragic deconstruction of the mask of innocence. He insists that art must preserve a counterworld in the midst of a world dominated by "an excessive inward misery."[56] But he also recognizes that this counterworld can exist only by an act of bad faith. Honesty thus compels him to see the work of art as also the embodiment of the world it is supposed to negate. Inevitably this leads to a self-contradictory and barely repressed favoring of Romantic dreamers over Apollonian poets, of Byron who vexes the will over Shakespeare who tranquilizes it.[57]

In his contradictory sense of art, as both revealing and concealing the world as will, Schopenhauer marks the penultimate stage in the movement of nineteenth-century German aesthetics from idyll to tragedy. Like Shelley, who defines art as at once a mirror and a lamp, Schopenhauer thus sees aesthetic representation as "only the objectification, the mirror, of the will, accompanying it to knowledge of itself," and at the same time "the most delightful, and the only innocent, side of life."[58] As we have seen, the crucial importance of this theory in the idealist debate derives from the fact that he defines will and representation as completely opposite in their effect on the reader, yet is forced to see them as identical in what they contain. Thus, almost unconsciously, he reveals as illusory the ideal of a naive art which is free of dissonance. Inasmuch as aesthetic representation is no more than an objective correlative for the will, the idealist separation of art from reality is not possible: the supposedly Apollonian world of art already contains the darkness of the world as will. The poem which was intended to celebrate Apollo, "a god . . . not of pathos and pathology or involvement, a god not of suffering but of freedom,"[59]

---

[56]Schopenhauer, *The World as Will and Representation*, I, 320.
[57]Ibid., II, 433.
[58]Ibid., I, 266.
[59]Thomas Mann, "Schopenhauer," *Essays*, trans. H. T. Lowe-Porter (New York: Vintage, 1957), p. 271.

turns out instead to contain the very suffering and mortality from which it was to provide a deliverance.

Because the awareness of suffering is supposedly alien to the work of art, its presence there is a covert presence, subversive of the destiny of art. It is Nietzsche who, in the realm of theory, provides a resolution to the dilemma of an aesthetics which is aware of destruction and death, yet unable to cope with its own knowledge. In *The Birth of Tragedy* he is concerned both to reexamine an interpretation of Hellenic culture which had formed the basis for the Romantic image of its own art, and to respond to the aesthetic theory of Schopenhauer, whose categories of will and representation are the metaphysical principles behind Dionysos and Apollo respectively.[60] The knowledge of "original pain . . . of eternal contradiction"[61] embodied in Dionysos is the knowledge which Shelley imaged in the form of a triumphal car with its captives. The fact that Dionysos shares with Apollo the sovereignty of the aesthetic world allows the awareness of destruction to become a constitutive rather than a blocking element in the work of art and permits the work of art to be openly a reflection of existence rather than a means to the ideal.

But what is perhaps more significant is that Nietzsche finds this awareness of the core of destruction in Greek culture, in the very culture which had been used by the Romantics as a tacit justification for an idealized theory of art, and which is now seen to provide a precedent for a very different image of art. Although the so-called naive art of Homeric epic had sought to affirm a golden world of gods and heroes against the darkness of reality, Greek tragedy had been a return beneath the ceremonies of innocence to the original roots of a culture whose knowledge of darkness preceded its creation of a Shape all light. Nietzsche shows both that consciousness did not originally exist in a state of purity and somehow "fall" into impurity, and that the earliness of

---

[60] It is important to bear in mind that Schopenhauer's metaphysics forms the background to Nietzsche's theory of tragedy, in order not to limit the debate between Dionysos and Apollo to the debate between frenzy and rationality depicted in Euripides' *Bacchae,* and in order not to identify Dionysos with something like Lawrence's blood-consciousness or Nietzsche's own subsequent will-to-power.

[61] Nietzsche, *The Birth of Tragedy,* p. 33.

classicism does not make it ontologically prior to Romanticism as substance is to shadow. Classical tragedy, as Nietzsche defines it,[62] comprehends both "the fair world of Apollo and its substratum, the terrible wisdom of Silenus," and makes us understand "how they mutually require one another."[63] Centuries before the Romantic period, it already recognized the impossibility of knowing "The pain alone; the joy alone; distinct" (*The Fall of Hyperion*, 1.174), and found in this vexation the source of its imaginative power. The tragedy of the Greeks thus provides Nietzsche with a means to fulfill the stated aim of his essay: to reexamine Greek culture with a view to legitimizing the pessimism of Romantic art, and then to show how there can be a "strong pessimism" which does not carry the taint of lateness and decadence.[64]

In his discussion of Romantic imagery Paul de Man suggests that there are a number of Romantic myths which recognize the basic structure of aesthetic consciousness as an "intentionality" or an emptiness, which seeks to coincide with a plenitude that it ascribes to something outside itself[65]—whether it be nature, Intellectual Beauty, or a Grecian urn. The Romantic myth of the Hellenic, the myth of a beautiful soul at home in a free land, is clearly one of these myths. It originates in the desire of aesthetic consciousness to draw closer to the Apollonian and objective, and enacts the failure of that desire, while preserving the myth of an ideal (if not actual) Apollonian discourse. It was Nietzsche's great achievement that he discovered the purely optative quality of Romantic myths of perfection, and so liberated Romantic consciousness from the shadow of a self-projected ideal. Failure to attain this ideal had turned silence and solitude into vacancy and had compelled Romantic poems to cast themselves in the mode of failure. Nietzsche's excavations in the archaeology of the Greek ethos diminished the crippling distance between the present and a supposedly perfect past by allowing the Romantic mind to see that the language of Apollonian classicism was itself a mask. In so

[62]Hegel, by contrast, sees Greek tragedy as moving beyond dissonance to a restored harmony. See *Hegel on Tragedy*, ed. Anne and Henry Paolucci (1962; rpt. New York: Harper, 1975).

[63]Nietzsche. *The Birth of Tragedy*, p. 33. For Nietzsche's account of the story of Silenus, see p. 29.

[64]Ibid., p. 4.

[65]De Man, "The Intentional Structure of the Romantic Image," p. 70.

doing they allowed the Romantic mind to consent to its own incompleteness, to become emancipated from the notion that its darker recognitions somehow made its own art abnormal in relation to a classical norm of poetry as the mode of humanists and physicians.

But this recognition had already been reached far earlier in the history of Romanticism, in the final poems of both Keats and Shelley. Like Nietzsche's essay, *The Fall of Hyperion* is a piece of archaeological research, an attempt by Keats to revisit the site of a personal and cultural past in order to find the divinities that shape his art. As it turns out, these gods are not Olympians but Titans, the gods of an excessive inward misery, an incurable pain, which it is the role of poetry to commemorate. Keats begins by defining art as the power that "vanquishes the suffering that inheres in all existence" and, in Nietzsche's words, glosses away the pain "from nature's countenance."[66] His definition of the poet resembles Schopenhauer's purely Apollonian definition of art as a deliverance from the will, and his reluctant admission that he is a dreamer is made in the same vein of renunciation as Schopenhauer's final, unwilling conclusion that an art which has failed to be a "quieter of the will"[67] must be rejected as having betrayed its high expectations. But he ends by creating a poem such as Nietzsche was to envision, a poem which draws its power from the recognition "that everything that is generated must be prepared to face its painful dissolution."[68]

The Fall of Hyperion, despite its early condemnations of the dreamer, gradually revalues his status, in the same way that Rousseau is rehabilitated in *The Triumph of Life*. As in Shelley's poem, the revaluation of a figure who has been symbolic of the Romantic failure becomes a way to transcend the crippling antithesis between a classical art that quiets the will and a Romantic art which sows seeds of misery. Of crucial importance to our sense of what distinguishes the second from the first version of Keats's Hyperion myth is the altered relationship between the Titans and the Olympians, equivalents for the dreamer and the poet. In *Hyperion* the presence of the Titans had been the evidence of a failure,

[66] Nietzsche, *The Birth of Tragedy*, p. 102.
[67] Schopenhauer, *The World as Will and Representation*, 1, 267.
[68] Nietzsche, *The Birth of Tragedy*, p. 102.

subversive of art, as the poet suggests in instructing his muse to leave them aside (III.3). In *The Fall of Hyperion* their experience has become a source of knowledge and vision, a mystery to be revealed only to the initiate. Here, finally, Keats recognizes his kinship with what he had rejected in *Hyperion*. Fifty years later Nietzsche, who unexpectedly links the rivalry of Apollo and Dionysos to the struggle of the Olympians and the Titans,[69] explains the place of the Titans in the theogony of creative consciousness. His statement can also stand as a gloss on the process of revision that takes place between Keats's two poems:

> The Apollonian need for beauty had to develop the Olympian hierarchy of joy by slow degrees from the original titanic hierarchy of terror. . . . The same drive which called art into being as a completion and consummation of existence, and as a guarantee of further existence, gave rise also to that Olympian realm which acted as a transfiguring mirror to the Hellenic will. . . . Whenever we encounter "naiveté" in art, we are face to face with the ripest fruit of Apollonian culture—which must always triumph first over titans, kill monsters, and overcome the somber contemplation of actuality, the intense susceptibility to suffering, by means of illusions strenuously and zestfully entertained. . . . yet [the Greeks] could not disguise from themselves the fact that they were essentially akin to those deposed Titans and heroes. They felt more than that: their whole existence, with its temperate beauty, rested upon a base of suffering and *knowledge* which had been hidden from them until the reinstatement of Dionysos uncovered it once more. And lo and behold! Apollo found it impossible to live without Dionysos.[70]

The Fall of Hyperion is not simply a redefinition of a Hellenic ideal regarded as normative for art. It also stands in a revisionary relationship to the assumptions of revolutionary optimism present in such works as *Prometheus Unbound* and Blake's *Milton*. Keats emerged from the first two books of *Hyperion* trapped by a disjunction between classical and Romantic art that condemned him to a poetry of exclusion. But he did not immediately turn toward a renunciation of idealism as the only norm for art. As

---

[69]In this respect Nietzsche seems to differ from the usual identification of Dionysos as an Olympian, a son of Zeus.

[70]Nietzsche, *The Birth of Tragedy*, pp. 30–31, 34.

Spengler has pointed out, the tripartite schemas of history developed by nineteenth-century idealism from Hegel onwards, in which a fallen present exists only to generate the hope of a more glorious future, "shattered the dualistic world-form" of previous eras by introducing a synthesizing era which could potentially give history "the look of a progression [toward]... a third kingdom [of] fulfilment and culmination."[71] The prophetic mode, in which poetry takes possession of the world-spirit in order to make itself the agent which discloses this third kingdom, is perhaps the most tenacious manifestation of the self-mystification by which Romantic art tries to recover a naive vision and hide from itself the knowledge of its radically temporal destiny. It has obvious affinities with post-Kantian idealism, which lays an epistemological claim to the cognition of ultimate reality and therefore to the achievement of a perfection which is no longer transcendent but immanent and imminent. The extent to which *Hyperion* commits itself to the assumptions of prophecy, and the extent to which this commitment is a compensatory redirection of a failed idealism, will be explored in the pages which follow. Also worth considering is the extent to which the fragmentary status of the poem, unintended as it may have been, supports the rhetoric of prophecy, by creating the sense of something to be completed in the future.

Keats presumably wrote *Hyperion* without reading *Prometheus Unbound*. Nevertheless Clymene's account of the "mouthed shell" which becomes filled with a "new blissful golden melody" (II.270–280) is curiously similar to Shelley's account of the "curved shell" in *Prometheus Unbound* "which Proteus old / Made Asia's nuptial boon, breathing within it / A voice to be accomplished" (III.iii.65–67). The letter on *Hyperion*,[72] concerned with both the Greek past and the revolutionary future, also provides evidence of Keats's affinities with the post-Kantian faith that art could combine with history in the legislating of a new world-order. Given Keats's lack of political interests, one is particularly struck by the reference to Napoleon, which assimilates the triumph of poetry to what can be described as a revolutionary paradigm of experience, obliquely suggested through the allusion to events in

---

[71]Spengler, *The Decline of the West*, p. 19.
[72]Cf. Keats, *Letters*, I, 207.

France. Napoleon for Shelley was a negative symbol of the tendency for revolution to be betrayed into counterrevolution and to perpetuate the cycles of history. Keats's notion of him seems closer to that of Byron, who implicitly makes a favorable link between Napoleon and Prometheus,[73] viewing the former as a frustrated and bound representative of a potentially valuable urge to transcend the temporal. Using Napoleon as a symbol of human limitation, Keats implies that poetry can take up where politics left off and complete the perfection of the world that could not be achieved through the French Revolution. Elsewhere he depicts Milton's career as enacting the same movement from pastoral to prophecy that he wanted to find in his own poem: Milton "had an exquisite passion for what is properly, in the sense of ease and pleasure, poetical Luxury; and with that it appears to me he would fain have been content . . . but there was working in him as it were that same sort of a thing as operates in the great world to the end of a Prophecy's being accomplished."[74] In his view of Milton as participating in an endeavor that extends beyond the bounds of his own will and conception, Keats is close to Shelley's concluding reference in "A Defence of Poetry" to individuals who are unconscious instruments of the spirit of the age.[75] But, more important, both poets reveal an affinity with Hegel's notion of a world-spirit that operates through a series of individuals, rupturing the calm surface of their lives, and then discarding them "like empty hulls from the kernel" when their purpose has been served.[76] The *locus classicus* for such a view within the poem itself is Oceanus' programmatic speech to the Titans, which at-

---

[73]"Ode to Napoleon Bonaparte" and *Childe Harold's Pilgrimage*, III.xxxvi. Cf. Harold Bloom, "Napoleon and Prometheus: The Romantic Myth of Organic Energy," *The Ringers in the Tower*, pp. 81–84. Bloom quotes Blake's description of his lost painting "The Spiritual Form of Napoleon": here Napoleon is a "strong energetic figure grasping at the sun and moon with his hands, yet chained to earth by one foot." Again, in contrast to Shelley, Hazlitt sees Napoleon as the champion of the Revolution: "the sword-arm of the Revolution which triumphed and perished with him" (*Life of Napoleon, Complete Works*, III, 38).

[74]Keats, "Notes on Milton's *Paradise Lost*," *The Poetical Works and Other Writings of John Keats*, ed. H. B. Forman (London: Reeves and Turner, 1883), p. 19.

[75]Shelley, "A Defence of Poetry," p. 297.

[76]Hegel's discussion of Napoleon as an instrument of the World-Spirit can be found in *The Philosophy of History*, trans. J. Sibree (1899; rpt. New York: Dover, 1956), p. 31.

tempts to rationalize the blind purgatory of Saturn's fall by assimilating it into a philosophy of creative evolution.

Perhaps for no other reason than the prevalence of biological metaphors in the Romantic period, the imagery of Oceanus' speech seems similar to the imagery of light and darkness used in Schelling's *Of Human Freedom*:

> From chaos and parental darkness came
> Light, the first fruits of that intestine broil,
> That sullen ferment, which for wondrous ends
> Was ripening in itself.
>
> [II.191-194]

As in Schelling's treatise, darkness is not the death of light but the hiding place of a future light, which lies buried within the darkness as the seed within the soil.[77] Hegel's image of the world-spirit as a kernel of infinity concealed within a limiting shell provides a further instance of a pattern of imagery which tries to distingush the spirit contained from the medium that contains it, and to suggest that the hidden *telos* of events develops the deeper truth of life dialectically from surface realities that seem to oppose it.[78] Thus it is possible for patterns of decline and defeat to enclose a future rhetoric of hope, which it is the function of poetry to decode and then to disclose. The famous image of the philosophical imagination as an air-sylph forming within the skin of the caterpillar, used by both Coleridge and Fichte, depicts the virtual inevitability of the process by which nature herself discloses the potential within the actual, and evolves perfection from imperfection: philosophy is "the power that shall first set free the imprisoned Psyche and

---

[77]Thus Schelling writes: "All birth is a birth out of darkness into light: the seed must be buried in the earth and die in darkness in order that the lovelier creature of light should rise and unfold itself in the rays of the sun. Man is formed in his mother's womb . . . " (*Of Human Freedom* [1809], trans. James Gutmann [Chicago: Open Court, 1936], p. 35). De Quincey likewise uses germinal imagery to describe historical processes ("Idea of a Universal History on a Cosmopolitical Plan," *Collected Writings*, IX, 442-443).

[78]Hegel, *The Philosophy of History*, p. 31. A variant of the biological metaphor which sees the germ of future perfection within present imperfection is the metaphor of the corrupt temporal body which encloses and disguises the eternal spirit within. Cf. *Prometheus Unbound*, II.60-65, *The Triumph of Life*, ll. 204-205; Schelling, *Of Human Freedom*, p. 40. What both metaphors have in common is a belief that corruption is not intrinsic to the soul, but is something external: the product of institutions or historical circumstance.

unfold her wings, so that, hovering for a moment above her former self, she may cast a glance on her abandoned slough, and then soar upwards thenceforward to live and move in higher spheres."[79] In this respect nature herself provides a model for the disclosing activity of poetry and poetic philosophy, whose sacred duty it is to liberate the inner shape of things through prophecy, rather than to limit imaginative vision to the mimesis of the actual.[80]

Schelling sees nature as a single and continuous creation, rising from the darkness of the material world "to complete unity with light," through a process of graded evolution in which each higher stage appears to be a negation of the preceding stage, but is in actuality a fulfillment of the hidden tendency within it.[81] In similar but less mystical terms Coleridge describes how "the maximum of each lower kind becomes the base and receptive substrate, as it were, of a higher kind, commencing through the irradiation and transfiguration by the higher power, the base of which it has become."[82] What is perhaps attractive about such schemas is that they seem to subsume rather than deny the more negative elements in nature and history. A common archetype emerges from such thinkers as Schelling, Fichte, and Hegel: that of human cultural development as possessed of a self-evolving energy that draws it teleologically toward the approachable but inaccessible goal of absolute freedom and completeness.[83] The letter on Apollo, considered alongside Oceanus' speech, asks to be

[79]J. G. Fichte, *The Vocation of Man* (1800), ed. Roderick M. Chisholm (Indianapolis and New York: Bobbs-Merrill, 1956), p. 144. Cf. also Coleridge: "They and they only can acquire the philosophic imagination, the sacred power of self-intuition, who within themselves can interpret and understand the symbol, that the wings of the air-sylph are forming within the skin of the caterpillar; those only, who feel in their own spirits the same instinct, which impels the chrysalis of the horned fly to leave room in its involucrum for antennae yet to come" (*Biographia Literaria*, ed. John Shawcross [Oxford: Clarendon, 1907], I, 167).

[80]Cf. Shelley's statement: A poet "not only beholds intensely the present as it is . . . but he beholds the future in the present, and his thoughts are the germs of the flower and the fruit of latest time: ("A Defence of Poetry," p. 279). Biological and evolutionary metaphors are frequent in Shelley, and link him clearly to the aesthetics of post-Kantian idealism.

[81]Schelling, *Of Human Freedom*, p. 38.

[82]Coleridge, *Theory of Life*, quoted by John Muirhead, *Coleridge as Philosopher* (1930; rpt. London: George Allen and Unwin, 1970), p. 126.

[83]Abrams, *Natural Supernaturalism*, pp. 172–179.

read with such an archetype of human progress in mind. The same biological monism which allows us to see matter and spirit as part of an ascending and continuous chain of being, stretching from root to flower, also permits us to see history as a single organism which derives the higher stages of its culture from its lower reaches. M. R. Ridley's intriguing suggestion that in Edward Davies' *Celtic Researches,* one of Keats's possible sources, the Titans and the Olympians were really the same people, is consistent with the idea of history as a narrative that has as its hero a single Universal Man, who is mankind at its various stages of evolution.[84] Keats, it would seem, planned a prophetic epic which would deal with the ascending march of time, and which would herald a new age through the figure of Apollo as both the hero and the shaper of the action. Interestingly, Apollo is described as "fore-seeing": the meaning of the name Prometheus.

Keats's letter is a somewhat confusing document. On the one hand it makes a distinction between a subjective, Romantic art and an objective, classical art, and thus locates the redemptive vision in a cultural past. On the other hand it seems to suggest that the goal of consciousness is a point in the future, necessitating an art that is prophetic rather than elegiac. In this respect the letter reflects both the problem of the poem itself and the historical dilemma of Romanticism, as a postclassical mode which initially defines itself in terms of loss and failure, and then tries to recover a sense of itself as a point of origin for future cultural development. Both Schiller and (at a certain point in his career) Friedrich Schlegel betray an ambiguity about whether to prefer a classical art that is seen as achieving a fulfillment denied to Romantic art, or a Romantic art whose incompleteness may herald the possibility of evolution and improvement.[85] This hesitation, in turn, reveals an underlying uncertainty about how Romantic art is to cope with the temporal rather than transcendent status of its language.

The myth of a modern or Romantic art that has become separated from a prelapsarian, classical art is already an acknowledgment by the Romantic mind of the temporality of its own language. Given a deep unwillingness to renounce a mode of vision

---

[84]M. R. Ridley, *Keats' Craftsmanship* (1933; rpt. London: Methuen, 1964), p. 65.
[85]Cf. A. O. Lovejoy, *Essays in the History of Ideas* (New York: Braziller, 1955), pp. 194ff., 210ff.

free of the problematical as normative for art, Romantic art has only two alternatives. It can accept its own temporality (although not that of art in general), and condemn itself to a poetics of exclusion and exile from the ideal, which remains intact but buried deep in a lost past. In this case the terrible doubt that all language (and not just Romantic language) may be temporal is always precariously close. Alternately Romantic art can commit the hubris of claiming to transcend its own condition, through a journey toward a new ideal that is projected upon the future.[86] The inherently sentimental structure of prophecy is thus more than apparent. The idea of a poetry whose drive toward the future makes the present "the elastic point of progressive development"[87] grows directly from a feeling that Romantic poetry can neither coincide with an Edenic classical past, nor accept the resulting temporality of language. Instead poetry opts for a new mode of vision which is prophetic rather than mimetic or tragic, and which becomes centered in such surrogates as Oceanus, who embodies the artist's power to move out of the temporal world of the poem and disclose the ultimate pattern of things from a point in the future. A new aesthetics of the infinite develops, in which the failure to have attained the ideal is rationalized by locating the ideal beyond rather than behind the aesthetic act. And this new aesthetics receives metaphysical sanction from the system of Fichte, which represents existence itself as the endless striving of the Absolute Ego toward an unattainable but approachable goal.

The letter on *Hyperion* remains cryptic because a number of ideas that have not been fully worked out are telescoped into a relatively short statement. But it seems that here, as in the wider arena of Romantic aesthetics, the millennial vision of poetry as marching onward toward the future arises partly as a compensatory response to an experience of failure encountered in *Endymion*. The letter thus anticipates the emotional dynamics of *Hyperion* itself, a poem concerned with acknowledging and circumventing the crisis of a logocentric Romantic vision. Through the fall of

---

[86] Here it is not so much the Romantic mode which becomes normative for art in general, as the apocalyptic act toward which it points.

[87] Friedrich Schlegel, *Dialogue on Poetry and Literary Aphorisms*, p. 144. Lovejoy interestingly notes that the "infinity" which is exemplified for Schlegel by Romantic poetry corresponds to Schiller's concept of naive poetry, rather than to his concept of sentimental or Romantic poetry (*Essays in the History of Ideas*, p. 225).

the Titans, Keats confronts the waning of beauty and the inability of imagination to construct a myth that will house its aspirations toward an ideal culture. The projection of power into the future permits him to move beyond the failure he has acknowledged, through the figure of a Promethean Apollo who, in suffering like the Titans and yet transcending that suffering, restores the link between humanity and divinity. It is a kind of radical poetics, which allows Keats not to see Romantic poetry as a fading coal, and which corresponds to the radical politics of other poets.

There are numerous parallels for Keats's attempt to build restorative patterns into *Hyperion*. A. W. Schlegel analyzes the teleological movement of the Aeschylean trilogy as a way of absorbing tragedy into epic. He sometimes sees tragedy as a form as structured around the ascent from the Titans to the Olympians: from the mind's dark gods to fuller consciousness.[88] There are also the Miltonic parallels that project a pattern in which the loss of paradise is seen in terms of a fortunate fall that points toward restoration. Neither of these triadic and incipiently Hegelian patterns is worked out with any degree of conviction in the first two books of the poem. Thus it is the arrival of Apollo in the third book to which one must turn if one is to argue the claim of *Hyperion* to be a logocentric poem, expressive of the Romantic spiral toward perfection. The incompleteness of this book has generally (and in the last analysis accurately) been seen as crippling the poem's drive toward synthesis. It does not follow, however, that Keats saw it in this way at the time he was writing it. We have already discussed the attempt of Romanticism to favorably revaluate its place in cultural history. As part of this attempt, post-Kantian aesthetics is also implicitly engaged in redefining the status of aesthetic endeavors that are in some way incomplete or inchoate, and in seeing the fragment as something more than the fading relic of a lost perfection.

Shelley's "Defence of Poetry" provides at least initial hints for an aesthetics of incompleteness. Despite an awareness of failure that comes out in such phrases as the description of poetry in terms of a fading coal,[89] it is a resoundingly prophetic document. There is a tendency to convert present imperfection—potentially

---

[88]A. W. Schlegel, *Lectures on Dramatic Art and Literature*, pp. 81, 79–80, 88, 93.
[89]Shelley, "A Defence of Poetry," p. 294.

subversive of hope—into a promise of future perfection, so that the failings of the present cease to be a falling away from original inspiration and become instead shadows of a reality to come. Images that see poetry as an enfeeblement of the ideal which precedes it are canceled out by images that see the unfinished quality of present language not as a sign of finiteness but as part of a drive to develop, in which "the future is contained within the present as the plant within the seed."[90] Thus it is possible for the vehicle of a vision to be imperfect without in any way affecting the vision itself, which points beyond its present embodiment toward a less limited future. Something of this rationalization of present imperfection is perhaps present in the third book of *Hyperion*. Although it has been argued that the poem breaks off because of a recognition that a restored harmony is incompatible with the suffering which must precede it, one can also argue that its incompleteness indicates a potential for further evolution, through the expansion of that new conception of human divinity which now exists only in embryo. Significantly, the poem breaks off on a climax, and not with the figure of Apollo "cursed and thwarted" (III.92). The new god may fail to convince the reader because Keats's conception of him is riven by hopeless contradictions. But the figure of Apollo may also be unsatisfying for more positive reasons: because the spirit that he embodies is, in Shelley's phrase, a lightning which has as yet found no conductor.[91]

There is thus more than one way to interpret the inability of Apollo to embody what Keats wanted him to embody. Hegel's Philosophy of Art reveals yet another aspect of the persistent debate between classical completeness and Romantic incompleteness.[92] In distinguishing between the two kinds of art within an ascending typology of cultures, Hegel speaks of the perfect harmony of form and spirit in Greek art, but justifies the disjunction between tenor and vehicle in the Romantic image by referring to an outer

---

[90]Ibid., p. 278.

[91]Ibid., p. 291.

[92]One may also point to A. W. Schlegel's characterization of Romantic art as a *Streben nach dem Unendlichen,* and to Friedrich Schlegel's description of it in terms of an aesthetics of the infinite: "the Romantic type of poetry is still becoming, its peculiar essence is that it is always becoming and that it can never be completed" (*Dialogue on Poetry and Literary Aphorisms,* p. 141).

reality which is incapable of fully representing spirit.[93] Like Schiller, he viewed the Romantic period as the disintegration of the classical ethos, but here the very characteristics that were thought to make Romanticism deficient become the source of its superiority in the grand march of Universal Man from nature to spirit, from finite to infinite. A model of history as progress rather than decline makes it possible to view even the failure of art to do what it is supposed to do in an affirmative light. Hegel discusses the problem of an art that is unable to satisfy its yearnings, and deliberately breaks with Schiller in not concluding that the gap between aspiration and embodiment converts the Romantic poem into a self-frustrated literary structure. On the contrary, he makes art's acknowledgment of its own inadequacies a gesture of triumph. Because the containing medium of Romantic art is finite, the work of art must become self-consuming, must die for the spirit within to find life in a realm beyond that of the poem itself. In his essay on Winckelmann, Pater recapitulates Hegel's typology of art and distinguishes between the Greek mind, which "begins and ends with the finite image," and the "overcharged symbols" of Romantic art, which are "a means of hinting at an ideal which art can not fitly or completely express" and in which "thought . . . outstrip[s] or lie[s] beyond the proper range of its sensible embodiment."[94] The poem itself is no more than the temporary vehicle of a vision that lies beyond it and becomes the sword of lightning that consumes the scabbard which would contain it.[95] The ultimate goal of consciousness is that which lies beyond the poem and to which the poem propels the reader.

Hegel did not set out to write a hermeneutics of the fragment form. Nevertheless what emerges from a juxtaposition of his theory with the large number of incomplete poems (and aphoristic forms of discourse)[96] in the early nineteenth century is a new

---

[93]Hegel, *Aesthetics*, 1, 77–81.
[94]Pater, "Winckelmann," *The Renaissance*, pp. 217, 218–219.
[95]Shelley, "A Defence of Poetry," p. 285.
[96]Blake annotated Lavater's *Aphorisms,* and his own *Marriage of Heaven and Hell* is cast in aphoristic form. Nietzsche comments on his own tendency to write in aphorisms and fragments, by defining the aphorism as ordinary consciousness raised to a higher power, where it comprehends through imaginative leaps: "In the mountains the shortest way is from peak to peak. . . . Aphorisms should be peaks—and those who are addressed, tall and lofty. The air thin and pure" (*Thus*

way of reading the literary fragment as something which stands as the formal equivalent of hope and potential. It becomes possible to see the breaking off of a poem as a high point, a moment of conversion in which the poem, by announcing its own finiteness, also makes known to the reader the infiniteness of that which it does not contain. Perhaps the best instance of a work that seems to bear out Hegel's theory is Shelley's *Epipsychidion*,[97] which concludes by celebrating a spirit that surpasses its sensible embodiment (ll. 587-591). The reader may be tempted to view the poem's failure to reach the far goal of time as something which negates the possibility of vision. But the poem is impelled forward by a sense that the very inadequacy of its medium validates a vision that lies just out of its reach, beyond the bounds of expression but still within the horizon of conception. Indeed, the incompleteness of the narrative—stemming from the fact that the intended journey of the lovers toward the ideal has not been made except in imagination—acts as a generating force in the poem, by setting up a challenge to be overcome in the open space beyond the final lines.

Such a reading of *Epipsychidion* is, of course, a rationalization of the poem's failure—one which salvages a celebratory and logocentric discourse from a narrative that is elegiac and therefore deconstructive of its own claims. But it is nevertheless a rationalization in which Shelley intends us to engage. Whether Keats meant the incompleteness of *Hyperion* to be read as a gesture of triumph or of defeat is more difficult to say. There is at least a precedent for a

---

Spake Zarathustra [1891–1892], trans. Walter Kaufmann [New York: Viking, 1966], p. 40). Some of Friedrich Schlegel's most pregnant ideas on art are cast in the form of aphorisms which convey the germinal energy of an idea rather than its discursive unfolding. Schlegel explicitly extends the principle of the energized fragment to his dialogues when he comments that "a dialogue is a chain or wreath of aphorisms" (*Dialogue on Poetry*, p. 137). A further comment that "a correspondence is a dialogue on an enlarged scale" (ibid.) may suggest the rationale behind a work such as Hölderlin's *Hyperion*, which is cast in the form of a correspondence.

[97]*Epipsychidion* is not, strictly speaking, a fragment. Nevertheless the "Advertisement" directs us to read it as somehow incomplete. The poem is described as "sufficiently intelligible to a certain class of readers," but presumably esoteric to other classes of readers. It "appears to have been intended by the writer as a dedication to some longer [poem]" (*Poetical Works*, p. 411). Also of significance is the fact that the writer died before embarking on his voyage, and that his home on the island was to have been the renovated ruin of an old building.

positive reading of incompleteness, in the view that Keats takes of
Endymion as not fulfilled within itself but fulfilled in the poem
beyond it.[98] *Hyperion,* moreover, does not actually seem to see
itself in tragic terms. Mention has already been made of the point
at which Keats chooses to break off *Hyperion.* It is evident in the
manuscript that Apollo is not on the verge of apotheosis but has
actually achieved it,[99] and possibly the poem stops at this point
simply because Apollo's deification leaves nothing more to be
said. The dots with which the poem concludes can be seen as
opening out into a broader space. From this point of view, the
poem remains incomplete only because of the impossibility of
bringing into the finite space of the narrative the infinite vista that
lies beyond apotheosis. Shelley, in fact, desribes a statue of Apollo
in terms of the "god-like animation" of its limbs, "the spirit which
seems as if it would not be contained."[100] And Schiller, discussing
the vocation of the artist, insists that the failure of the present to
incarnate the future is no obstacle: for the "pure moral impulse . . . the future is its present, . . . direction is also completion,
and the road has been travelled when once it has been chosen."[101]

The penultimate lines bear out the more positive interpretation
of the poem's incompleteness at least as much as the final lines
point toward *The Fall of Hyperion*:

> "Creations and destroyings, all at once
> Pour into the wide hollows of my brain,
> And deify me, as if some blithe wine
> Or bright elixir peerless I had drunk."
>
> [III.116–119]

The "knowledge enormous" that Apollo receives here (III.113)
differs from the later "power of enormous ken" in being epic and
apocalyptic rather than tragic: more an encounter with the spirit
of prophecy than a tempering awareness of the core of fierce

---

[98]See *Endymion,* IV.774, where Keats refers to his plans for *Hyperion,* and the
letter to Haydon (already cited) where *Hyperion* is seen as taking up where *Endymion* left off.

[99]There is no authority for Woodhouse's addition of the words "Glory dawned,
he was a god," but the manuscript does contain the words "and lo he was the God!"
(*Hyperion: A Facsimile of Keats' Autograph Manuscript*).

[100]Shelley, "Notes on Sculptures in Rome and Florence," *Prose,* p. 347.

[101]Schiller, *On the Aesthetic Education of Man,* p. 53.

destruction. Apollo's vision of events and rebellions is felt as a vertiginous expansion of consciousness beyond its finite limits, which elevates him from the hero of a private visionary quest to the vehicle of something like the Hegelian world-spirit. Apollo's deification climaxes Keats's attempt in the third book to impose on his poem a forcible shift in mode. In this canto Keats moves, experimentally, toward the form used by Blake and sometimes by Shelley. The mythological prophecy, which tries to secularize the Miltonic, logocentric epic by using a classical or personal rather than a Christian pantheon, claims for the poet and for his human discourse unmediated access to, or even identity with, a transcendental source. The assumptions behind such a form are radically humanistic. Indeed, since myth is a divinatory and hence divine medium,[102] mythological poetry occupies a central place in the rhetoric of a natural supernaturalism.

Behind the conclusion of *Hyperion* lies a model of experience which tries to reverse the failure to recover an ideal past by displacing the ideal toward the future. Abrams has discussed at length such tripartite visions of time in which an innocence that is vulnerable to experience is reaffirmed on a higher level, after being strengthened by experience.[103] Blake is the prime exponent of a poetry that tries to recover the lost language of pastoral in prophecy, the innocence given by nature in a transcendence created by the mind through rhetorical self-apotheosis. But Hegel, Friedrich Schlegel, and, to some extent, Schiller also seek to create schemas that have in common a structure that absorbs and compensates for the anxiety of existence in a historical world. Such schemas permit the mind to relocate, without having to question, the utopian impulse which is the driving force behind much Romantic literature.

The third book of *Hyperion* recapitulates in miniature this movement from pastoral to prophecy that assumes the Hegelian movement from nature to spirit. For Hegel and Schiller the struggle of the Titans and Olympians is, in fact, symbolic of the movement from nature to spirit,[104] and it is worth noting that while Keats's Titans are repeatedly associated with natural

[102]F. Schlegel, *Dialogue on Poetry,* p. 88.
[103]Abrams, *Natural Supernaturalism,* pp. 141ff.
[104]Hegel, *The Philosophy of History,* pp. 244–246. Cf. also Schiller's comment:

forces,[105] Apollo rejects the green turf (III.94) because, as Bloom puts it, "he is immediately destined for higher vision,"[106] The third book begins by depicting an Apollo who is immersed in a world of sensations, tended by a Mnemosyne who watches over his physical needs and progress (l. 70). But it concludes with a vision of imaginative apocalypse that will restore the pleasures of imagination on a less sensuous level, having triumphed over the encounter with dejection. This dejection exists not to negate vision, as in the first two books, but as a contrary which makes progression possible. In some miraculous way, the power that is restored beyond the poem's boundaries will have gained by having subsumed the experience undergone by the Titans, and yet will remain immune to the consequences of that experience.

In retrospect, the incompleteness of *Hyperion,* alternately ruined and prophetically unfinished, becomes one of the elements that commits the poem to the myth of a recoverable perfection. The fragmentary status of the poem, which mirrors the status of the Titans themselves as fragments of a lost order, asks the reader to approach the poem in the spirit that Shelley approached the relics and broken statues of a lost Greece, glimpsing somewhere in the space behind them the perfection that survives in a form "whose very fragments are the despair of modern art."[107] Unlike the critic of a merely imperfect work of art, the viewer of a broken statue assumes for it an original perfection which it is his function to reconstruct mentally. The emotional drive behind the fragment form is thus holistic and sentimental: even as it acknowledges the force of time, it does so in a manner that keeps alive the myth of an anterior wholeness that partly cancels out its own condition. Its purpose in the rhetoric of the poem is to preserve, in the mode of nostalgia, "the sleeping, the cold, the buried image of the past"[108] which can be awakened into the perhaps equally illusory mode of hope. The purpose of the

---

"The empire of the Titans fails, and infinite force is mastered by infinite form" (*On the Aesthetic Education of Man,* p. 121).

[105]*Hyperion,* I.21, 57–60, 341–342; II.153.
[106]Bloom, *The Visionary Company,* p. 387.
[107]Shelley, "Preface to *Hellas," Poetical Works,* p. 447.
[108]Shelley, "A Defence of Poetry," p. 294.

third book is to transform the nature of the poem's fragmentariness by moving forward to embrace that hope.

There are obvious problems with this reading. Hegel's definition of Romantic art within an aesthetics of the infinite had been born of a desire to rationalize a kind of art which seemed to offer less than a more perfect and more harmonious, art. Keats's thrust toward apocalypse is even less able to hide the anxiety of living in a historical world betrayed by the very fact that there is a need for apocalypse. The question inevitably arises of how there can be a synthesis of Apollo's innocence with the Titans' experience, and of whether it remains useful to speak of the accommodation reached beyond the gate of death in terms of a restored innocence. In its avoidance of this question, *Hyperion* resembles other texts of Romantic idealism, which also project syntheses of innocence and experience that refuse articulation except in a white radiance beyond the words. Keats later came to recognize this problem when he made it clear that *Hyperion* was an abortive attempt rather than a deliberate fragment.[109] But it is worth stressing that the poem was published in its unfinished form during his lifetime, and that he may initially have felt that it was capable of standing as a fragmentary intention of man's infinite destiny.

If Keats's decision to explore the myth of the Titans points toward Nietzsche's deconstruction of a logocentric, Hellenic myth associated with Apollo, it also brings to mind the very different sentimental assumptions of Romantic Titanism. Thomas Burnet's *Sacred Theory of the Earth* presents an early version of a millennial vision, which begins with an antediluvian earth that is smooth and regular and ends with the return of mankind to this original purity, when the sons of earth or the "giants" have been overcome by the sons of heaven.[110] In his strange combination of biblical and Titanic myths within a triadic pattern of history, Burnet can

---

[109]On being unable to complete *Hyperion*, Keats gave the manuscript to Woodhouse in April 1819. He later renounced the poem in a letter to J. H. Reynolds (September 21, 1819), but only when he was already at work on *The Fall of Hyperion*. Thus it would seem that it is his involvement in the later poem which clarifies for him the contradictions of the earlier poem, and brings him to recognize that the illusion of apocalypse in the last lines hides a moment at which his art comes face to face with its own darkness.

[110]Thomas Burnet, *The Sacred Theory of the Earth* (1685; rpt. London: Centaur Press, 1965), pp. 374-376.

be said to anticipate the Romantics. But he remains relatively orthodox, both in emphasizing the darkened present and in assigning a negative value to the Giants, associated with the merely human self. As early as Collins' "Ode to Liberty," however, we see the beginnings of a myth which favorably associates the Giants with the fragments of a potentially recoverable perfection (ll. 18–21), with a fallen but once unified *human* culture whose present Titanic and flawed status represents a historical and imposed rather than an essential condition. Shelley's *Prometheus Unbound* makes a far more radical claim in inverting the traditional hierarchy of the Titans and Olympians, and in making the Titanic or earthbound self the agent of an immediate redemption.[111] Romantic Titanism makes the same humanistic assumptions as Romantic Hellenism: it is Romantic Hellenism driven into an adversarial position, and therefore waiting to be unbound. The Romantic revision of the status of the Titans results from the sentimental assumption that the human is, in fact, a fallen form of divinity. Consequently, narratives that deal with Titanic heroes subtend a discourse which is potentially, if not actually, transcendent. They blind themselves to their own awareness of temporality by reacting to this awareness sentimentally, rather than tragically, as something thrust upon them by Necessity or History.

Romantic Titanism, therefore, is one expression of the refusal of a post-Kantian natural supernaturalism to see the mortal and the divine as mutually exclusive. There are myths of the Titans' return from exile to godhead—at another time, perhaps in another form—that have been linked with Keats's intentions in *Hyperion*.[112] Such myths bring to mind Frye's notion of a "buried innocence trying to push its way into experience,"[113] an innocence that has been driven underground rather than corrupted or revealed as illusory. Although they may seem to reveal the illusoriness of beauty, Keats's Titans, guiltless of their own fall, are also representatives of the radically innocent self which makes hope seem a matter of justice, and the communication of that hope an

[111]Cf. also Blake, "A Descriptive Catalogue," No. v; *Milton*, 1.36–39; Friedrich Hölderlin, *Hyperion* (1797–1799), trans. Willard Trask (New York: Signet, 1959), pp. 166, 31.
[112]Hungerford, *Shores of Darkness*, pp. 138–139.
[113]Northrop Frye, *The Stubborn Structure* (London: Methuen, 1970), p. 188.

aesthetic duty. *The Fall of Hyperion* will prove remarkable chiefly
for its refusal to yield to such fictions about the occultation of
innocence. Keats will not allow the fallen Titans to become identified with the myth of a Promethean imagination imprisoned
underground and waiting to be liberated in the resurrection of
Albion and man.[114] His use of the Greek myth will stand as an
allusion to the assumptions of revolutionary Titanism as well as to
those of Romantic Hellenism. And in both cases the aim will be to
temper the sentimental idealism of the prevalent myths of human
culture.

It may at first appear that the hope of evolution from mortality
to godhead embodied in the figures of Prometheus and Apollo is
still present in *The Fall of Hyperion*. The ascent of a stairway as an
image of the progressive stages of creative consciousness[115] seems
to imply a movement from dreamer to Apollonian poet that is
structurally similar to the evolution from the Titans to the Olympians anticipated in *Hyperion*. The harsh condemnation of the
Dreamer,[116] moreover, suggests that the ability to transcend the
miseries of the world is still the norm by which poetry is to be
judged. It is apparent, however, that no such progress takes place
in the poem. The stairway, which is a major structuring image in
Dante's *Purgatorio*,[117] is introduced at the beginning of Keats's
poem (1.90,128) but never makes a reappearance. The speaker's
sojourn in the ancient sanctuary breaks up the sense of progress
with a series of abrupt alternations between godhead and
mortality: between a sense of weakness and accesses of vision that
put him in possession of what De Quincey, using the same image
of Jacob's ladder, was to call the literature of power:

> I strove hard to escape
> The numbness, strove to gain the lowest step.

[114]Cf. also Shelley's lines in *Epipsychidion*, describing the island: "It scarce seems
now a wreck of human art, / But, as it were Titanic" (ll. 493-494).
[115]Abrams, for instance, takes a progressive view of the poem, in which the
speaker evolves in orderly fashion from dreamer to poet (*Natural Supernaturalism*,
p. 128).
[116]I have used the word Dreamer (with a capital "D") to distinguish the narrator
of the poem from the "dreamer" as defined by Moneta.
[117]Cf. Henry Francis Cary, trans., *The Divine Comedy of Dante Alighieri* (1814;
rpt. London: G. Bell, 1896), XII.107-112; XIII.1-3).

> Slow, heavy, deadly was my pace; the cold
> Grew stifling, suffocating, at the heart;
> And when I clasped my hands I felt them not.
> One minute before death, my iced foot touched
> The lowest stair; and as it touched, life seemed
> To pour in at the toes. I mounted up,
> As once fair Angels on a ladder flew
> From the green turf to Heaven.
>
> [I.127–136]

The power, once gained, is in constant danger of again giving way to impotence. Evidence of its precariousness can be found in the ambiguous status of the speaker, who is at once superior and inferior to those who find "a haven in the world" (I. 150). Nowhere is there any evidence that the Dreamer will achieve the essentially clarified vision claimed by Wordsworth on Mt. Snowdon: a vision in which the abyss lies below the poet as something which is only the distant origin of a light that moves beyond it to find its home in the ethereal vault, beyond either encroachment or loss (*The Prelude*, XIV.39–74).

As we have suggested, the inability of the Dreamer to become a poet is initially seen as a failure which reflects on the status of Romantic texts in general within a literary hierarchy whose norms condemn them as self-frustrated enterprises. But almost from the beginning, a strong sense of identity pushes against the corrosive self-doubts of this poem. The Dreamer's very mortality, more similar to Cain's knowledge of death than to Apollo's dying into life, is seen as a source of strength:

> "Thou hast felt
> What 'tis to die and live again before
> Thy fated hour. That thou hadst power to do so
> Is thy own safety."
>
> [I.141–144]

A shriek had marked Apollo's rebirth in the third book of *Hyperion*. The corresponding shriek is significantly earlier in *The Fall of Hyperion*, and suggests that it is the Dreamer's mode of vision which permits rebirth into a new sense of poetic vocation. Stuart Sperry, one of the many critics who see the poem as an existential (though not necessarily a literary) failure, comments on Keats's inability to follow Milton in moving from the unreconstructed hopelessness of the first Adam as he contemplates the triumph of fallen history, to the redemptive promise of the second Adam as he is taught hope by Michael. *The Fall of Hyperion*, he concludes, "fails through the inability to evolve a framework for transcending process."[118] But it seems rather that the refusal to proceed from the vale to the mountain is deliberate, and answers Keats's earlier question as to whether Milton's lesser anxiety for humanity proceeded from "his seeing further or no"[119] than the Romantics. As one of the bards of elder time, Milton symbolizes the prophetic myopia of a naive vision: the belief that artists are among the sacred few who can see beyond the images of infected will that they depict.

At the beginning of the poem Keats too seems to share this myopia, as he unfavorably contrasts his own immersion in the misery of the world with the healing detachment of the poet. That these words come from the mouth of Moneta, a figure who is herself described in terms of misery and sickness (1.258), is one of the first indications that the self-lacerating contrast of poets and dreamers is inadequate to deal with the aesthetic problems raised by this poem. Elsewhere, the Dreamer who is here condemned is singled out for praise, as one of the few who have passed the test necessary to enter the fane and receive an esoteric knowledge like that imparted to the epic hero in his descent to the underworld:

> "None can usurp this height," returned that shade,
> "But those to whom the miseries of the world
> Are misery, and will not let them rest.
> All else who find a haven in the world,
> Where they may thoughtless sleep away their days,
> If by a chance into this fane they come,
> Rot on the pavement where thou rotted'st half."
>
> [1.147–153]

Moneta is, in fact, disturbingly contradictory in her pronouncements, suggesting that she is not so much an external goddess or muse as a projection that constellates for the speaker his own simultaneous sense of self-doubt and visionary power. At one

---

[118]Sperry, *Keats the Poet*, pp. 331–332, 336. Among the few critics who do not see the poem as an existential failure are Morris Dickstein (*Keats and His Poetry*, pp. 242–263), and Irene Chayes ("Dreamer, Poet and Poem in 'The Fall of Hyperion,'" *Philological Quarterly*, 46 [1967], 499–515).

[119]Keats, *Letters*, 1, 278.

moment she is critical of those who find "a haven in the world." Yet only a few lines later she accuses the speaker of being a dreaming thing unable to find a "haven" in the ordinary world (1.168–171). She suggests both that the state of being in harmony with oneself is inferior to the misery of the sacred fane because it is too simplistic and thoughtless (1.147–152), and alternately that the movement from harmony into self-division is a fall from a state of Apollonian innocence where nothing is sought beyond the human face (1.163). A kind of logic can be imposed on Moneta's statements by arguing that she has in mind an ascending scale of value, in which the dreamer is superior to the torpid multitude that sleeps away its days, but inferior to the poet and humanitarian activist above him. Yet the reader inevitably asks why those who are at the top of the scale and those at the bottom are alike described as finding a haven in the world. He asks whether there is not an implication that the poet's immunity from the fever and the fret is also a kind of thoughtlessness or escapism, and whether there is not a partial favoring of the dreamer over the poet.

It is perhaps closer to the truth to suggest that Moneta's contradictory views stem from Keats's own uncertainty as to whether the naive vision of the poet is a mark of superiority or deficiency. Like *The Triumph of Life*, *The Fall of Hyperion* is a poem of revaluation and reassessment, which is in the process of revising the assumptions about the role of poetry in relation to reality with which it begins. The contradictions of the poem are thus part of Keats's struggle to accommodate himself to a new image of art, with which he still feels insecure, because in so many respects it appears to do violence to the old image of art. There is no theoretical statement of this new image, corresponding to Moneta's characterization of poetry as a balm. Rather it emerges implicitly and, as we shall see, from the very form of the poem.

That there is some reassessment of the initial condemnation of the speaker is difficult to deny. In imagery that links him to the fallen Titans and links the poet to Apollo, the Dreamer contrasts himself with the poet as vultures are contrasted with eagles (1.189–192).[120] Yet he also justifies his sickness as "not ignoble" (1.184), and

---

[120]The images of the eagle and vulture are used interchangeably in the manuscript version of II.8–9. In the manuscript (1.21) Saturn is described as an old eagle "moulting his plumage." Apollo is associated with "eagles golden-feathered" (II.226).

goes on to speak of himself as seated "Upon an eagle's watch" (1.308–309). As the poem progresses, the speaker gains in self-assurance and power. He ceases to be entirely a passive, dreaming thing, and is pictured actively and aggressively, as one who grasps for knowledge as a miner "twing'd with avarice" digs for gold (1.271–277). His evolution has sometimes been seen as a sign that he has ceased to be a dreamer and become a poet.[121] Yet it is apparent that his mode of perception is very different from that of the poet, whose art is a palliative to anxiety rather than a vision which sows the seed of misery in writer and reader. The "sickening east-wind" which blows across the ancient sanctuary echoes and alters a passage from Dante's *Purgatorio* which promises unequivocal renewal, and suggests that Keats's purgatory will be very different from Dante's, and will not point toward a paradise that heals the miserable self.[122] Although Moneta initially tells the Dreamer that his insight into the mysteries of existence will be free of pain (1.242–248), such a description hardly fits his month-long vigil (1.392) in one of the desolate places of history. Even as she makes this promise, the Dreamer's anticipated mode of perception is contrasted unfavorably with her own. He is to experience as a "wonder" what she experiences as a "curse"; but she is after all immortal, whereas he is merely mortal. The equation of painlessness and mortality, and suffering with immortality, reveals at least some ambiguity toward the former. By implication it is the poet, who sees without vexation and venom, who is being criticized. And when the Dreamer actually comes to contemplate the history of the Titans, his suffering is an indication that he has moved away from the poet and drawn closer to Moneta in stature, closer to that power of unmediated vision which sees things without the narcotic of Apollonian illusion. Significantly, he is *capable* of gazing directly into Moneta's brain, as though confronting the dark memories of his subconscious without the protection of the painted veil. If there is finally an element of wonder as well as

[121] Abrams, *Natural Supernaturalism,* p. 128.

[122] The lines in Cary's Dante read "As when, to harbinger the dawn, springs up / On freshen'd wing the air of May, and breathes / Of fragrance, all impregn'ed with herbs and flowers" (*Purgatorio,* XXIV.145–147). The corresponding lines in Keats are "When in mid-May the sickening east wind / Shifts sudden to the south, the small warm rain / Melts out the frozen incense from all flowers" (1.97–99).

accursedness in his vision, it is because Moneta, like the poet, represents an extreme of vision that does not quite express the delicate balance between release and suffering which Keats is seeking. Thus she can be a source of vision to those who encounter her terrible knowledge, yet is herself "visionless entire" (1.267).

Moneta, it is apparent, represents what she herself condemns: the dreamer who suffers without mitigation the venom and vexation of life. Yet clearly the speaker who acquires a privileged status as the possessor of the poem's purgatorial wisdom is not quite the dreamer described by Moneta. The fact that Keats must set up a series of inconsistent dichotomies—blindness versus vision, poetry versus dreaming, humanitarian activism versus suffering passivity—suggests that what he is looking for is a third category of poetic vision which eludes classification in such standard antitheses.[123] One perhaps turns to Arnold for an explicit typology of creative artists which supplies the category missing from Keats's own dichotomies. In "The Strayed Reveller,"[124] Arnold distinguishes among three modes of vision, all of which attempt to avoid the excessive inward misery of the art which fuses completely with the flux of life. There are the gods who live in Olympian happiness, and "see below them / The earth and men" (ll. 130–134). There are the bards who share the vision of the gods but not their detachment, and who must "become" what they sing as the price of vision (ll. 208–234). There is finally the reveller himself, a *strayed* reveller, who achieves through narcosis a kind of joy in bad faith, which permits him to see without pain and labor (l. 274). Although the poem moves toward a wishful identification with the reveller, the logic of its categories points in another direction. Clearly, in the context of the human world it is the bard who

---

[123]One finds a similarly restless movement between impossible opposites in Shelley's *Alastor*. The preface points to two equally unsatisfactory ways of relating the ideal to the real. There is little to choose between a multitude that cannot rise above the lasting misery and loneliness of the world, and a visionary whose single-minded dedication to the quest for perfection causes him to ignore the reality surrounding him. Because it is recognized that both modes of existence involve a kind of blindness, the poem and the preface are left emotionally unresolved.

[124]Matthew Arnold, *The Poems of Matthew Arnold*, ed. Kenneth Allott (London: Longmans, 1965).

has the stature of the gods, and not the reveller whom Circe has allowed to simulate a painlessness alien to his own, human condition. The bard is neither Keats's poet (who partly finds his equivalent in Arnold's reveller), nor is he Moneta's dreamer. Rather he represents a type of vision between the two, a vision which cannot achieve the pure detachment of the gods, but also one which is not reduced to the suffering which it must endure in the process of creating art.

The following pages will attempt to show how Keats moves toward this third kind of vision, and how the speaker's fluctuations between power and inadequacy are fundamental to a vision that rises above the triumph of life yet never knows the security of the gods. Unlike Blake's Olympian bard, who is monarch of all he surveys, the Dreamer is from the outset humiliated and made to feel his pettiness. He is, in all respects, belated. Others have preceded him in the sanctuary and make him no more than the latest in an anonymous series of dreamers. He has come too late to the initial feast (1.31-32) and he comes too late to the sacrifice (1.241). He comes too late to the war "Foughten long since by giant hierarchy" (1.223), and requires an interpreter to decipher the text of a past that far exceeds his comprehension. He suffers from a sense of temporal dislocation, and the meaning of the ritual that he witnesses at several centuries' remove partly eludes him, even as he recognizes that through it he is approaching the hiding places of man's power.

A curious change between the two Hyperion poems is the replacement of direct presentation of the history of the Titans by the more elusive mode of indirect representation or reenactment. Keats presents not Saturn or Thea themselves but images or statues of them[125] which, for much of the time, are either silent or distant and are explicated by Moneta to the Dreamer. The curious fact that these figures are images suggests that the poem is engaged in reflecting on itself as an act of aesthetic perception, and is specifically concerned to explore the relationship of aesthe-

---

[125] At first there seems to be some ambiguity about whether Saturn is an image: "Onward I looked beneath the gloomy boughs, / And saw what first I thought an image huge, / Like to the image pedestalled so high / In Saturn's temple" (1.297-300). But Moneta makes it quite clear that this is a likeness of Saturn: "*So* Saturn sat . . . " (1.301). Cf. 1.336, 383, 391 ("the three *fixed* shapes").

tic representation to the world that is represented. The past is presented through layers of indirection as through a film: to someone who sees it in a dream, by way of an interpreter who shows him, perhaps within the mind, the semblances of something which once happened. The figures may be images preserved in a temple to commemorate an event of immense and humbling significance. Alternatively, the reader may be meant to think of the use of masks in ritual enactments of tragedy (1.277) where the rigid, nonorganic quality of the figures acts as a barrier to comprehension, and suggests the impossibility of knowing the ultimate truths of which we see only the simulacra. In either case, the use of representation rather than presentation makes us aware of a mystery which cannot entirely be captured in the brazen vessels of art. The act of representing, of making an image for something, is an attempt at either exorcism or domestication of the alien. And the Dreamer is made aware that this attempt to move beyond the dark passages in life, to rid ourselves of our specters by attempting to know what is behind the images we make of them, never entirely succeeds.[126]

There is more to the Dreamer's ordeal than humiliation, however. The fallen Titans, who at first are merely cold images, seem to be partially awakened into speech (1.354ff.), as a result of the long meditative vigil of the Dreamer, in which his memory searches back into the buried depths of the psyche. Moreover, the very distance which makes it impossible for the Dreamer to search the entrails of the past and lay bare its knowledge also permits him to see events in a perspective that is denied to Saturn, a mere actor in the tragedy and at times a pathetic figure. Although the Dreamer is initially a "stunt bramble by a solemn pine" (1.293), in the end he also sets himself upon an eagle's watch, above the vale of Saturn's solitude. He is in some way higher than Saturn, able to grasp, at least with his "outward eye," the size and shape of what he sees (1.305–306). Given the tremendous initial height of the

---

[126]Geoffrey Hartman takes up related questions in "Spectral Symbolism and Authorial Self in Keats' 'Hyperion,'" (*The Fate of Reading* [Chicago: University of Chicago Press, 1975], pp. 57–73), but concludes that Keats's quest for authorial identity is frustrated by the fact that he "fails to move his images" and so liberate himself from them: "We await an enlightenment or transformation which does not come" (pp. 58, 66, 68).

temple and its statues, this is no mean achievement. Variations of perspective and height and alternations between prostration and ascent (1.122–135) convey the emotional rhythm of the Dreamer's responses, which are simultaneously those of humiliation and triumph. The figures that he sees are distant from him, as gods are from the human worshipers who behold only their images. But these figures are also, in a sense, the images of his own mind: inhabitants of the dead, silent places in his imagination, whom he has brought to the level of consciousness, made articulate, and partly tamed. Without him these dead images would be unable to tell their dreams, and would only "dream all night, without a noise" (1.374). The new ability to see and "seeing ne'er forget" (1.310) marks the crossing of some kind of threshold in the process of self-cognition, by which a knowledge buried in the racial memory is made fully conscious and recovered for the future. Of particular importance is the bold and rather difficult conceit of a brain from which the veils are withdrawn (1.255–277): strictly speaking, Moneta's brain, but also the Dreamer's brain, inasmuch as she is the guardian of his memory and therefore an aspect of himself. It appears that although Moneta is herself a figure within the huge sanctuary, the sanctuary and the history it encloses are also in some sense within her mind. The image suggests how the ancient sanctuary which so completely surpasses the Dreamer's imagination in temporal and spatial extent is also reducible to the theater of his mind, which has grown partly able to contain the initially crushing force of death.

The ability to contain and comprehend death is what distinguishes the living Dreamer from the entropic statuary of the past. But this is in no way the ability to move beyond death to the total assumption of power envisaged in the concept of a fore-seeing Apollo. The web of history will always remain no more than "half-unravelled" (1.308), oppressing the mind with a core of mutability that cannot be absorbed into a pattern and therefore anesthetized. One thinks, by contrast, of Blake's Bard, whose vision encompasses all of time and proclaims the power of the mind to master and reshape the material of history from the higher vantage point of prophecy. Wordsworth on Mt. Snowdon is more tentative, but is still above experience, gazing down on the landscape with its subject mountains from a point in infinite space.

Keats's Dreamer, however, is closer to the spectator in Schopenhauer's theory of the sublime, whose visionary power stems not from an undarkened Olympian contemplation which cancels the cycles of time and will, but from an involvement in those cycles which is not pure immersion in their blindness. A discussion of the sublime may seem, at this point, a digression. But Schopenhauer's theory, a precursor of Nietzsche's concept of tragedy, is fundamentally a phenomenology of creative perception which tries to locate the source of aesthetic exaltation or "sublimity" and thus to define the nature of imagination. Conventionally, theories of the sublime assume an aesthetic experience that is a revelation of the infinite. But following the distinction that he himself makes between the knowing and suffering selves,[127] the distinction that Yeats was later to make between clarified spirits who own the truth and those of us who receive as agents only,[128] Schopenhauer suggests that the spectator of the sublime is at once a knower and a sufferer, contained within the history that his mind comprehends:

> [in the sublime experience] our will that is broken... appear[s] clearly before our eyes. Yet as long as personal affliction does not gain the upper hand, but we remain in aesthetic contemplation, the pure subject of knowing gazes through this struggle of nature, through this picture of the broken will, and comprehends calmly.... Then in the unmoved beholder of this scene the twofold nature of his consciousness reaches the highest distinctness. Simultaneously, he feels himself as individual, as the feeble phenomenon of will, which the slightest touch of these forces can annihilate... a vanishing nothing in face of stupendous forces; and he also feels himself as the eternal, serene subject of knowing, who as the condition of every object is the supporter of this whole world, the fearful struggle of nature being only his mental picture or representation.[129]

So also the Dreamer sees from a height and yet endures the vale and all its burdens, combining panoramic vision with dramatic

---

[127]Schopenhauer, *The World as Will and Representation*, I, 207.

[128]Yeats, *Explorations* (London: Macmillan, 1961), pp. 301–302.

[129]Schopenhauer, *The World as Will and Representation*, I, 204–205. Cf. also the description of St. Peter's cathedral, I, 206.

experience. He is at once a detached spectator of Saturn's tragedy, and an actor and victim in his own tragedy, which repeats in an aesthetic dimension the Greek god's submission to the chariot of life.

Schopenhauer's theory of the sublime differs from that of Kant in telescoping together the two moments which in the latter are consecutive: the moment of absolute prostration before something which surpasses and humiliates the temporal self, and the moment of mastery over this alien force.[130] In his almost unconscious revision of Kant (and indeed of himself), Schopenhauer questions the possibility of an art that can acknowledge pain and yet move toward the goal of an absolute freedom that has transcended the world as will. The experience of the sublime thus stands as a model for art in general, acknowledging as it does a liberating power in aesthetic perception that is nevertheless not the power to unbind Prometheus from the procession of life. The liberating element is no longer the ability to transcend or transform the actual, but the ability to *represent* it, to make it the object of human knowledge. One thinks of Arnold's distinction between the gods who see the earth below them without feeling pain, and the bards who must become what they sing. Schopenhauer's artist is not simply an Olympian spectator, but is at once spectator and actor in the scene he depicts.

In a similar vein Nietzsche describes how the "mirror of appearance" protects the poet "from complete fusion with his characters" and yet forces him to "become his images," to recognize them as "objectified versions of himself."[131] The interaction

[130]Kant, *Critique of Judgment*, pp. 100–104.
[131]Nietzsche, *The Birth of Tragedy*, p. 39. At this point Nietzsche is trying to distinguish, rather confusingly, between a poetry of contemplation and a poetry of immersion. But it is clear elsewhere that he sees lyric poetry as involving both kinds of experience: the Apollonian and the Dionysiac. The lyric poet is "first and foremost, a Dionysiac artist, become wholly identified with the original Oneness, its pain and contradiction, and producing a replica of that Oneness as music . . . however, this music becomes visible to him again, as in a dream similitude through the Apollonian dream influence" (p. 38). Elsewhere he says of the lyric poet that "to the extent that he interprets music through images he is dwelling on the still sea of Apollonian contemplation," but at the same time, "when he looks at himself through that medium he will discover his own image in a state of turmoil: his own willing and desiring" (p. 45).

between visionary and spectacle is such that the act of perception is immersive, leading the visionary to find his own image in the world that he sees, and detached, leading him to recognize a saving distance between himself and the images he projects. Rossetti, in his cryptic and suggestive poem "Aspecta Medusa," provides a very apposite commentary on the simultaneously immersive and distancing functions of the mirror of aesthetic representation. The poem centers around the Gorgon's head: a figure like De Quincey's *Mater Tenebrarum*, the purveyor of a terrible, necessary, yet destructive knowledge. Not to know death, not to eat of the forbidden tree, is to shirk the knowledge of one's humanity. Yet the knowledge of death will inevitably prove, as in Byron's *Cain,* a kind of suicide. Perseus therefore permits Andromeda to see the core of destruction, the "death she lived by" (l. 5), but to see it only indirectly, "mirrored in the wave," as a "shadow upon life" (ll. 4,8).[132]

Mirror, shadow, and veil are all analogues for the act of aesthetic representation, which points to a knowledge deeper than "the untumultous fringe of silver foam" ("Epistle to J. H. Reynolds," l. 91), without actually plunging into what Novalis called the destructive element. One can see the difference between such an art, and one which keeps a bower quiet for the mind or reshapes the external world by projecting its own inner radiance onto it. The new concept of art is committed to the inevitability of knowledge rather than the fulfillment of desire. The mirror does not beautify what it is supposed to reveal, and the veil does not suggest that the knowledge behind it is other than what it is. The

---

[132]Rossetti's poem runs

> Andromeda, by Perseus saved and wed,
> Hankered each day to see the Gorgon's head:
> Till o'er a fount he held it, bade her lean,
> And mirrored in the wave was safely seen
> That death she lived by.
> Let not thine eyes know
> Any forbidden thing itself, although
> It once should save as well as kill: but be
> Its shadow upon life enough for thee.

(*The Collected Works of Dante Gabriel Rossetti*, ed. William Michael Rossetti [London: Ellis and Elvey, 1901]).

function of mirror and veil is to mitigate the almost unendurable knowledge that they disclose, to furnish a means of surviving the encounter with darkness.

Schopenhauer and Nietzsche represent stages in a movement toward the recognition that the work of art is partly a meeting with what De Quincey called the Dark Interpreter, who reveals "the worlds of pain and agony and woe possible to man—possible even to the innocent spirit of a child."[133] Given an acceptance of such a concept of art, Keats's problem was to achieve an engagement with reality that would not cripple his art by reducing it to the abject dejection of the Titans. Shelley's problem too, in *The Triumph of Life*, was to gain knowledge without capitulating to the corrosive light of the new chariot of revelation. It is for this reason that both poets have recourse to a kind of frame device, in which a narrator sees the dark core of history in a dream, and through the mediating eyes of a surrogate figure such as Rousseau or Moneta. The dream serves the function of the mirror of Nietzsche and Rossetti, permitting vision through a protective but transparent barrier. In his waking identity the Dreamer remains outside his dream, even as he projects himself into it as dreamer for the purpose of gaining knowledge. The perceiving self is thus doubled and split, becoming both passive and active, both the contemplator and the sufferer of what occurs. This simultaneously immersive and distancing effect is further built into both poems through certain structural repetitions. Rousseau's life and its rupture by the Shape in the Car is repeated in Shelley's life and its rupture by the encounter with Rousseau. The Dreamer's encounter with his aesthetic failure is repeated in the encounter of the Titans with their historical failure. The effect is of doubled or concentric experiences, as in Nietzsche's idea of an aesthetic experience in which there is first "a reflection, without image or idea, of original pain," and then a "second reflection," which permits one to contemplate what was at first only raw anguish.[134] The doubling of each poem's central experience of dejection and failure, doubles the self into actor and spectator, and more or less

---

[133]De Quincey, *Suspiria De Profundis, Posthumous Works*, ed. A. H. Japp (London: Heinemann, 1891), I, 12.

[134]Nietzsche, *The Birth of Tragedy*, p. 38.

enacts the dialectic of cognition to which Rousseau points when he enjoins Shelley to give up his contemplative position and become an actor in the procession "and what thou wouldst be taught I then may learn / From thee" (*The Triumph of Life*, ll. 305–308). It can reasonably be argued that the very act of retrospective narration, in which both Keats and Shelley engage, serves a similar doubling function. Like structural repetition, narration too is a mirroring or imaging of an original experience without image or idea. It is a repetition of this experience at a distance which allows for reflection, but also a repetition which insists on what Eliot calls the rending pain of reenactment, presenting the Dreamer with "the image which now reveals to him his oneness with the heart of the world."[135]

In his comments on Shakespeare, who occupies the position of a normative ideal in Romantic literary mythology, Coleridge speaks of the "utter aloofness" of the artist from those feelings of which he, as a "superior spirit," is the painter and analyst.[136] The use of the dream-vision made in the last poems of both Keats and Shelley involves a reassessment of canonical assumptions about the artist as one of the sacred few, detached from ultimate participation in the procession of images he projects.[137] As such, it serves as an implicit commentary on the mode of perception involved in aesthetic representation, and goes beyond the debilitating antithesis of classical and Romantic poetics suggested by Moneta in her distinction between poets and dreamers. The narrator of *The Fall of Hyperion*, like Shelley/Rousseau at the end of *The Triumph of Life*, eschews the aloofness from reality characteristic of eagles and Olympian poets. But he also avoids the excessive inward misery that wastes those who merge completely with the bacchanalian dance of life, and consent to view the Gorgon's head directly. The contradictions of Moneta's distinctions, which alter-

---

[135] Ibid.

[136] Coleridge, *Notebooks*, ed. Kathleen Coburn (London: Routledge & Kegan Paul, 1957–1973), 4115.f.26^v–f.27^v.

[137] Typical of such assumptions is Schopenhauer's desire for an art that is objective and detached, even as he admits that subjective experience is the only authentic mode of knowledge. His treatment of the sublime obviously transcends the distinction between objective and subjective that elsewhere cripples his argument, and it thus points toward Nietzsche's sense of aesthetic perception as involving both Dionysiac emotion and Apollonian detachment.

nately favored and condemned both poet and dreamer, had made clear the need for a third category of vision: one that would provide an alternative between a poetry that escapes from reality to the haven of the ideal, and one that is still haunted by the ideal but so aware of the real that it can only frustrate its readers. The use of dream-vision implicitly develops a poetics which answers this need. It suggests that art is a kind of purgatory: neither godlike and foreseeing nor infernal and poisoned, neither a medium of pure knowledge nor one of pure suffering.

In his discussion of what he calls "the poetry of experience," Robert Langbaum points to the pivotal position of Nietzsche in the genesis of such an aesthetic: "Nietzsche's Apollonian-Dionysian dichotomy corresponds to our distinction between the poetry of meaning, which the reader understands through judgement [and as] . . . an abstraction from experience . . . [and] the poetry of experience, which the reader understands . . . through finding by an effort of creative insight his own life in the otherwise incomplete images or events."[138] The relationship of the reader to the text is analogous to the relationship of the poet to the experience which he attempts to "read," and suggests the process by which reader and poet complete and comprehend the images which they see only by renouncing the security of distance and involving themselves in these images. Equally important, however, is the process by which immersion in the contradiction of life is followed by a partial reestablishment of distance. In the dialectic of cognition outlined by Rousseau, Shelley is enjoined to become an actor in the tragedy of life so that Rousseau can take Shelley's place as spectator: there is to be a reversal of roles between the two, which indicates not the replacement of an aesthetics of detachment by an aesthetics of immersion, but the need for both men to play the roles of actor and spectator. The aesthetics of the dream-vision therefore cuts across the standard distinction

[138]Langbaum, *The Poetry of Experience* (1957; rpt. New York: Norton, 1963), p. 232. Whether Langbaum is aware of the extent to which Nietzsche seeks a fusion of the Dionysiac and the Apollonian is not clear. In identifying the Dionysiac-Apollonian dichotomy with his own distinction between the poetry of experience and the poetry of meaning, he seems to see Nietzsche as purely Dionysiac. Yet he also distinguishes Nietzsche from the modern cult of the irrational, pointing out that for him the movement is "toward formulation" (p. 235).

between objective and subjective poetry (or classical and Romantic poetry). However, it does not do so in order to collapse classical detachment into Dionysiac involvement, but rather in order to recognize the claims of both kinds of vision. The bards of Arnold's "Strayed Reveller," to return to our earlier example, are not the polar opposite of the gods, related to the gods as Keats's Dreamer to his poet. As we have suggested, they have the stature of gods in the human world, but with the single difference that they must suffer what they depict, must combine a Dionysiac identification with the flux of history and an Apollonian breadth of vision. The context of values changes from the divine to the human world, and the pure detachment which seems appropriate to Olympian gods seems irresponsible in human revelers.

It is possible to see the enterprise in which Keats and Shelley were engaged as part of debate that was to persist throughout the nineteenth century, and return in the work of such twentieth-century writers as Conrad and Thomas Mann.[139] Arnold's *Empedocles on Etna,* which has as a major concern the relation of the singer to the darkness of experience, is torn apart by its inability to find a compromise between the Apollonian impulse represented by the naive singer Callicles, and the Dionysiac impulse represented by the philosopher Empedocles. Ultimately the poem sets up an impossible choice between an awareness of dejection which becomes a commitment to death, and a need for innocence that is too much aware of its contrary to be evidence of anything other than bad faith. An analogous problem recurs in "The Lady of Shalott," where Tennyson acknowledges the destructive force of contemplating life without the protective mirror of aesthetic representation, and yet is driven toward the knowledge that comes from breaking the mirror, a knowledge as inevitable as growing up. Tennyson too permits no alternative way between a commitment to death, and an art that achieves detachment only by limiting itself to pure illusion and solipsistic dream.[140]

---

[139]Thus Aschenbach in *Death in Venice* is polarized between the Apollonian and Dionysiac impulses. *Buddenbrooks* insists that the heightening of artistic talent is accompanied by a decline from health into morbidity. To have artistic vision is basically to commit oneself to a destructive, Faustian fate.

[140]Of related interest is George Eliot's story "The Lifted Veil," in which the extrasensory power developed by the sensitive Latimer, after an illness, allows him

As he confronted the crucial question of whether to seek an ideal Apollo or consign himself to the living death of the Titans, Keats too faced the problem of whether to make his art evasion or martyrdom. The end of *Hyperion* does not answer the doubts about an ideal poetry that the narrative has raised, and Apollo's deification resembles nothing more than Callicles' vision of an Apollo who leads his choir up to the mountain, forgetful of the hollows in the landscape of vision which include the flaying of Marsyas and the destruction of Empedocles. The desire to create a poetry that is celebratory and positive is so strong in Keats that contrary evidence, which has pushed its way into the poem, must be ignored. This is because there is as yet no way of facing this evidence without being destroyed by it, as Rousseau was by his initial encounter with the Car of Life, and as Hyperion is at the end of the second book, where, at the sight of the Titans, his very brilliance is made to reveal "a vast shade / In midst of his own brightness" (II.372–373). Art, the poem's conscious awareness of itself as an act of vision or an act of retrospective narration, provides such a way, tempering the knowledge with which it infects those who submit to its harsh discipline.[141] If the terrible vision of *The Triumph of Life* is bearable, it is partly because it is described in aesthetic metaphors of embroidery and dance (ll. 446,444)— because, frenzied and destructive as the poem's dance of death is, the mind has hammered its blind fury into form. Schopenhauer implicitly recognized the role of aesthetic representation when he commented, "without the representation, I am not knowing subject, but mere, blind will. . . . As soon as knowledge, the world as representation, is abolished, nothing in general is left but mere will, blind impulse."[142] Where he erred, in the context of his own

---

to see the corruption and darkness behind surfaces of beauty. Here the power of vision is something corrosive, pathological, something which leads only to misery. Yet to return to the haven of the ordinary world, after the painted veil has been lifted, is to engage in an act of bad faith. There is thus no alternative between a power of vision that is destructive, and an illusion that is no longer blind, knowing itself to be illusion. The Romantic concept of art attempts to find such an alternative.

[141]All art is in some sense an act of representation, an imaging of original oneness. My comments apply only to works that somehow thematize the act of vision, as Keats and Shelley do by making use of the dream-vision form.

[142]Schopenhauer, *The World as Will and Representation*, I, 180.

metaphysics, was in expecting too much of representation, in imagining that it could deliver him from the bitter furies of complexity for which it could do no more than provide an objective correlative. If there has been a major revision in Keats's concept of dreaming between *Endymion* and his final poem, it is in the direction of the recognition Schopenhauer could not face. When Endymion dreams, he is liberated from the pressure of reality into a vision of his epipsyche. The speaker of *The Fall of Hyperion* finds no such private and sectarian paradise—only a dream which is a repetition of reality.[143]

[143]The argument of this section assumes that *The Fall of Hyperion* is thematically complete, even though literally speaking it is an unfinished poem. A comparison of the two Hyperions suggests that the substantial changes and additions are in the discussions of poetic vocation and the indirect manner in which the Titans are presented through an interpreter. It seems, from the few lines that we have of the second canto, that Keats had made very few changes in the actual narrative of the Titans and the Olympians, and at this point was simply repeating the earlier poem. Since *Hyperion* assumes a progress from the Titans to the Olympians that is analogous to a movement from mortality to godhead, this narrative would obviously have proved incompatible with the kind of accommodation Keats reaches implicitly through his use of the dream-vision: an accommodation which argues for a never-ending purgatory of the imagination rather than a rebirth into Olympian power. However, one must distinguish here between problems of vision and problems that are merely technical and structural. The problems Keats would have faced in deciding what to do with the remainder of *Hyperion* fall into the latter category. The poem, as it stands, more or less resolves the problem of reaching an adequate sense of what poetic vocation is.

CHAPTER 5

Image and Reality in Coleridge's Lyric Poetry

And art thou nothing?

—Constancy to an Ideal Object

In his late poem "Constancy to an Ideal Object" Coleridge recognizes something inescapably illusory and phenomenal in the images constructed by art. The shape all light that he sees while climbing a mountain succeeds in manifesting the ideal that he pursues, and attests in a strange way to the power of imagination to overcome distance and difficulty and envision as present something which is always beyond the horizon of ordinary vision. Yet the poem also recognizes the naiveté of believing that imaginary representation actually makes present something which is only a projection of desire and which, in a literal sense, is not there at all. The poem gives itself and does not give itself to its own illusions. The sophisticated mind responds with irony to the rustic's sense that the ideal is more than the self-created sustenance of a lonely mind. Yet as Wordsworth well understood, the urge to become like a rustic, to become simple again, is a powerful one, so powerful that it constantly unsettles our attempts to accept ourselves as we are.

Modern theorists such as Derrida, de Man, and Sartre all question the view of language as something in which the imaginary sign becomes the object it seeks to evoke, and point instead to the radical nothingness of aesthetic images, as products of consciousness rather than nature. Sartre argues against the confusion of imagination with perception, consciousness with the external world, and defines the image as "an act which envisions an absent or non-existent object as a body, by means of a physical or mental content which is present only as an 'analogical representative' of the object envisioned."[1] Because the image which seeks to make the imagined object appear can never deliver that object except as absent, imagination is an activity that dematerializes itself. Derrida likewise describes aesthetic representation as an ambiguous process which implies the absence of that which would not have to be *re*presented if it were actually present.[2] The image, by its very nature, cannot constitute a plenitude. As an intentional structure it is never simply an image, but always an image *of* something which it is not: it necessarily posits its object as being outside itself, absent from itself, rather than as a content of the image.[3]

But such recognitions are already latent in the eighteenth-century use of a vocabulary of absence and presence as the basis for distinctions among perception, imagination, and memory. This fact makes the Romantic espousal of an idealist poetics a sentimental rather than a naive gesture, and suggests that the recognition confronted in "Constancy to an Ideal Object" simply makes explicit a knowledge always latent in those lyrics concerned with the epistemology of vision. Typical of the increasing separation between images and being is Beattie's sense of the difference between perception and memory on the one hand, and imagination, in which "we contemplate a certain thought . . . without referring it to past experience or to real existence."[4] Coleridge himself will later distinguish between "Presentation" or "Perception blended with the sense of real Presence," and imaginary or mnemonic "Representation" in which "Definites [are] combined with a sense of their Absence"[5] It must be added that by and large eighteenth-century imaginative theory and the works which derive from it—poems such as Samuel Rogers' *Pleasures of Memory*, Thomas Campbell's *Pleasures of Hope*, and the sequence that Coleridge himself planned under the title of "The Soother of Absence"[6]—ignore the deconstructive potential within the notion

[1]Sartre, *The Psychology of Imagination*, p. 25.
[2]Derrida, *Of Grammatology*.
[3]Sartre, *Imagination*, pp. 131–132.
[4]James Beattie, "Of Memory and Imagination," *Dissertations Moral and Critical* (London: Strahan and Cadell, 1783), p. 8.
[5]Coleridge, *Notebooks*, 3605, 4058.
[6]The title refers to a series of poems planned on the solaces that the natural world and outward events offer for personal deprivations. The poems were to focus partly on Asra, partly on landscapes of plenitude which would serve as

of imagination as re-presentation, and see poetry as a compensatory reduplication which renews and therefore guarantees the absent or unreal. But already in the notion of a poetry which "enshrine(s) . . . the spirit of the Past / For future restoration" (*Prelude*, XII.284–286), Wordsworth admits (in the description of poetry as shrine rather than celebration) the paradox at the heart of Keats's urn, which designates art as a form constructed around its own deconstruction. The lacuna that imagination encloses within itself as a result of positing the objects of desire as ideal or imaginary rather than actual is increasingly a problem for the major Romantic poets.

Much Romantic theory, with its reabsorption of imagination into perception and its claims for the fusion of subject and object in the act of perception, reveals itself as regressive in relation to the understanding of representation that emerged in the eighteenth century. Michel Foucault has described the dissolution in the classical (or post-Renaissance) period of a "culture in which the signification of signs did not exist, because it was reabsorbed into the sovereignty of the Like."[7] In the seventeenth and eighteenth centuries, according to him, the "ancient solidity of language as a thing inscribed in the fabric of the world" gave way to an awareness of language as "unfulfilled by any similitude," as a system of signs without foundation in the world of things.[8] For Milton's Adam at the Creation, names correspond intimately to the things they signify. The sacramental concept of nature, in which "the forms of matter" also double as words in the language of God,[9] reabsorbs signs and things into each other. But for Hobbes and Locke linguistic signs, even if imposed by God, are part of an arbitrary code, dependent for their existence on common con-

---

"some one spot of cloudless and fixed sunshine in the memory of Consciousness" (*Notebooks*, 3404. Cf. also 1225, 1541, 1937, 2035, 2062, 2224, 2336, 2953, 2980, 3404).

[7] Michel Foucault, *The Order of Things: An Archaeology of the Human Sciences* (1966; New York: Pantheon, 1970), p. 43.

[8] Ibid., pp. 43–47.

[9] Coleridge, *The Philosophical Lectures,* ed. Kathleen Coburn (London: Pilot Press, 1949), p. 367. Coleridge's interest in a sacramental language is also apparent in *Lectures 1795 on Politics and Religion,* ed. Lewis Patton and Peter Mann (London: Routledge & Kegan Paul, 1971), p. 339. Jean-Paul's *School for Aesthetics* is an instance of a Romantic aesthetic system based largely on a theory of correspondences.

sent rather than innate significance.[10] It is against this awareness of words as arbitrary mental structures that we must view the attempt of Wordsworth and Coleridge to see the material world as instinct with the signatures of consciousness. Thus the Romantic claim of a marriage between mind and nature, often considered revolutionary in its implications, can also be seen as a conservative and sentimental attempt to revive a Renaissance or hermetic system of correspondences, in a world which has already been revealed as discontinuous.

Shelley actually claims that the imagination "reproduces all that it represents."[11] And Blake clearly reveals the conservative basis of much Romantic aesthetics, in denouncing the post-Lockian dissociation of "mental deities" from their "objects," and celebrating a naive ideal of poetry as something which "animate(s) all sensible objects with Gods or Geniuses."[12] But more sophisticated theorists such as Coleridge and Schelling are careful not to claim this naive fusion of image with thing. Thus Coleridge directly takes up the terminology of the eighteenth century:

> Hard to express that sense of the analogy or likeness of a thing which enables a symbol to represent it so that we think of the thing itself, yet knowing that the thing is not present to us. . . . known and felt not to be the thing by that difference of the substance which made every atom of the form another thing, that likeness not identity—an exact web, every line of direction miraculously the same, but the one worsted, the other silk.[13]

---

[10]Locke notes that there is no "natural connection . . . between particular articulate Sounds, and certain *Ideas,* for then there would be but one Language amongst all Men" but rather "a voluntary Imposition, whereby such a Word is made arbitrarily the *Mark* of such an Idea." That words "*signifie* only Men's peculiar *Ideas,* and that by *a perfectly arbitrary Imposition,* is evident, in that they often fail to excite in others (even that use of same Language) the same Ideas we take them to be Signs of" (*Essay Concerning Human Understanding* [1690; rpt. Menston: Scolar Press, 1970], Book III, ch. 2, pp. 187–189). A similar point is made by Hobbes (*Elements of Philosophy,* in *The English Works of Thomas Hobbes of Malmesbury,* ed. Sir William Molesworth [1839; rpt. Aalen Scientia, 1962] Vol. I, Pt. I, ch. ii). Cf. also Coleridge, *Aids to Reflection,* p. 202.

[11]Shelley, "A Defence of Poetry," p. 282.

[12]Blake, "The Marriage of Heaven and Hell," Plate 11.

[13]Coleridge, *Anima Poetae,* ed. E. H. Coleridge (London: Heinemann, 1895), p. 87.

This claim of a likeness which is not identity finds expression in a series of water-images that deal with the reflective transposition of sensuous experience into words. Jean-Paul describes how "at the edge of still water the real tree and its reflection seem to grow from a single root toward two heavens" so that they become "limitless continuations" of each other.[14] In a more famous passage Wordsworth uses the image of rams inhabiting separate but congruent worlds to suggest that, in Schelling's words, "the ideal world of art and the real world of objects are . . . products of one and the same activity,"[15] but yet "Antipodes unconscious of each other" (*Excursion*, IX.449):

> In a deep pool, by happy chance we saw
> A twofold image; on a grassy bank
> A snow-white ram, and in the crystal flood
> Another and the same!
>
> [IX.439–442]

But though such images may seem to keep sign and reality separate, their purpose is a hypostasis of the fictional, a blurring of the line between imagination and perception. In another instance of the same image, where he speaks of losing the line "That parts the image from reality" and the water from the shore (*Recluse*, I.571–579), Wordworth reveals how easily the vocabulary of parallelism can be absorbed into that of identity. Romantic theory may seem to distinguish representation from presence. But it also designates it as the exact reflection, the perfect double of presence, separated from the latter in a way that does not force it to pay the price of separation. A similar equivocation is apparent in Coleridge's famous definition of the imagination in *Biographia Literaria*, which is also concerned with the relationship between source and emanation established by imaginative repetition.[16] On the surface, the distinction between primary and secondary imagination seems reminiscent of Addison's Lockian distinction between the primary pleasures of imagination deriving from perceived objects and the secondary pleasures deriving from remem-

---

[14]Jean-Paul, *Horn of Oberon*, pp. 43, 25. Cf. also Coleridge, *Notebooks*, 2600.

[15]F. W. J. Schelling, *System des transzendentalen Idealismus* (1800; rpt. Hamburg: Felix Meiner Verlag, 1957), p. 17. Translation mine.

[16]Coleridge, *Biographia Literaria*, I, 202.

bered or absent objects.[17] But the poetic imagination seems to transcend its nominal secondariness, in becoming a repetition of the act of perception, which in turn repossesses the central life to which imagination and perception are both concentric, and hence "connatural" or "consubstantial."[18] From here it is but a short step to a much larger claim which allows Coleridge to "Mix up Truth & Imagination, so that the Imag. [sic] may spread its own indefiniteness over that which really happened, & Reality its sense of substance & distinctness to Imagination/."[19] Impossibly, this confusion of the absent and the present allows the imaginary to acquire the reality of perception, without limiting perception to what is real.

The ambiguities that haunt imaginary representation are nowhere more evident than in Wordsworth's strange poem "The Two April Mornings," which explores the question of whether images, as duplications of something absent, are to be taken literally or figuratively. The poem is explicitly about Matthew's encounter with the double of his dead child. But it raises questions of whether the image in which the object of desire presents itself is actual or illusory, whether it reincarnates a lost beauty and becomes an intimation of immortality, or merely represents something which is not there at all. The miraculous apparition in the graveyard of a girl "whose hair was wet / With points of morning dew" (ll. 43–44) seems actually to bring back from the dead the child whose presence it recreates only analogically. It seems to claim for imagination a power beyond that of mere memory: a power that transcends the separation of fiction from reality and imposes its desire on the world of fact. In a sense the poem argues that the mind must resist this seduction into illusion, and that to believe that the image preserved for so long in dream and memory can again become real would be to cross the thin line that divides vision from pathology. As we know from so many of the darker poems of imagination that precede *The Prelude*, the figures who (like Keats's Isabella) try to materialize an imaginary object in the prose of the world are guilty of a blind fixation. There is

---

[17]Addison, *The Spectator*, IV, No. 411.

[18]Coleridge, *The Philosophical Lectures*, p. 114; *Unpublished Letters of Samuel Taylor Coleridge*, ed. E. L. Griggs (London: Constable, 1932), II, 262.

[19]Coleridge, *Notebooks*, 1541.

something sterile, as Auden says, in substituting "identity for analogy,"[20] as Narcissus did in trying to merge with his image. Nevertheless, the living girl does not wholly give up her identity with the dead girl. The strange experience in the graveyard refuses to be reduced to what it literally is: an instance of paramnesia or the deceptive association of something remembered with something perceived. The meaning of the poem does not reside in Matthew's rejection of illusion and his return from the realm of the uncanny to the ordinary world. Rather it emerges from that ambiguous moment in the graveyard when the lost child seems to be there and yet not to be there: when the possibility of her renewed life also reawakens the possibility of her death, dematerializing the object of desire in the very moment of its restitution.

At issue in this temporal duplication is the imitative nature of poetry, as a claim to recapture "the spiritual presences of absent things" and to "arouse the sensual from their sleep / Of Death" (*Excursion*, IV.1234; "Prospectus", ll. 60–61). Romantic theory tends to range life-oriented terms such as "genius," "organic," and "vital" against their mechanistic opposites, and to accord poetry a privileged position in this secular debate between body and soul. But it is not so easy to say whether poetic reproduction is an "imitation" which masters the very "essence" of the object of desire, or a "copy" which merely represents it and therefore reveals "an emptiness . . . an unreality"[21] within the fabrications of language. Wordsworth's poem, as one which explores the relationship between copy and original, says something about the uncanny resemblance between signs and objects: a resemblance which is less than identity but more than analogy. Merleau-Ponty's description of the ambiguity of images is relevant here: "In a singular way the image incarnates and makes appear the person represented in it, as spirits are made to appear at a séance. Even an adult [as opposed to a child] will hesitate to step on an image or photograph; if he does, it will be with aggressive intent . . . the image is never a simple reflection of the model; it is, rather, its 'quasi-presence.' "[22] Words such as "image," "phantom," "echo,"

---

[20] Auden, *The Dyer's Hand*, p. 70.
[21] Coleridge, "On Poesy or Art," *Biographia Literaria*, II, 257.
[22] Maurice Merleau-Ponty, *The Primacy of Perception*, ed. J. M. Edie, trans. J. M. Edie et al. (Evanston: Northwestern University Press, 1964), pp. 132–133.

"apparition," and "reflection" recur throughout the poems of Wordsworth and Coleridge and are the means by which language explores its own illusoriness. But images are not wholly unreal: they are "the half embodyings of thoughts."[23] More importantly, the point at which they touch reality is also the point at which they become exposed to the knowledge of their own nothingness. Matthew is aware of this as he turns away from the graveyard, and Wordsworth, less naive than he seems, recognizes that images are not simply phantoms of delight, but products of the mind's dusk as well as its dawn. They rule at the blind point of ordinary vision, caught up in the interplay of life and death, the illusory and the real.

Revenants and surrogates—whether they come back literally, or metaphorically like Lucy and the Boy of Winander, whom the poet summons back through an act of orphic commemoration—speak for the power of imaginary representation, but also for the duplicity of its substitutions. As figures who are both youthful and dead, they seem to know less and more of experience than the poet himself: they bring back a dream of innocence whose naiveté they expose by refusing the poet their literal presence. Less overtly, the same dialectic of absence and presence occurs in such poems as "Tintern Abbey" or the "Immortality" ode, where a later experience is made to signify or stand for an earlier one which it can replace but cannot entirely bring back. Because Wordsworth's poems return again and again to a concern with the role played by substitution and compensation in experience, they reflect indirectly on the paradox of imaginary signs. As Derrida remarks, "when the present does not present itself, then . . . we go through the detour of signs," which "represent the present in its absence [and] take the place of the present."[24] It is because he knows that in the economy of signs there is no verbal currency which can be unequivocally exchanged for what it designates, that Wordsworth so often approaches innocence obliquely: through naive beings with whom the poet cannot merge, and who only represent what is denied the confirming immediacy of first person presentation.

[23]Coleridge, *Coleridge's Shakespearian Criticism*, ed. T. M. Raysor (London: J. M. Dent, 1960), I, 35.
[24]Derrida, *Speech and Phenomena*, trans. David B. Allison (Evanston: Northwestern University Press, 1973), p. 138.

Romanticism is reluctant to admit that the external world—history or nature—may not be the materialization of a mental deity, and that words may be unable to reproduce desire as fact. The conversation poems—among which we can include *The Prelude*—are born of a utopian drive to identify imagination and perception. Coleridge alludes to a passage from Jean-Paul's *Titan* on man's desire "to see his ideal outside himself as a physical presence, an idealised or imagined body."[25] The auditor in the conversation poems is meant to objectify the poet's vision and thus to deny the insistent fissure between thought and being. On the other hand, certain passages in *The Prelude* which present a silent or unresponsive auditor, and certain late poems by Coleridge which address themselves to an absent auditor, seemingly controvert the assumptions of the conversation mode. "Constancy to an Ideal Object" and "The Pang More Sharp Than All," like Renaissance love poems dealing with the absence of the beloved, in which Coleridge was interested,[26] explore the problems of an experience which is simulation rather than enjoyment, nothingness rather than being. Inevitably—like the Renaissance poems in question—they thematize the problems of poetry itself, which cannot confirm its representations as present, and is constantly thrust back into a sense of its own textuality. But in removing the auditor these later poems only draw attention to a sense of the intentional structure of poetic vision that is already latent in the conversation poems, which are monologues rather than conversations, attempts to create a self-confirming poetry through "a species of ventriloquism, where two are represented as talking, while in truth one man only speaks."[27] The dialogue that takes place in Coleridge's career between the conversation poems and their later deconstructions thus raises dilemmas crucial to Romantic poetry. It is with these poems and others, as they bear more generally on the problems of a visionary poetics, that the remainder of this chapter will be concerned.

Certain similarities are immediately apparent among the con-

[25]Coleridge, *Notebooks*, 4276n.
[26]Ibid., 2428. Instances of such poems are Donne's valedictions, Spenser's *Epithalamion*, Shakespeare's sonnets on the theme of absence, and Sidney's *Astrophil and Stella.*
[27]Coleridge, *Biographia Literaria*, II, 109.

versation poems: a group which includes "Tintern Abbey" and later inversions of the mode such as "Dejection: An Ode" and "To William Wordsworth," as well as the poems normally considered part of the canon.[28] The poems usually begin by emphasizing the alienation of the speaker, through physical or temporal separation, from some primal scene of nature envisaged as past or future rather than present. They usually end with a benedictory address which reabsorbs the speaker into the "one life," abolishing absence and loss, and enabling him to recover vital incentives within himself. The goal of these poems is thus the sentimental one of reabsorption and reintegration into the naive. They acknowledge a dichotomy between subject and object, which they seek to transcend through an act of vision that fuses imagination and its object.

But perhaps the most crucial feature, in establishing this communion between the centering self and its universe, is the inclusion in the poem of a naive auditor who receives the poet's words not as written text but as living communication. Wilhelm von Humboldt describes the activity of conversation as a dynamic process, in which speaker and listener discover that they are animated by "the same essence" through the fact that "a signal, created out of the deepest and most personal nature . . . is a sufficient mediator to stimulate both of them identically."[29] Conversation, as a mode of communication in which two people are immediately present to each other, seems to deny the skepticism inherent in modes such as inscription, elegy and commemoration, which introduce a temporal lacuna between presence and representation. At least as it is conceived in Romantic theory, conversation arises directly from the One Life.[30]

The ideal landscape projected in these poems is one of plenitude, and indeed the *locus amoenus* described in "The Eolian Harp" (ll. 3–4), as one critic points out, is reminiscent of the bower

---

[28]The group includes "The Eolian Harp," "Frost at Midnight," "This Lime-Tree Bower, My Prison," "The Nightingale," "Reflections on Having Left a Place of Retirement," and "Lines Written in the Album at Elbingerode."

[29]Wilhelm von Humboldt, *Linguistic Variability and Intellectual Development* (1836), trans. George Buck and Frithjof Raven (Coral Gables: University of Miami Press, 1971), pp. 36–38.

[30]Friedrich Schlegel, *The Philosophy of Life and The Philosophy of Language*, trans. A. J. W. Morrison (London: Henry Bohn, 1847), pp. 388, 390–391.

of Adam and Eve before the Fall.[31] "This Lime-Tree Bower, My Prison" concludes in a landscape which affirms the radical innocence of life, because it allows the poet to say that there is "No waste so vacant, but may well employ / Each faculty of sense" (ll. 62–63). And the Wye country, which forms the setting of "Tintern Abbey," was actually associated by contemporary writers with the naive world of Greek pastoral.[32] But the most interesting of these landscapes occurs perhaps in "The Nightingale," which depicts an idyllic existence in which there is no distance between presence and representation: the questions and responses of the many birds in the grove (l. 58) are absorbed into a single "choral minstrelsy" (l. 80) in which the original voice and its secondary repetition are inseparable. So also in Wordsworth's "There Was a Boy," the boy himself is seen as one of the voices of an infinitely self-echoing and therefore self-producing nature. And toward the end of "Frost at Midnight" the clouds are reflected in the lake and the lake is reflected in the clouds (ll. 55–57), making of the discourse of nature one that summons image and substance into intimate relationship.

Because "The Nightingale" is the only poem which Coleridge actually called a conversation poem, the landscape at its center is of particular significance. Ideally conversation is the human approximation of the interchange between the birds, who cause the many and dispersed parts of the universe to converse, to answer and reverberate to one another across time and space. It is of importance that nature is depicted as reflecting and echoing itself, because it would otherwise be a primitive and undifferentiated world of sensation, rather than a highly organized system of "Multeity in Unity" which can serve as the goal as well as the origin of consciousness.[33] But we recognize in this holistic sense of nature's reflectiveness the very anti-type, and therefore the cure,

---

[31]A. J. Harding, *Coleridge and the Idea of Love* (Cambridge: Cambridge University Press, 1974), p. 46.

[32]See Thomas Dudley Fosbroke, *The Wye Tour; or, Gilpin on the Wye, with Historical and Archaeological Additions . . .* (W. Farror, 1818), pp. v–vi.

[33]Coleridge, *Biographia Literaria*, II, 232. Cf. the tendency of thinkers including Hegel, and sometimes Schiller, to condemn nature as inferior to consciousness. Coleridge himself reveals similar hesitations in his condemnations of pantheism, and it is therefore important to note that the "Nature" of the conversation poems is at once sensuous and reflective, naive and highly organized. On Coleridge's

of human reflectiveness. By "duplicating itself in a mirror" the world, as Foucault notes in his discussion of Renaissance similitudes and correspondences, "abolishes the distance proper to it,"[34] rather than splitting itself into image and truth. Echo and origin are almost simultaneous, the response to one bird's call being at the same time the call to which another bird responds:

> But never elsewhere in one place I knew
> So many nightingales; and far and near,
> In wood and thicket, over the wide grove,
> They answer and provoke each other's song.
> ["The Nightingale," ll. 55-58]

The basis for a hermeneutics of conversation as a self-duplication, which transcends solipsism, yet heals and absorbs duality, is discernible in some comments of Schelling at the beginning of his *Ages of the World*. He speaks of the "silent dialogue," the "inner art of conversation" which finds its formal counterpart in dialectic, and which separates the self into an asking and responding self, "an ignorant one" and a "knowing one which, however, does not know its knowledge," like the naive self of Coleridge's conversation poems. The dialogue between selves also takes place across time, as the present self returns through recollection to the origins of its selfhood and converses with the past so as to bring it into the consciousness of the present. Through knowledge conceived as conversation, the inward and superior self becomes manifest to the self-conscious and sentimental conversant: it acquires "another in which it can view itself, represent and become intelligible to itself," and thus be raised from unconsciousness. But through this conversation the lower and superficial self is also led back "to just that innermost part of [its] nature which is . . . the living witness of all truth." Through the dialogue between the fallen self and its inward witness man "rejuvenates himself again and again," bringing together the internal and external worlds, the past and the present, the ideal and the real.[35]

---

relation to pantheism, see Thomas McFarland, *Coleridge and the Pantheist Tradition* (Oxford: Clarendon, 1969).

[34]Foucault, *The Order of Things*, p. 19.

[35]Schelling, *The Ages of the World*, pp. 85-88.

Perhaps of use in understanding the implications of the conversation mode for Romantic poetry as a whole is Derrida's critique
of the persistent tendency to value oral over written language, in
terms of its greater proximity to an aesthetics of presence and
origin. He describes how Rousseau distinguishes between the
unmediated presence of the self to its own voice, and the reflective distance that separates this self from the written word. The
written text empties out "the interiority of the soul," whereas
"natural writing" is "immediately united to the voice and to
breath . . . hieratic, very close . . . to the voice one hears upon retreating into oneself."³⁶ Although literature arises from the absence of presence, its purpose (as Derrida interprets Rousseau) is
reconstitutive: it seeks, in forms which approximate the ideal
order of voice and song, to recover what it imagines itself to have
lost. Such forms include hymn, prophecy, perhaps lyric itself.
Coleridge too will speak of this language heard when "the Soul
seeks to hear; when all is hush'd, / And the Heart listens" ("Reflections on Having Left a Place of Retirement," ll. 25–26). The conversation poem, it might almost be said, is an attempt to abolish
the radical fissure in being which Rousseau symbolizes through
the distinction between *parole* and *écriture*. Hence it seeks to create
a form of writing that is not written but oral: to imagine the voice
once again made present to itself through communication to a
second self who promises to renew the original experience or
enact what never was.

Whereas painting, in Rousseau's words, is "often dead and in-
animate, . . . vocal signs . . . announce to you a being like yourself.
They are, so to speak, the voice of the soul."³⁷ The emphasis on
voice and sound as directly joined to life, because they proceed "as
does respiration itself, from the breast . . . from the interior of a
living creature," is also found in Humboldt's treatise *Linguistic
Variability and Intellectual Development.*³⁸ Humboldt's essay is
largely concerned with assimilating Herder's theory of cultural

³⁶Derrida, *Of Grammatology*, pp. 34, 17.

³⁷Jean-Jacques Rousseau, *Essay on the Origin of Language* (1772), in *On the Origin
of Language: Jean-Jacques Rousseau, Essay on the Origin of Languages and Johann
Gottfried Herder, Essay on the Origin of Language*, trans. John H. Moran and Alexander Gode (New York: F. Ungar, 1966), p. 63.

³⁸Humboldt, *Linguistic Variability*, pp. 36, 34.

pluralism to a Hegelian vision of the evolution of consciousness. But he is also one of the earlier theorists of a hermeneutics of presence associated with Wilhelm Dilthey and Friedrich Schleiermacher, and condemned by modern writers such as Hans-Georg Gadamer as a false "Romanticism of immediacy" derived from an "aesthetics of genius."[39] Like other Romantic writers including Friedrich Schlegel, Humboldt conceives of language as process rather than product, communication rather than script. Sound emanates from the inwardness of the vital self and represents interiority to the world, but in such a way that it "reproduces the evoked sensation simultaneously with the object represented." Written language is no more than "an incomplete, mummified preservation" of this life that links man to the world around him, necessary only in the sense that it is the sole means to "again render perceptible the living speech concerned."[40]

Considered as part of this endeavor, the conversation poems take their place in a more general attempt to create a language that is literal rather than figurative. We need not confine ourselves to theories of voice and script. The valorization of presence over representation is prefigured in the Abbé du Bos's insistence that painting is superior to poetry because the latter makes use of "artificial signs," where the former employs "natural signs" and indeed passes entirely beyond the realm of signs to exhibit "nature herself . . . to our sight."[41] The specifics of these typologies of the arts are unimportant. Indeed Wordsworth, in his criticism of the picturesque, suggests that it is painting which limits itself to reduplication, and poetry which sees into the life of things, possessing the landscape as an interior presence rather than an external scene.[42] What is important is the belief that there is a form of art which can free itself from the reflexive awareness of itself as sign and discourse. The very phraseology used by Wordsworth in his description of Coleridge, as denied access to "Nature's living

---

[39]Hans-Georg Gadamer, *Truth and Method* (1960), trans. Garret Barden and John Cumming (New York: Seabury Press, 1975), p. 361.

[40]Humboldt, *Linguistic Variability*, pp. 35, 27.

[41]Jean Baptiste du Bos, *Critical Reflections on Poetry, Painting and Music* (1719), trans. Thomas Nugent (London: John Nourse, 1748), I, 321–323.

[42]Wordsworth's note to l. 284 of "Descriptive Sketches (1793)" (*Poetical Works*, ed. Ernest de Selincourt and Helen Darbishire [Oxford: Clarendon, 1966], I, 62).

images" and forced to substitute "words for things," reveals this paradoxical belief in a language which can absorb language into nature.

"Tintern Abbey," Wordsworth's only lyric in the conversation mode, brings out the assumptions and problems of the form. As a poem concerned with memory, and therefore with the significa- tion of something absent by its mental image, it is centrally in- volved with questions of presence and absence as they relate to the attempt to represent what may not be there. Memory, Beattie notes, is the power "to recall past sensations and thoughts, and make them again present." But though it differs from imagina- tion in constituting its object as past rather than nonexistent,[43] it remains haunted by the gap between epiphany and the text of reminiscence. The preface to *Lyrical Ballads*, like "Tintern Abbey" itself, seems to concede and then deny this gap. Wordworth's state- ment on the manner in which emotion is recollected in tranquil- lity[44] parallels his earlier description of the manner in which the poetic act includes reflection as well as sensation, the original "feeling" as well as the later "thought" which "represents" without ever actually becoming that feeling.[45] Poetry is clearly distin- guished from nature in which, as Coleridge observes, "there is no reflex act" but rather a "coinstaneity of . . . the Thought and the Production."[46] But in line with the primitivist notions that per- vade the preface, Wordsworth goes on to argue for a "species of re-action," which causes the "tranquillity" that separates mind from nature to disappear, and yield to the rapture of the original emotion.[47]

"Tintern Abbey" can be seen as a dialectic between two on- tologies of the image: one involving the sense of negativity and distance consequent upon writing in the mode of memory, and the other involving an attempt to annihilate this distance through the mode of the conversation poem. Repeatedly in the course of

[43]Beattie, "Of Memory and Imagination," pp. 8–9. Cf. also Sartre, *The Psychology of Imagination*, p. 236.

[44]Wordsworth, "Preface to *Lyrical Ballads* (1800)," *The Prose Works of William Wordsworth*, ed. W. J. B. Owen and Jane Worthington Smyser (Oxford: Clarendon, 1974), I, 148.

[45]Ibid., p. 126.

[46]Coleridge, *Notebooks*, 4397.

[47]Wordsworth, "Preface to *Lyrical Ballads* (1800)," p. 148.

the poem the speaker draws attention to his inability to "paint /
What then I was" (ll. 75-76), to convert image into thing and thus
to write a logocentric poetry. But more and more he sees himself
as having transcended the limits of mere pictorial reduplication
(l. 61), as having been "laid asleep / In body, and become a living
soul" (ll. 45-46). He claims to have recovered "The language of
my former heart" (l. 117): a language deeper than discourse,
which closes the fissure created by time within the self, and makes
the poet present to himself within his feelings. Of crucial importance
to this illusion of self-communion is the introduction of Dorothy
into the poem. Dorothy is, in Shelley's words, the other who responds to the speaker with "the voice of his own soul" (*Alastor*, l.
153), and makes otherness (the otherness of time as well as self)
into identity. It is through her "voice" (l. 116) that he recovers an
inner language which reawakens the "inland murmur" (l. 4) of the
scene itself.

The conversion of text into conversation and of thought into
life is central to the view that Wordsworth's poem seems to take of
poetry. Like the two trees growing from the same root toward
similar heavens, the imaginary repossession of a lost harmony
achieved by Wordsworth's poem and the actual repossession of it
by Dorothy are envisaged as in all respects congruent. The real
experience confirms the imaginary one, and confirms the power
of the imagination to repeat in the finite mind that impossible
condition which Stevens calls the first idea behind the merely
invented world. One of the poem's paradoxes is that, as Kaplan
puts it, it "proclaims the poem as a victory over the poet's dependence on memory,"[48] or at least seems to do so. Memory, in
Proust's words, enmeshes the mind in the strange contradiction of
survival and nothingness.[49] In accomplishing its return to the
hiding places of man's power not through recollection alone, but
also by reincarnating the past in a living person and by returning
to a landscape that is no longer simply imagined but also real,
"Tintern Abbey" claims that poetry can free itself from the
ambiguities of existing in an imaginary mode. It claims to have

---

[48]Fred Kaplan, *Miracles of Rare Device* (Athens: University of Georgia Press,
1974), p. 43.
[49]Marcel Proust, *A la recherche du temps perdu* (1919-1927; rpt. Paris: Pléiade,
1954), II, 759-760.

cleansed the doors of invention and found a language that is innocent of the divergence between sign and thing.

But the poem only seems to make this claim, because the concluding benediction, so apparently untarnished by the fallings and vanishings that "disturb / Our cheerful faith" (ll. 132–133), once again reimplicates epiphany in the ambiguities of memory (ll. 139–141). There is a recognition, absent from the more simplistic conclusions of Coleridge's poems, that Dorothy is not really a naive being, and that for her too the physical presence of the landscape will be displaced by its imaginary representation, as the past which has been recovered in the future is again lost in the past. The insistent possibility of a rejuvenated imagination, which will have recovered its capacity to perceive naively, is always complicated by the knowledge that the lines of communication between innocence and experience are of dual direction. Wordsworth as a theorist tends to claim that poetry can abolish the separation between image and presence. But his poems seem deliberately to structure themselves around this separation: to generate in the mind of the reader a debate between naive and reflective consciousnesses that coexist in the same moment, without bringing about the reconversion of sentimental into naive poetry.

Nevertheless, "Tintern Abbey" makes clear a certain intention which is also the thrust behind Coleridge's conversation poems. These poems are less willing to doubt than Wordsworth's poem is, and also less able to believe. The attempted absorption of text into voice can take many forms, and that Coleridge should have chosen to develop the conversation mode rather than the prophetic mode used in "Religious Musings" is revealing. Both modes seek to create the illusion of a poet who is immediately present to his audience, and thus able to communicate and hypostatize a vision of the imminent renewal of consciousness. But Coleridge lacked the sublime confidence of Blake, who chose as the vehicle of his affirmations a hierarchical mode of utterance, in which the poetic voice simply imparts a higher truth to a silent auditor. Prophecy is the formal equivalent of a radical idealism, which holds that the human mind is the source of vision, and that the external world can be reconstituted in accordance with patterns imposed by man's imagination. Conversation, by contrast, is dialogical and therefore inherently self-doubting. On the surface, it seems to pursue the same goals as prophecy in a more genuinely dialectical manner, entertaining doubts that are finally resolved and incorporating points of opposition to a truth that is developed rather than imposed. But underneath, it is an incipiently skeptical mode, troubled by questions of the source and authority of vision. Its very acknowledgment of the need to secure the assent of an auditor—dramatized by the failure of a poem such as "The Eolian Harp"—betrays an uneasiness about the reality of its affirmations. Whereas the rhetoric of prophecy seems self-authenticating, the language of conversation is always complicated by questions of the dependency and autonomy—hence also the secondariness and primacy—of poetic imagination.

The current of insecurity that underlies the conversation poems is apparent if we read some of Coleridge's notebook entries on the need to recreate inner experience in the external world. In these he returns again and again to his sense of existing "almost wholly within myself, in *thoughts* rather than in *things.*"[50] He speaks of seeking in external nature "a *symbolical* language for something within me,"[51] and of needing "an outward Interpreter" for the music of his heart.[52] The subjectivity of mental representations and the need to generalize them into some kind of Concrete Universal are constant concerns of Romantic philosophy. Thus Hegel attributes to language an externalizing and self-confirming role, through which the ego constructs itself as an object "existing *for others,*"[53] and he extends this formulation to art, which confirms the private vision by producing it in the medium of "external things."[54] For Coleridge, however, language points solipsistically to the world of desire, rather than beyond itself to that miraculous self-presence which comes only from the communion with another person in which "each contemplates the Soul of the other as involving his own, both in its givings and its receivings ... and thus still keeping alive its *outness,* its *self-*

[50]Coleridge, *Collected Letters of Samuel Taylor Coleridge,* ed. E. L. Griggs (Oxford: Clarendon, 1956–1971), II, 881.
[51]Coleridge, *Notebooks,* 2546. Italics mine.
[52]Ibid., 2035. Cf. also 524, 1554.
[53]Hegel, *The Phenomenology of Mind,* pp. 660–661.
[54]Hegel, *Aesthetics,* I, 31.

oblivion."[55] Of particular interest to the problematical status of poetry is a long entry in which Coleridge explicitly relates language and human community as modes of externalization:

> All minds must think by some *symbols* . . . something that is *without,* that has the property of *Outness* (a word which Berkley preferred to "Externality"). . . . every generous mind . . . feels its *Halfness*—it cannot *think* without a symbol—neither can it *live* without something that is to be at once its Symbol, & its *Other half.* . . . Hence I deduce the habit, I have most unconsciously formed, of *writing* my inmost thoughts—I have not a soul on earth to whom I can reveal them.[56]

Here the insecurity of language is apparent. It can symbolize, but it cannot confirm itself by being its own other half. It is essentially a substitute for something else, unable to give a foundation to what it projects except insofar as it can rejoin the living outwardness which sanctions its existence as representation, dependent for its autonomy on something outside itself.

Coleridge wrote "This Lime-Tree Bower, My Prison" when a minor injury prevented him from accompanying his friends on a walk. The poem envisages from a distance a landscape of communion with nature and communication between friends: a landscape which the friends reenter after a circuitous journey from the unsunned dell to the wide heaven, and the repossession of which confirms God's omnipresence. But behind the poem is a sense of privacy and exclusion. It seems that this vision can have no value unless it is hypostatized as a memory of something actually seen, and communicated to those friends whose absence casts in doubt the reality of both communion and community. Thus the separation of the reflective consciousness, of Coleridge himself, from the friends who are actively and sensuously present to nature throws into relief the question of whether language can guarantee the experience of epiphany against the possibility of its literal absence.

For Coleridge, as for Rousseau, language has an ambivalent status. It is, first of all, the sign of the poet's separation from nature: a medium he resorts to only because he cannot participate

[55]Coleridge, *Notebooks,* 2540.
[56]Ibid., 3325. Cf. also Friedrich Schlegel, *The Philosophy of Language,* p. 371.

with Lamb in the living images of nature. But it is, more important, the medium by which this loss is recovered: the medium
which claims to represent a world beyond the dejected self. Yet
between representation and presentation there is a crucial difference, as Coleridge was later to point out. Representation
creates a world of things "not combined with the sense of real
Presence:"[57] it imagines a scene precisely because that scene is not
present to it. Arising as it does from the gap between consciousness and things, it can never be the means to close that gap. Such
indeed is the meaning of the poem's central image of a place
which is at once a bower and a prison. Although the act of writing
the poem somehow releases the poet from the emptiness of his
own subjectivity and allows him to enter a natural plenitude beyond himself, the recreation of that brighter world remains imprisoned within the imaginary.

It might almost be said that the poem rests with a certain ambiguity, recognizing that poetic language does not so much provide a bridge between the inner world of dream and imagination
and the world of actuality[58] as exist at the suture of the imaginary
and the perceived. Such is not the case, however. It is important
for an understanding of these poems that they are not simply
poems, but conversation poems that confirm the truth of the fictive by identifying it with a person who exists outside the realm of
the fictive. Like Adam, who awoke to find a second self which
made his dream seem true, Coleridge's poems seek an *alter ego*
which is "the supplement and completion" of the speaking
voice.[59] Through this other half they claim to emerge from the
limiting enclosure of reverie into the open space of the real, to
make of the poet a man speaking to men rather than a dreamer
who projects the form of his desire onto a blind world. Epistolary
novels such as Senancour's *Oberman* or Hölderlin's *Hyperion* develop through a largely one-sided correspondence that acknowledges something unreciprocated and unrealized in the dialogue

---

[57]Coleridge, *Notebooks*, 4058.
[58]Cf. *Notebooks*, 4397, for Coleridge's argument that poetry mediates between
painting, which is purely external, and music, which is purely internal: that it is "a
middle nature between a Thought and a Thing."
[59]Coleridge, "The Improvisatore," *Poetical Works*, ed. E. H. Coleridge (Oxford:
Clarendon, 1966), I, 465.

with the ideal. They recognize, through their very form, the subjectivity of those fictions of perfection that the mind may construct only "to feed itself in its destitution, . . . to survive within a
voiceless Nature."[60] In Coleridge's poem, however, private vision
claims to rejoin the real world at the point where a rook seen by
Lamb is also seen by Coleridge (ll. 68–74).

Through this movement from mental representation to presence, Coleridge creates the illusion of a poem that has expanded
the limits of poetry and represented the infinite within the finite.
Yet we should not ignore a crucial difference between "Tintern
Abbey" and this poem: the fact that the speaker only 'deems' (l.
70) that Lamb has seen the bird. By making its liberation from the
imaginary dependent on a constitutive act of imagination the
poem, in effect, curves back into the ambiguities of its own private
space. Yet, seemingly, Coleridge does not recognize the extent to
which his hesitations about the self as a source of visionary authority have only been allayed by a projection of himself onto another
being. This fact will prove of crucial importance in the later
poems, where language is constantly seen as a narcissistic structure.

In "Frost at Midnight" too, there is an acknowledgment of the
isolation of the imagining consciousness and a similarly problematical attempt to achieve an experience of communion which
will make nature thought and thought nature. The frost, secret
and inaccessible, embodies the spontaneous, productive energy of
nature as it both creates and reflects, hanging its icicles up to the
gaze of the moon. It is "Unhelped by any wind" (l. 2), dependent
on nothing outside itself, and intimately linked through its secrecy
and silence to the very continuum of life itself. The babe, as a
breathing but not a thinking creature, is a part of this *plenum* and
participates at a level deeper than consciousness in "the number-
less goings-on of life, / Inaudible as dreams" (ll. 12–13). Only the
poet, the "sole unquiet thing" in nature (l. 16), seems estranged
from a life that is vital rather than exhausted and flickering. He
seeks to move from mental to sensuous consciousness, to find in
the external world the echo or mirror of himself, in order to

[60]Etienne Pivert de Senancour, *Oberman; lettres publiées par M. . . . Senancour*
(1804; rpt. Paris: Bibliothèque 10/18, 1965), pp. 46–47. Translation mine.

produce his own "Abstruser musings" (l. 6) in the medium of things, as the frost does.[61] But his consciousness turns solipsistically back on itself, caught in the inevitable narcissism of its attempts to grasp the external world as an object in relation to a subject rather than as a purely objective reality. The film on the grate, a residue of desire rather than evidence of the genius that joins the subjective to the objective world, seems to image the emptiness of the imagining consciousness. It dreams but does not produce anything, imagines and heralds a life beyond itself, but does not make it present except as an echo.

The images of the mind are thus without natural similitudes, suspended within themselves. But the other side of the solipsism of consciousness is that nature is without human similitudes, pristine yet uncompanionable. The coldness and silence of the frost, which refracts but does not absorb light, reveals the resistance of the external world to the conversation of eye and object.[62] Yet if communion is to take place, it is not only the mind which must give itself to nature, but also nature which must allow itself to be internalized as human experience. If the process seen in *Biographia Literaria* as intrinsic to perception—the process by which "the spirit in all objects which it views, views only itself"[63]—is here seen as solipsistic, it can only be because experience puts in doubt the theoretical consubstantiality of thought and thing. The marriage between the spirit of desire and the body of the world, often taken for granted in post-Kantian idealism, proves precarious and inevitably brings human creativity up against a radical self-doubt.

[61]Cf. Hegel's statement: "Spirit does not stop at the mere apprehension of the external world by sight and hearing; it makes it into an object for its inner being which then is itself driven, once again in the form of sensuousness, to realise itself in things, and relates itself to them as *desire*" (*Aesthetics*, 1, 36).
[62]There are at least two other instances of the frost image in Coleridge's poetry. In the opening paragraph of the prose section of "The Blossoming of the Solitary Date-Tree," the image is used to suggest imaginative sterility: the failure of inner and outer worlds to coincide. In "The Two Sisters," the mind's reflection of an ideal that is not possessed is paralleled to the manner in which the winter sun is reflected on ice that has not thawed.
[63]Coleridge, *Biographia Literaria*, 1, 184. Cf. also Hegel, according to whom man must "recognise himself alone alike in what is summoned out of himself and in what is accepted from without. . . . This aim he achieves by altering external things whereon he impresses the seal of his inner being and in which he now finds again his own characteristics" (*Aesthetics*, 1, 31).

As if to escape from the loneliness of the present, where promise is not fulfilled and vision remains unconfirmed, the poet returns to similar scenes in the past and to the Wordsworthian hypostasis of imagination through memory. He recalls how he sought, even as a child, the stranger whose arrival was portended by the film in the grate: "Townsman, or aunt, or sister more beloved, / My play-mate when we both were clothed alike!" (ll. 42–43). This being was to have been the double or similitude of desire, incarnating it in the actual world. Paracelsus speaks of the universe conceived as a system of correspondences in terms of two twins "who resemble one another completely, without its being possible to say which of them brought its similitude to the other."[64] The sister, clothed identically to Coleridge yet other than him, allows vision to externalize itself without ceasing to be present to itself. Conversely, as a stranger she brings before him a world that is not initially companionable and, in Hegel's words, strips this "external world of its inflexible foreignness" by revealing it as a mere "external realisation of himself."[65] In her, as in the Shelleyan epipsyche who is at once an objective being and the innermost voice of the poet's soul, the internal and external worlds are so intimately combined that they melt into each other. Vision and fact touch on their inner side, separated from each other only by a fold in being.

But for Coleridge, unlike Wordsworth, there is nothing to remember because the twin never materialized. The primal unity of desire and its object, which the poet can only imagine in the present, was always an imaginary and narcissistic construct rather than a recollection of something that once existed. In the creative sequence of Coleridge's world it is not being which precedes nothingness, but emptiness which precedes and generates the compensatory projection of plenitude. The doubling of the present in the past, through an act of memory that promises liberation but narcissistically repeats the loneliness of the present, thus deconstructs the multiple attempts in this poem to actualize desire in the medium of time, nature, or human community. It is in the light of this recognition that we must read Coleridge's attempt to transfer

---

[64]Paracelsus, *Liber Paramirum*. Quoted in Foucault, *The Order of Things*, p. 20.
[65]Hegel, *Aesthetics*, I, 31.

the locus of the ideal from the past to the future, as he seeks through his child to recover the failure of imagination and memory in the equally illusory and intentional mode of hope. The child too is the twin of the poet's desire, but paradoxically he is a twin who bears no resemblance to him, being the very opposite of what Coleridge was as a child (l. 51ff.). Toward the end, the poem moves beyond the isolation of consciousness from nature symbolized by winter, to a spring landscape in which the child is part of the natural scene. In the concluding lines, moreover, it returns to the initial image of the frost in order to cancel out its sterility and negativity in a celebration of the sweetness of all seasons. By association, the poet too enters this imagined innocence, in which there are no longer any vacant spots in the *plenum* of psychic time, and in which the ambiguous silence of nature has been transformed into the articulate sounds of a human presence.

So persuasive is Coleridge in imposing hypothesis as fact that a critic such as Reeve Parker actually sees the poem as moving from the "superstitious solipsism of a depressed sensibility, toying with a companionable form, to the apprehension of a regenerate companionship, based not on superstition but on substantial belief."[66] To some extent it is true that the speaker believes himself to have rejoined a naive existence. But it is worth pointing out that there is, and can be, no conversation between the poet and the child, whose attraction is precisely that it inhabits a language earlier than articulation. Like nature herself, the infant is silent, oblivious to the poet: it neither confirms nor denies the vision that Coleridge projects onto it, and thus refers him back to that very sense of vision as musing and fantasy that he had sought to escape in associating his hopes with a real being. Thus the imagination remains at the end of this poem what it was at the beginning: an ideal and self-echoing faculty, which has to project itself into the external world in order to "find" itself there, and which is trapped in a kind of circularity.

The continued separation of vision from fact shows itself in the peculiar way in which Coleridge, unlike Wordsworth, imagines the landscape of communion: namely, as completely external to

[66]Parker, *Coleridge's Meditative Art* (Ithaca: Cornell University Press, 1975), p. 127

the self who celebrates it. In the final lines Coleridge imagines a world of presence, but he himself is not present in it. In this transformed and renewed world the clouds and lakes, the icicles and the moon, are mirrored in one another (ll. 55-58, 73-74), but do not include the poet in their conversation. The much proclaimed fusion of subject and object in the act of perception[67] therefore never takes place, as subjective meditation gives way entirely to the objectivity of second-person address. The inaccessibility of the landscape projected arises from the essentially despairing way in which Coleridge conceives the relationship between present and future, and therefore between the real and the ideal. While the hope that Wordsworth projects onto Dorothy is confirmed by its duplication in his own past, the segments of human time in this poem are radically discontinuous. Repetition and renewal, the organizing principles behind Wordsworth's poetry, and the apparent impetus behind this poem that links father to son, can only make of the future a return to the frustration that existed in the past. Thus if regeneration is to occur, the future's relationship to the present must be seen as revolutionary and antithetical rather than continuous. But revolution (whether imaginative or political) is a lonely and unconsciously skeptical form of idealism: an insurance policy taken out on the future against the doubts and insecurities felt in the present. The revolutionary mind simultaneously claims everything and nothing. It allows itself completely to transcend actuality, but because it also destroys all transitional ground between the future and the present in which it must remain, it never allows itself to possess this transcendence as fact.

Whether Coleridge is aware of this irony implicit in the fact that his poems are structured in terms of reversal rather than development is difficult to say. Perhaps one of the most interesting features of the affirmative conversation poems is the fact that they always seem to claim an experience of epiphany, but to do so only vicariously, through an *alter ego* who is ambiguously Yeatsian mask and Shelleyan epipsyche, therefore ironic and sentimental. More than one critic has pointed to something borrowed, secondary in Coleridge's experience of epiphany. Hartman remarks

[67]Coleridge, *Biographia Literaria*, I, 174.

that "his relation to writing of all kinds is more embarrassed than that of Keats and more devious than that of Akenside. His imagination sees itself as inherently 'secondary'—."[68] Bloom talks of "a failure in priority, a failure to have begotten himself."[69] And Coleridge himself speaks of seeing himself as "an herbaceous Plant, as large as a large tree . . . but with *pith within* the Trunk, not heart of Wood . . . an involuntary Imposter."[70] More significantly, he contrasts himself with Monk Lewis: "The simplicity & naturalness is his own, & not imitated . . . [I] cannot attain this innocent nakedness, except by *assumption*."[71] The vicarious enjoyment of epiphany through a surrogate self merely takes further a dissociation between image and presence that already existed in the self-conscious language of "The Eolian Harp" and Coleridge's earlier lyrics in the style of eighteenth-century loco-descriptive poetry. In "The Eolian Harp" Coleridge had seemed to celebrate through the wind-harp a completely spontaneous and natural art, yet his own language had been artifical to the point of describing the elements of the natural scene as "emblems," literary representations "of Innocence and Love" (l. 5). In both cases the feeling of communion with nature is evoked analogically, either through an image that represents epiphany without becoming it, or through a surrogate self with whom the speaking voice cannot fuse. It is as though the experience is not possessed literally, and as though there is a latent recognition that poetry cannot become the unequivocal reappropriation of presence. The existence of a surrogate self, through whom the poet must represent himself in a place where he is not, points in turn to the surrogate status of literary signs, which also seek to take the place of the absent and to represent something which they cannot recapture.

Such a statement may seem paradoxical, in view of the fact that the conversation poems make use of a naive auditor precisely in order to literalize the imaginary. It is, as Derrida says, part of the

---

[68]Hartman, "Reflections on the Evening Star," in *New Perspectives on Coleridge and Wordsworth: Selected Papers from the English Institute*, ed. Geoffrey Hartman (New York: Columbia University Press, 1972), p. 111.

[69]Bloom, "Coleridge: The Anxiety of Influence," in *New Perspectives on Coleridge and Wordsworth*, ed. Hartman, p. 258.

[70]Quoted in George Whalley, "Coleridge Unlabyrinthed," *University of Toronto Quarterly*, 32 (1962–1963), 343.

[71]Coleridge, *Collected Letters*, 1, 379.

strategy of signs that "the substitute [should] make one forget the vicariousness of its own function," and should make itself pass for the experience itself.[72] But somehow Coleridge's poems draw attention to their strategy in a way that inhibits the suspension of disbelief which allows the conversion of images into realities. His auditors are sometimes indirect rather than direct auditors, like Lamb who is physically absent although he is the object of a direct address. Where Wordsworth stands beside Dorothy and experiences a reunion with nature both directly and through her, Coleridge remains physically isolated from the being on to whom he projects his own naiveté, able to live his dreams only through another and at a distance that seems to negate his claim of proximity to this being. In part, the conversation poems seem genuinely blind to the fictitiousness of this communion between a self-conscious mind and a completely spontaneous being such as the harp or the babe. But in another sense Coleridge's vicariousness, as Bate astutely points out in connection with his plagiarisms, is the product of an inner censorship which makes him reach out for another to take his place and serve as "usher for what he cannot feel completely free to advance himself."[73] Like the self-conscious language which qualifies and sees through the imaginary paradise of "The Eolian Harp," the vicariousness of these poems reveals (perhaps half-consciously) Coleridge's own insecurity about the naive claims made by his language. To recover a "primary intuition" of nature,[74] to recreate "the original, as yet unconscious, poetry of the spirit" which Schelling recognizes in the external world,[75] might be to reduce the self-consciousness of mind to the unconsciousness of nature. Coleridge's philosophical uncertainties about the pantheistic fusion of thought and nature have as their corollary a doubt about the poetics of presence that never ceases to haunt these seemingly naive poems.

The shift in the latter part of the eighteenth century from an aesthetics of imitation to one of genius is largely an attempt to overcome the representative and therefore secondary status of

---

[72]Derrida, *Of Grammatology*, p. 144.
[73]W. J. Bate, *Coleridge* (1968; rpt. New York: Collier Books, 1973), pp. 137–138.
[74]Coleridge, *Notebooks*, 4186.
[75]Schelling, *System des transzendentalen Idealismus*, p. 17. Translation mine.

language. Vatic and sublime poems such as "Religious Musings" and Blake's prophecies are a direct product of this shift, and claim the immediate presence of a vision that is validated by the living, the original and originating voice of the poet. It is perhaps in the context of this drive toward a repossession of the productive energy of nature[76] that we should view Coleridge's impulse toward vicariousness and plagiarism, which are simply more overt and despairing versions of imitation. "Imitators," according to Edward Young, "only give us a sort of Duplicates of what we had, possibly more better, before."[77] Vicariousness, like imitation, is the language of a mind which can see the forms of beauty but cannot feel them except ambiguously, and which recognizes something substitutive and sentimental in the claim of poetry to possess the plenitude it designates. It arises from the emptiness of imaginative dispossession, and is the form taken by imitation in a period which condemns as illegitimate the deviation of presence into representation.

Yet it would be wrong to conclude that this aspect of the conversation poems constitutes a deliberate deconstruction of their assumptions. Coleridge's vicariousness involves a complex mixture of what psychologists call projection and introjection: he at once attributes to another what he wishes to disown, and claims as his own what he cannot have. In a very real sense, vicariousness can be seen as a sentimental form: a way of keeping innocence recoverable by entrusting it to someone else. Yet it is also a tortured, self-doubting form which constantly reveals the hollowness of such recovery. Its use in these poems allows deconstructive and self-mystifying tendencies to coexist, by a kind of automatonism, without being accommodated to each other. By projecting naiveté onto someone else, Coleridge betrays a duplicity at the heart of imaginative faith, which can constitute the ideal only as existing outside itself, and yet avoids a complete deconstruction of innocence.

Coleridge's uncertainty about whether to accept or question the aesthetics of genius persists even in a later poem such as "Dejec-

---

[76]Edward Young actually characterizes original genius as being "of a vegetable nature" (*Conjectures on Original Composition*, p. 12).
[77]Ibid., p. 10.

tion: An Ode," where the failure of communion between eye and landscape, and of conversation between the poet and his naive *alter ego,* radically calls into question the vision of life eddying "from pole to pole" (l. 135) projected in the concluding benediction. Although the poet imagines a period when dejeçtion did not exist, he also seems deeply uncertain whether he actually possessed at birth that "shaping spirit of Imagination" (l. 86) which he claims to have betrayed. In a revealing image he describes how "hope grew round me, like the twining vine, / And fruits, and foliage, not my own, seemed mine" (ll. 80–81). It seems that the emptiness of the self may always have been more primary than a visionary power which was always partly borrowed. In these lines the poem approaches an astonishing conclusion: namely, that poetic genius does not arise like a natural or 'generated' object, "representative of its own cause within itself . . . and resembl[ing], not represent[ing]," but that it is partly fabricated, invented, "representative always of something not itself."[78] The curious fact that Coleridge sees himself as imitating or following the Wordsworth group, even though the conversation poems were actually written before "Tintern Abbey," suggests that his vicariousness is not so much a matter of literary indebtedness as of a feeling that vision itself is incapable of self-authentication. Yet the poem as a whole remains sentimentally committed to the very myth that its existence exposes. Its sentimentality is now defiant rather than repressive. In using the form of the verse-letter rather than the conversation, Coleridge concedes the absence of his auditor and gives up the subterfuge of an indirect auditor in order to admit the estrangement of text from voice. In finally opting for the ode, he renounces all hope of the intimacy of conversation. Yet in celebrating Asra (in one version Wordsworth), he continues to insist that there exist peculiarly privileged people whose joy is intrinsic, and modes of poetry similarly privileged in their immunity from the doubts and vanishings of human experience.

"To William Wordsworth" is also a poem concerned with the activity of genius, and specifically with reading aloud: with the

[78]Coleridge, *Notebooks,* 2444. Note that in contrast to Coleridge's usual tendency to classify art as an organic and not a mechanical product, it is precisely an aesthetic object (a statue) which is here used to exemplify "Fabrication" (a child is used as an instance of "Generation").

production of vision as fact through the conversion of script into voice. But the poem, which contains all the elements of a conversation poem (the auditor, the vision of the One Life, the benediction), inverts them in a peculiar way. As a text which is addressed not by the poet to his auditor but, from a passive viewpoint, by the auditor (Coleridge) to the poet (Wordsworth), it seems to throw into relief a one-sidedness in the projection of vision always latent in the conversation poems. The assent of the auditor is obtained here, but only because Coleridge consents to Wordsworth's curious way of grounding his vision in the real world by arguing that the light projected from within is really generated by a cooperation of reflected and bestowed lights. In fact there is no cooperation in this poem, which constantly deflects conversation into ode or hymn, the presence of vision into its transcendent inaccessibility. The conjunction between vision and actuality achieved in the poem is described through two despairing images: the strewing of flowers over a bier (ll. 71-75), and the powerful surge of the ocean which washes over a drowned man (ll. 62-63) and awakens just enough of death in life to make life die again. The obvious estrangement of Coleridge from Wordsworth leaves the latter's affirmations unfulfilled, almost meaningless, in a world which still desires the temporal union of consciousnesses through conversation, rather than the hopelessness of faith. Yet significantly, the inversion of the conversation mode does not explicitly deconstruct its assumptions, but rather confirms, from a position of complete despair, a vision which Coleridge is content to celebrate in the mode of exile.

Curiously, Wordsworth's poetry itself (the object of Coleridge's nostalgia in this poem) shows some awareness of how vulnerable its vision is. Although Coleridge tries to use *The Prelude* as Keats uses the nightingale (in order to explore sentimentally the gap between the intended and actual status of his own art), Wordsworth's poem, considered as an intertext for the reader of Coleridge's conversation poems, functions much like Keats's urn, and casts doubt upon the very notion of art that Coleridge is concerned to project upon it. At first sight, Wordsworth's text seems to follow, in extended form, the conversational model established in Coleridge's poems. It argues for a communion between self and nature that is confirmed by its transmission to Coleridge, whose presence as reader and friend is meant to create "Kindred mutations" that enable the poet "To hold fit converse with the spiritual world, / And with the generations of mankind" (xiv.94, 108–109). But the presence of other implied readers in the subtext of the poem challenges this assumption that discourse is the manifestation of community rather than alienation. In certain episodes—the encounters with ruined figures such as the Discharged Soldier, the Blind Beggar, and the maiden seen near the murderer's gibbet—Wordsworth seems to question and see through his own view of poetry as a unifying communicative act, and to feel himself thrust back into the privacy, indeed the irrelevance, of his vision. Because these figures come from the margins of society and refuse the conventionalities of social intercourse, they suspend our sense of the poet as a man speaking to men within a community that actualizes his vision. They nearly always exist in landscapes that are colorless or denuded of natural imagery. They are either blind or silent, refusing vision and speech. Thus they seem to block the dialogue of reception and bestowal essential to Romantic theories of communication and perception. They represent a certain recalcitrance of the universe of things toward penetration by the light of imagination: a limit at which poetic representation finds itself exposed and unable to insist on itself as truth. It is against these lacunae in the harmony of experience that the rest of *The Prelude* takes shape, as an Apollonian surface that has discovered within itself a vital crevice.

Of particular interest in this regard is a related poem, "The Old Cumberland Beggar." The beggar represents an absence, a vacant spot in perception, which the mind must fill if it is to preserve its vision of the natural economy as one in which nothing is wasted or unemployed. He represents something in society, and also in the self, with which one cannot communicate. Charity is essentially a way of reintegrating him into the community and thus reaffirming that everything has its place in the Great Chain of the organic society (ll. 73–79). Yet there is something one-sided, hence insecure, in the process of giving as it emerges here, and therefore in the dialogue between the self and what resists domestication into the intimacy of conversation. The giving does not enrich the recipient, except momentarily. The speaker does not communicate with the beggar. Rather he communes, in a mood of "self-congratulation" (l. 125) with the gratitude he projects onto a man who does not respond one way or the other, and neither confirms nor denies the poet's vision of things. The narcissistic structure of philanthropy comments, in turn, on something unfulfilled in the very nature of vision, which knows itself to be a solipsistic, projective activity. Sometimes (as in this poem) Wordsworth is unable to absorb the knowledge contained in such incidents. He insists nervously that the ruined figure explain his existence and fill the silence with conversation, eliciting from him a tale whose "strange half-absence" (*Prelude*, IV.443) reveals only the irrelevance of words to the world of things. But at other points he seems to accept the stubborn muteness of the objective world, and the ambiguity of these dispossessed figures who, like Keats's Titans, reveal both the survival and the erosion of vision in such a world. In these moments he experiences a curiously unrapturous epiphany: a "visionary dreariness" or a "bleak music" (*Prelude*, XII.256, 320) which arises from the poet's ability to find a language that respects silence, rather than from the sublimity which subdues the external world to the will of imagination.

While Coleridge did not borrow the conversation mode from Wordsworth, his development of the form seems to have coincided with the start of a friendship which revolutionized his sense of what poetry should be. The poems are full of references to the Wordsworth group and are partly understood as Coleridge's attempt to draw closer to a natural and naive poetry identified with Wordsworth. Yet Wordsworth himself, in *The Prelude*, doubts the "communicativeness and *utterancy* of heart and soul"[79] which is the goal of the conversation poems. In the Matthew poems ("The Two April Mornings" and "The Fountain") he similarly questions the attempt to perceive the imaginary by finding a real surrogate for the dead child who lives only in Matthew's imagination. As Nietzsche recognized in *The Birth of Tragedy*, where he looks more closely at the supposed sweetness and light of Hellenic literature, the primary texts to which the later, sentimental mind has recourse in order to assure itself of the possibility of a naive poetry prove to be as beset by complications as the later texts themselves. A reading of Wordsworth would reveal the extent to which Coleridge's dialogue with a Wordsworthian poetry, like Keats's dia-

[79]Coleridge, "The Improvisatore," *Poetical Works*, I, 464.

logue with his fiction of Greece, is the dialogue of a mind with a self-projected and almost impossible ideal. It was not easy, however, for Coleridge to accept this fact. The poems we have considered so far vacillate between a repressive and a defiant sentimentality. The poems of Coleridge's later years, having approached but failed to achieve the desolate strength of irony, are more reluctantly sentimental. Living with the discontinuity between language and its object, and making of poetry something more than an uneasy lodger in an age which will not allow the blind literalizing of imaginary constructs, are the dilemmas that confront the poems of Coleridge's later years.

In a famous definition in *The Stateman's Manual,* Coleridge distinguishes between symbol and allegory, emphasizing the superiority of what he will elsewhere call a "tautegorical language,"[80] a metonymic sign which abolishes the dualism of presence and representation:

> Now an Allegory is but a translation of abstract notions into a picture-language which is itself nothing but an abstraction from objects of the senses; . . . On the other hand a Symbol . . . is characterized by a translucence of the Special in the Individual or of the General in the Especial or of the Universal in the General. Above all by the translucence of the Eternal through and in the Temporal. It always partakes of the Reality which it renders intelligible; and while it enunciates the whole, abides itself as a living part in that Unity, of which it is the representative.[81]

It is therefore strange to find that a number of Coleridge's later poems use allegoric figures such as Faith and Hope, and that others—such as "The Pang More Sharp Than All," "Love's Apparition and Evanishment," and "Time Real and Imaginary"— actually describe themselves as allegories or allegoric romances. Through their subtitles these poems explicitly reflect on their own mode of production and make aesthetic representation one of

[80]Coleridge, *Aids to Reflection,* pp. 181–182. Note that Coleridge in *Aids to Reflection* prefers allegorical to tautegorical language.

[81]Coleridge, *The Statesman's Manual, Lay Sermons,* ed. R. J. White (London: Routledge & Kegan Paul, 1972), p. 30. Cf. also *Notebooks,* 4503.

their primary concerns. The allegorical sign is an empty sign, in which the separation of tenor from vehicle announces a radical discontinuity between desire and its object. De Man has, in fact, seen in the Romantic use of allegory, particularly by Rousseau in the context of a confessional language, a deliberate irony toward the notion of language as a plenitude. The prevalence of allegory, according to him, "always corresponds to the unveiling of an authentically temporal destiny" and constitutes a renunciation of "the nostalgia and the desire to coincide."[82] Its use by Coleridge, at the very least, seems to correspond to an increasing awareness of the impossibility of an aesthetics of presence, an increasing doubt about the post-Kantian denial, through immediate vision, of the lacuna between image and substance.

Equally striking is the fact that the late poems seem to regress, behind the natural diction sought in the conversation poems, to a dissociative eighteenth-century diction which Coleridge dismisses as that "amphibious something made up half of image and half of abstract meaning."[83] The Romantic drive toward an aesthetics of presence and fusion is apparent in his criticisms of William Bowles, whose heart and mind fail to become "*intimately* combined and *unified,* with the great appearances in Nature—& not merely held in solution & loose mixture with them, in the shape of formal Similies."[84] Yet it is precisely simile and simulation which characterize Coleridge's later poems. These are second-rate poems, surprisingly similar in some ways to the derivative and self-conscious efforts of his youth, to the point where "The Pang More Sharp Than All" actually seems to rework two earlier poems entitled "The Sigh" and "The Rose." But these poems are also separated from the early work by Coleridge's theoretical writings, which make a highly sophisticated attempt to work out a hierarchy of styles that will purge the language of genius from that of secondary talent. Through distinctions between symbol and allegory, imagination and fancy, imitation and copy, Coleridge seems voluntarily to give us tools that can be used to dissect his own poetic production. Thus there is implicit in the later poems a tendency to

---

[82]De Man, "The Rhetoric of Temporality," pp. 190–191.
[83]Coleridge, *Biographia Literaria,* I, 15–16.
[84]Coleridge, *Collected Letters,* II, 864.

self-deconstruction which results from their conscious secondariness. The pre-Romantic forms of moralized landscape, sentimental effusion, and the loco-descriptive poem, functioning as they do within the framework of Addisonian theory, recognize something projective and secondary in the pleasures of imagination. As Wasserman says, though in a critical vein, such poetry "both pretends to a relation between subject and object and yet keeps them categorically apart."[85] By impeding the absorption of vehicle into tenor it draws attention to the element of fiction and representation in literary language. Much of Coleridge's later work is, of course, simply bad poetry. But his use of a dissociative diction also says something about the limits of representation, as an attempt to materialize the absent in the space of the poem—something which is stated more explicitly through the thematic concern of the poems with solitude, sterility, and absence.

The central fact of poems such as "Love's Apparition and Evanishment," "The Pang More Sharp Than All," and "The Blossoming of the Solitary Date-Tree" is the absence of a sympathetic auditor, which confirms the separation of vision from allegory by exiling conversation into soliloquy. The late poems are obsessively concerned with their own status as pseudo-poems, with the falsity of a poetry that finds itself without the sustaining interchange between image and reality furnished by a world in which the text of hope can converse with actuality through the medium of an auditor. Often, as in "Duty Surviving Self-Love," the poem will be prefaced by an apology pointing to its ineffectuality. At other points, as in "The Blossoming of the Solitary Date-Tree," half of the poem will be in the form of prose. Through the use of prose Coleridge acknowledges a collapse of faith in the power of the poet as maker rather than analyzer. The embarrassment of a rhetoric that does not convince even itself, the constant need for apology and self-justification, reveal a poetry corroded by the illegitimacy of its own illusions. The critic who points out the sheer badness of much of Coleridge's later poetry must, however, recognize that this inferiority is at least partly the product of his honesty. Coleridge cannot share in Blake's grandiose claims for

[85]Earl Wasserman, "The English Romantics: The Grounds of Knowledge," *Studies in Romanticism*, 4 (1964), 20–21.

the reshaping power of human imagination. He sees through the naiveté of such claims, and makes them in a language that is aware of the gap between poetic intention and the real act. "The Pang More Sharp Than All" is explicitly concerned with the emptiness of poetic signification. The tone of the poem is almost impossible to sum up. It seems pathetic, an evasive and self-pitying attempt to falsify an unbearable emptiness by blaming someone else for the betrayal of hope (l. 50). It seems to use language to hide from itself. Yet one might almost say that the poem is ironically about the kind of emotional and linguistic counterfeiting in which it finds itself trapped. Unlike philanthropy, which pretends to an involvement with others, the internalization through self-pity of a communion known not to exist in the external world is under no illusions as to the narcissism of its attempts to falsify and relieve the bitterness of fact. Coleridge's insight is apparent in the recurrence of twins, simulacra, and magic balls in the poem: objects which reflect or repeat other objects and lay bare the element of duplicity in the twinning of image and reality or poet and auditor vital to the Romantic theory of poetry as a conversation with truth. What the poet experiences is never love, but an emotion which substitutes for the former in its absence (l. 58). What he envisions is never the magic child, but its illusory repetition in the mirror of his mind. The crystal ball of the magician, to which the imagination is here compared (ll. 39-41), deceives the eye by engendering a perception which has no object, or has only an unreal object. Through the crystal ball, Coleridge seems to thematize the dilemma of a language that must falsely create an object out of itself—a child or a figure of hope—in order to confer on itself a reality that is immediately put in question by the illusoriness of the object created.

Yet to see through the phantasms of hope is not necessarily to renounce them. The later Coleridge wants desperately to make the transition from youth to maturity, from Romantic idealism to religious orthodoxy, or from self-love to duty. A stylistic feature such as the envoy at the end of "Love's Apparition and Evanishment" is a stoic device, which tries to simulate through the structural detachment of the moral from the fable a separation of knowledge from desire that the poem belies. But as James Boulger notes, the universe of Coleridge's later years seems "theoretically determinate . . . but practically indeterminate."[86] De Man has commented on the uncomfortable tendency of language to relapse "into the figure it deconstructs" and thus to regenerate what it seems to undermine.[87] The very fact that Coleridge returns again and again to a medium in which he has so little personal faith builds up a theoretical faith in the structures of signification. The simulacrum which is poetry does not reduce to an empty sign. Or to put it differently, absolute negativity, the ironic self-rejection of discourse through the unending deconstruction of fictions, proves impossible to achieve. Similarly, the pseudochild in "The Pang More Sharp Than All," never actually perceived and existing only in the realm of reflection, nevertheless leads a phantom life in the mirror and seems to point toward a real child and a real poetry which it copies and betrays. The ambivalent mood of these poems is apparent if we consider that they are not simply allegories and soliloquies, which concede a distance between word and presence, but also poems written in a confessional style. Confession is the language of a sentimental despair, which vests the possibility of active faith elsewhere. It empties itself out partly in order to await passively the reversal of circumstances promised in the purgatorial hierarchy of its address to an auditor. It is renunciatory, but also eschatological.

The same ambivalence can be seen in Coleridge's allegories, which to some extent see through the self-mystification of language by throwing into relief a tendency to substitute words for things which is characteristic of all language, but which also recognize the sentimentality, the metonymic and therefore holistic impulse behind all substitution. "The Pang More Sharp Than All" and "Love's Apparition and Evanishment" deal with allegory on a thematic as well as a formal level. Their concern with feelings that take the place of other feelings, with kindness or hope counterfeiting love, reflects back on the very nature of allegory itself as a process of figural substitution and, by setting allegory in the context of love, recognizes that signification is inseparable from the desire to coincide. Although de Man sees allegory

[86] James Boulger, *Coleridge as Religious Thinker* (New Haven: Yale University Press, 1962), pp. 196, 199.
[87] De Man, "Political Allegory in Rousseau," p. 674.

as a form of language which has renounced the desire to coincide with plenitude, its problematical status among the modes of Romantic literary consciousness stems precisely from the fact that it does not result in a literature of deconstructed signs. The phantasms of "Love's Apparition and Evanishment" are both annunciatory and deceptive: the bridesmaid Hope heralds the coming of Love (ll. 17–19), but the love itself is unconsummated. Like the love that is the focus of the poem, allegorical language is a language which appears and vanishes, which promises and denies. Its essential characteristic is not to deny meaning, but to designate as available somewhere else a meaning that it cannot make immediately present. The sense that language is a pledge of significance, ultimately reconvertible into its effective content, never ceases to haunt a style of awareness which does not so much deconstruct as defer meaning. Thus the allegorical image materializes the husk of the ideal object, without ever delivering the inner core which the husk's presence seems to promise.

What is ignored in de Man's account of allegory is that the confessional use of allegory implies at least a latent eschatology: an irony, certainly, but one that is not disengaged from a certain utopianism.[88] The poems in question are perhaps not "generative" and "productive" texts in the sense envisaged by de Man in his discussion of texts that relapse into what they deconstruct; unlike poems such as *Epipsychidion* and *Alastor,* they do not hold up an ideal and argue for it in the face of its demonstrated impossibility. But they remain condemned to reproduce the shadows of illusions they see through. Although it is possible to envisage a

---

[88]It is apparent that even in the confessional use of allegory, Romantic literature is not wholly ironic. But it should further be noted that in choosing as his example of an allegorical text a passage from Rousseau that is associated with the assumptions of Augustinian confession, de Man prejudges the whole question of Romantic allegory ("The Rhetoric of Temporality," pp. 185–188). Had he chosen to note that Shelley's *Prometheus Unbound* also uses allegorical personifications such as Love and Hope, his conclusions might have been slightly different. It is clear that the allegory in the latter case admits a temporary separation of image from reality, but is also strongly eschatological. Thus we may conclude that allegory does not inevitably renounce all desire to fulfill its signs as truth. This is not to deny that allegorical language is also a discontinuous language through which the mind questions the fusion of sign and thing. But Romantic allegory, it seems, shares with other Romantic modes a tendency both to deconstruct and reconstruct the notion of a unity between desire and its object.

deconstructed poetry, it does not seem possible to write it. Irony can never purge itself of a certain sentimentality. By its very existence as an articulate rather than a mute structure, a poem resists the knowledge of its own impotence, and wakes "just enough of life in death / To make Hope die anew" ("Love's Apparition and Evanishment," ll. 27–28).

The indeterminacy of these poems as a group is further increased by the fact that there is another side to Coleridge's use of borrowed styles of awareness, already evident in the two conversation poems which reveal doubts about a naive poetry. "Reflections on Having Left a Place of Retirement" encapsulates and rejects the standard features of the conversation mode: the depiction of an idyllic scene, and the address to a person who incarnates this scene as human (and not simply natural) presence. But it does so in terms of an essentially Renaissance convention of the superiority of the active to the contemplative life. In "The Eolian Harp," through the image of the harps, the speaker envisions nature as an organic unity in which souls, though diversely framed, vibrate in sympathy. The original title of the poem, "Effusion xxxv," already acknowledges the tenuousness of this vision. It sets the poem's reverie within the epistemology of the eighteenth-century sentimental effusion, which recognizes something private in the affective projection of feeling onto the world of primary fact. But the failure of the desired communion between speaker and auditor openly challenges the vision of the harps, and makes explicit a dissociation of rhetoric from fact already implicit in the poem's self-consciously metaphorical language. Nevertheless, although the landscape of vision remains unconfirmed by the world, it is rejected in a vocabulary of religious orthodoxy (ll. 50–55) whose borrowed nature makes the demystification of vision as uncategorical as the vision itself is unconvinced. It is as though by attributing his own doubts to the reproving voice of a superego, Coleridge is spared the internalizing of doubt and is able to turn it into a ritual social gesture. We find a similar strategy in some of the later poems which are concerned with the renunciation of love, and by implication, with the rejection of a poetry that seeks to consummate its vision in the real world. "Reason for Love's Blindness" might almost be imitated from a Renaissance sonnet sequence, and two other poems ("Lady, to Death we're doomed . . . ," and "Farewell to Love") are in fact adapted from

Marini and Greville. Where Coleridge is not actually imitative, he is second-rate, given to transparently pathetic or melodramatic utterances. Yet another tactic is the prose disclaimer, where Coleridge undermines his own argument by pointing to the literary worthlessness of his own poem. By the use of such a device in "Duty Surviving Self-love," he is able to divide his allegiances, to stand within and outside the stoical position he seems to take up. The language of renunciation in the late poems, perhaps even more than that of romantic illusion, seems banal and inauthentic, without personal authority. Coleridge apparently chooses it because it allows him to see through his own illusions, but in a manner so stereotyped as to leave him the option of reconstructing, perhaps in another poem, a hope which is nevertheless unsanctioned by the discipline of reality.

It is not so much that Coleridge actually continues to hope, as that the borrowed or disclaimed nature of his renunciation reveals an uneasiness in his commitment to despair. The stylistic restlessness of his poetry, which seems half-heartedly to try out various positions,[89] stems from a sense of the inadequacy of univocal styles of awareness to express the contradiction of human creativity, which seems to feel both the nothingness and the reality of its visions. At the root of this dilemma is a division between head and heart which leads either to the repression of skepticism in the conversation poems or to the unconvinced attempt at self-criticism characteristic of the late poems. The need for a creative skepticism is the subject of one of Coleridge's finest poems, "Constancy to an Ideal Object."

> And art thou nothing? Such thou art, as when
> The woodman winding westward up the glen
> At wintry dawn, where o'er the sheep-track's maze
> The viewless snow-mist weaves a glist'ning haze,
> Sees full before him, gliding without tread,
> An image with a glory round its head;
> The enamoured rustic worships its fair hues,
> Nor knows he makes the shadow, he pursues!
>
> [25–32]

---

[89]Schulz's book, *The Poetic Voices of Coleridge* (Detroit: Wayne State University Press, 1963), deals with this tendency to experiment with several voices, but does not see it as a sign of emotional indeterminacy.

The Brocken-specter described here is the image seen by a man at sunrise when, in climbing a mountain, he comes upon a shadow projected onto a bank of mist, magnified and illuminated. As Coleridge says in *Aids to Reflection,* it is both specter and mental deity.[90] Like "The Pang More Sharp Than All," this poem contains within itself an illusory self-projection through which it explores the duplicity of its own mode of being. Unlike the former, it moves beyond the self-imposed sentimentality of personal complaint to recognize that the privacy and self-doubt, so often felt in the late poems to be betrayals of an ideal existing somewhere else, are intrinsic to the imagination. The poetic image is always a coronation of one's own desire, a self-projection which must remain ironically aware of the distance between beauty and truth. That knowledge does not consume innocence, that the imagination finds a way to be at once ironic and egotistically sublime, is perhaps the singular achievement of this poem.

Like other late poems, "Constancy to an Ideal Object" starts with the absence of conversation and community. The speaker finds himself in a foreign country, and addresses from a distance a being who does not reply, who can be made present only in the mind, and then too as a thought or a glory but never as an actual face. One of the curious facts about this poem is that the object of desire is never directly named within the text, and it is only obliquely that we become aware of someone who is absent even from the words of the poem. The sense of a public and communal poetry implicit in ode, hymn, and conversation seems to have given way to a sense of literature as unheard by its auditor, and as communicating only indirectly to its reader. The enforced solipsism of the text forces on it a sense of the idyllic scene it projects (ll. 16–18) as dream rather than poetry. At first the poet asks why he should not despair and become (in the words of Shelley's "Mont Blanc") "reconciled" to the wilderness where everything seems impermanent. Like other Romantic poems which ascend the mount of vision ("Mont Blanc," *The Fall of Hyperion, The Prelude*), this poem is concerned with the limits and extent of the mind's transcendence of mutability and death. The presence of ideals that have no basis in experience seems at first to complicate

---

[90]Coleridge, *Aids to Reflection,* p. 220. Cf. also *Notebooks,* 258, 430. In the second entry Coleridge quotes a German account of the phenomenon, in which the shadow is only a specter, without a glory round its head.

life. But gradually the poet comes to feel that the obstinate tendency of the mind to reconstruct illusions that it should see through is precisely what makes man superior to brute nature. The ideal object is epistemologically less real than nature, being mental rather than empirical. But it is also more real, being the only source of "constancy" and value in a world where all things "veer or vanish" (l. 2). The act of signification is not tautegorical, but neither is it self-emptying. Although Asra is never present in the glory which seems to represent her without in any way resembling her, the image enjoys a mysterious intimacy with its object: "She is not thou, and only thou art she," (l. 12).

In a way, the poem curbs the self-consuming doubt of the later poems by finding in the silence which despairs of conversation a compensating mythopoeic power. But Coleridge also seems to allude back to the radical idealism of his earlier poem on the Brocken mountains, "Lines Written in the Album at Elbingerode," which had claimed for the imagination the capacity to evaporate disagreeables and replace the real scene by a mental or "ideal" representation of home and England. The fact that the image with a glory is no more than an atmospheric illusion makes the ideal transparent to the very reality which it seeks to shut out. This reality, the "sepulchral form" of a foreign mountain ("Lines Written in the Album," l. 6), continues to provide the viewpoint from which the mind constructs the ideal, as a transcendence of the real which is all the more illusory because the medium in which it is accomplished is a bank of mist. The glory that suddenly lights up sterility and appears, delivered from the facticity of the mountain and suspended in pure air, could not appear if the poet did not continue to stand on the mountain where all things "veer or vanish." It is a fact of the poem's optics that if the self were to merge with its ideal, the ideal would disappear. It is the self, from within which the specter of desire is projected onto the world, which makes possible an act of creation that must therefore point back to the isolation and hopelessness in which it has its genesis. Moreover, as Prickett points out, the halo around the ideal object is visible only to the person who projects it.[91] Others see only the spectral shadow.

[91]Stephen Prickett, *Coleridge and Wordsworth: The Poetry of Growth* (Cambridge: Cambridge University Press, 1970), p. 26. Prickett's analysis of this poem is probably the most thorough and interesting one available. However, he tends to over-

The culminating image of Coleridge's poem, which seems to refer to Wordsworth through the figure of the rustic and to Shelley through the image of the rainbow, clearly intends some kind of revision of an image of art that perceives its self-projections as truth. Arising as it does from the gap between perception and imagination, the image knows within itself a certain futility: the purpose of the image, as Sartre notes, is "to make an object 'appear', [but that] object is not before us, and we know it is not."[92] Yet even a theorist like Sartre, who tends to polarize percept and image, concedes the existence of phenomena that mix presence and absence, being and pure, imaginary unreality. Faces seen in the fire "have for their material a pure appearance," but the absent object of a painting is "present by proxy" and the image therefore "knows a certain fullness together with a certain nothingness."[93] It is therefore significant that the aesthetic analogue envisioned in this poem, a Brocken-specter rather than a crystal ball, a natural phenomenon rather than a glass artifact, reproduces desire outside rather than inside the mind. As Keats points out, there are things real, things semi-real, and nothings. From an awareness of the divergence between imagination and perception arises a sense of the image as a nothing, given value only by an ardent and ultimately fanatical pursuit. This had been the conclusion of "The Pang More Sharp Than All." Like the Brocken-specter that seems to see through the Shelleyan epipsyche, the magic child in the magic glass had seemed ironically to deconstruct those many Romantic images of vision as a revelation, through hope, of a perfection that lies hidden within the mind: images such as Shelley's crystal sphere in which the Spirit of the Earth is laid asleep like a child, or his Chariot of the Hour which contains a winged infant and a landscape composed of "shapes in an enchanter's glass" (*Prometheus Unbound*, IV.266–268, 206–227).

---

emphasize the sudden transformation of illusion into reality, and to underplay the ironic element which continues to complicate the constitutive authority of imagination even at the end.

[92] Sartre, *The Psychology of Imagination*, p. 24.

[93] Ibid., pp. 48, 107. This "presence" in the painting arises only because paintings possess a certain rudimentary physical existence that distinguishes them from poetry and music, which are purely unreal. The painter's canvas is something we perceive as well as imagine. What Sartre says of painting, however, would seem to me to apply in some degree to literature as well.

But it seems that imaginative epiphany, as the Romantic mind rediscovers it beyond the crisis of demystification, is what Keats calls a semi-real thing. In this poem Coleridge finds that such epiphany neither creates an experience of plenitude nor betrays the mind into dryness and impoverishment. Paradoxically it recognizes both love's apparition and its evanishment, and achieves the difficult peace which eluded Coleridge in his poem of that name.

The increasingly frequent comments in Coleridge's notebooks on problems of absence and presence add up to no unambiguous position.[94] They recognize in practice that the imaginary is a loss of presence, and that it is an act of envisioning that to some extent transects and annuls its own nothingness: "Even as when travelling toward a Palace or Mountain, now 20 miles off & now but 3, even such is my feeling when absent & present/-."[95] But insofar as these comments have a direction, they show Coleridge aware of and wanting to get beyond what he will recognize in "Constancy to an Ideal Object" as the insubstantiality that troubles all fictions of presence. Thus, while he sometimes seeks to renounce illusion, at certain points he envisages a poetics of pure representation, freed from all need for presence, and argues that the mind can project its ideals without any need of a confirming response. In discussing the absence of a beloved object, he speaks first of how light is more than half projected, and then of "the *incorporeity* of true Love in absence—Love per se—a Potassium/—it can subsist by itself—." The secondary "reflected Light" of the moon that represents in its absence the presence of the sun, seems itself to acquire a kind of primacy in the realm of the unreal.[96] Similar in its tenor is the peculiarly idealistic skepticism characteristic of Shelley's theory of signs, which deliberately misreads eighteenth-century skepticism so as to retain its terms while reversing their meaning. Shelley dispenses with the Romantic notion of a parallelism between language and nature, but in order to disguise and not to expose the cleavage between perception and imagination recognized by the skeptics. That "language is arbitrarily produced by

[94]Coleridge, *Notebooks*, 1334, 1541, 3247, 3256, 3508, 3605, 4058.
[95]Ibid., 3512.
[96]Ibid., 4036 f34ᵛ. See also the poem "Duty Surviving Self-Love."

the imagination and has relation to thoughts alone,"[97] that it bypasses the mediation of the real in its journey toward the ideal, is a fact which is used to deny the limitation of the imaginary by the real, and not to deny the reality of the imaginary.

In "Lines Written in the Album at Elbingerode," Coleridge had seemed to make such a claim for the power of imagination to constitute its vision regardless of presence. In contrast to the conversation poems, and like the late poems, this poem envisages the goal of the imaginary act as lying outside the landscape of the perceived: in "recollection and hope" rather than "in the scene which is present," as A. W. Schlegel says in distinguishing Romanticism from classicism.[98] The foreign setting thematizes the dilemma of Romantic poems, which must create an experience of epiphany within an alien world, where the actual and the ideal have become discontinuous. Thus the imagination becomes something that seeks to negate the real scene, to create across distance and absence a vision of England that eludes physical visualization. From the belief that external reality is a world of "cyphers" given value only by the "Life within" (ll. 18–19), Coleridge argues for the power of imagination to project into the clouds the "sands and high white cliffs" of another, unreal country (l. 28). The actual German scene is conjured away "like a departing dream" (l. 32), and is replaced by an English scene that is quite literally not there at all. The capacity to imagine something that is absent becomes a sign of the mind's capacity to deny, and liberate itself from, the necessity of perceiving something that is present, and therefore of submitting to the actual.

The belief that absent or distant objects are more vivid than present ones,[99] and that ideals are truer than realities, arises in a world where the present is no longer the materialization of desire

---

[97]Shelley, "A Defence of Poetry," p. 279. Cf. also Shelley's statement that "All things exist as they are perceived . . . 'The mind is its own place, and in itself Can make a Heaven of Hell, a Hell of Heaven'" (p. 295). Here the connection between Shelley's skepticism and his idealism (in an epistemological sense) is apparent. The fact that the mind has no certain knowledge of the world outside itself leads not so much to radical uncertainty, as to a sense that the external world is reducible to mental certitudes.

[98]A. W. Schlegel, *Lectures on Dramatic Art and Literature*, p. 27.

[99]Coleridge, *Notebooks*, 308. This is not an uncommon view. Cf. also Campbell, *Pleasures of Hope*, 1.1–8.

and has become the scene of man's estrangement from the ideal. But such a claim is no more than the other side of a poetics of presence, a displacement of this poetics from the naturalist mode, in which the ideal is actually possessed, to the visionary mode, in which it is possessed in the mind. Thus it too fails to come to terms with the ambiguities inherent in aesthetic representation. Between a radically "subjective" Romantic poetics which claims the power to constitute the absent or unreal as real, and an "objective" classical poetics which does not have to use the detour of substituting imaginary signs for realities, there is only the distance that separates the sentimental from the naive. Classical literature, as envisaged by the Romantics, was a literature of natural signs. Romanticism accepts the arbitrariness of its own signs, yet constantly seeks ways to deny the traumatic implications of this recognition. No longer able to literalize the imaginary as in "classical" poetics, it seeks to accomplish the same end by denying the real as a place of realization, and thus making the unreal into the only reality.

But such an elision of actuality is impossible. In Romantic aesthetics from Hegel to Jean-Paul and Coleridge himself, there exists a significant oscillation between definitions of art as mediating between thought and thing, and as existing in the mode of the egotistical sublime: projecting its vision onto a world whose conformity to the imagination is either assumed or deemed unnecessary.[100] In the *Aesthetics*, Hegel celebrates poetry as the "art of the spirit which has become free in itself and which is not tied down for its realization to external sensuous material." But in *The*

[100]In his notes for his essay "On Poesy or Art" Coleridge first defines poetry (in contrast to painting) as "purely *human*—all its metaphors are *from* the mind, and all its products are *for* the mind." But he goes on, in the same passage, to describe it as a "middle nature between a Thought and a Thing," intermediate between mind and nature, the inwardness of music and the outwardness of painting (*Notebooks*, 4397 f48–49). Jean-Paul, who generally sees poetry as mediating between the objective and subjective, inconsistently defines it in idealist terms: "in sculpture reality creates the imagination, whereas in a poem the imagination creates reality" (*Horn of Oberon*, p. 297). Geoffrey Hartman has in effect traced this kind of oscillation in Wordsworth, between the mediatory mode of *akedah* and the sublime mode of *apocalypse* (*Wordsworth's Poetry, 1787–1814* [1964; rpt. New Haven: Yale University Press, 1971]). My own sense would be that the oscillation reveals not so much a repression of or anxiety about apocalypse, as a deep anxiety about whether the self can be absorbed into Being—whether this be the Being of nature (*akedah*) or Absolute Being (*apocalypse*).

Phenomenology of Mind he argues against the one-sided Romanticism of the beautiful soul and Rousseauist ethics, in which the self abstracts itself from the world.[101] Such oscillations betray, in their turn, the compensatory element in both alternatives. From the failure of mediation arises a declaration that the imagination is something transhistorical, that it can exist regardless of presence. Kant gave the name of sublimity to this capacity of the mind to separate itself from the world of facticity. But the vocabulary of mediation itself arises from a recognition that there is something one-sided, hence profoundly vulnerable, in an ideal that is guaranteed solely by the mind.

We have already noted that the conversation poems show a deep vacillation about the source, and therefore the authority, of poetic vision. At certain points in "This Lime-tree Bower," Coleridge seemed to argue for the autonomous power of imagination to deny physical limitations and restore landscapes that were not present, but seemed to make this renewal dependent on the presence of a real auditor. And conversely, he seemed to base the truth of the imagination on a real auditor whose presence could be represented only by a constitutive act of imagination. Both formulations circle round a lacuna in imaginative experience, preferring either pure reality or pure ideality to the complicated linkage between the real and the ideal that characterizes imagination. But the manner in which each formulation is constantly relapsing into the other reveals a deep anxiety about whether there is any vocabulary sufficient to guarantee a myth of total satisfaction. So also in "Lines Written in the Album," the claim made for imagination turns out to be complicated and contradictory. The inward orientation of reverie is uncertainly combined with the outward orientation of conversation. In the final lines Coleridge finds it necessary to confirm the autonomy of his vision by presenting it to an auditor who, as stranger rather than friend and countryman, only confirms that solipsistic estrangement of vision from actuality which the poem proclaims but does not really want.

One of the central ambiguities in "Dejection: An Ode" arises from an uncertainty about whether epiphany is created by a

---

[101]Hegel, *Aesthetics*, 1, 89; *The Phenomenology of Mind*, pp. 664–679.

cooperation between the light reflected and the light bestowed, or by a projection of light from within. The crisis of the poem arises precisely from a failure in mediation: the failure of the landscape, whose beauty is only the calm before the storm, to provide for the poet's feelings an outward language that is continuous rather than intermittent. What is apparent in the poem is that all seasons are not sweet, as Coleridge had once claimed. Thus the poet seeks to separate himself from nature, to take onto himself the blame for his dejection in order to reclaim the initiative of renewed vision. In the concluding celebration of Asra he claims for imagination the power to transcend distance and sterility, and to represent an ideal that is absent through an act of unmediated vision. Such vision is purely inward, liberated from the need for physical perception, and therefore from the reality which might confirm it but might also expose it.

It is often observed that the paradox of this poem lies in Coleridge's ability to create despite his professed inability to do so. But in fact almost the reverse is true. The dilemma of the poem is that there is no consolation in the power of imagination to constitute an ideal that is not fulfilled in the prose of the world. The poet is able to "give" life to Asra, but does not receive it back into the creating self, which remains estranged from the radical innocence that it projects. The existence of this dejected self constitutes a denial of the "life" given by it, and constantly exposes the ideal as illusory from the vantage point of the real. Precisely because he has liberated the imaginary from the real, the poet has made impossible the remarriage of vision and actuality demanded by the mediatory assumptions of the conversation mode, if not by poetry itself as a communicative mode. Or, to put it differently, such mediation is achievable only at the cost of reimplicating the desire for the imaginary in the knowledge of the real.

"Dejection" goes considerably further than other poems in recognizing the impotence of radical idealism: in recognizing, with Hegel, that the act of envisioning a nonexistent ideal is, in its very nature, "a dual state of mind" rather than a liberating act.[102] Other Romantics tacitly admit this linkage between desire and knowledge in imaging hope and despair as twins rather than anti-

---

[102]Hegel, *The Phenomenology of Mind*, p. 513.

theses, as shadow and substance or concave and convex. To imagine an ideal that existed in an autonomous realm of illusion would be to imagine that impossible phenomenon which Sartre calls a "shut imaginary consciousness." Such a consciousness is completely unconscious of anything outside itself, and is therefore without "being-in-the world." Because it exists in a purely imaginary world turned in on itself through dream, death, or fiction, without any conception of reality, it is closed to the insight that might perceive it as illusory.[103] But what is apparent in a poem such as "Dejection," and more explicitly in the late poems, is that there is no such state of consciousness. The imagination can construct an ideal that does not exist, but it must then deconstruct this ideal from the vantage point of existence. A poem either accepts this deconstructive potential within imagination or condemns itself to be a self-frustrated literary structure, which projects within itself aesthetic norms that are discontinuous with the experience it dramatizes.

Our analysis of Coleridge has taken us back to those problems in the psychology of Romantic idealism with which we began, and which reveal the latent affinity of Romanticism to existentialism. Although Romantic theory attempts to conceive of signs as either autonomous or natural entities, Romantic poetry reveals a constant sense of their intentionality. What is implied in the phenomenological insistence on the intentionality of signs is that while the imagination can "constitute regardless of presence" (as de Man says),[104] its ideals are not for this reason unbound to the real and able to subsist in their own fictive counterworld. Unlike the autonomous sign envisaged by Schiller and other idealists, the intentional sign is always oriented toward meaning, directed to the thing to which it refers and therefore linked to the actual world. Unlike the natural sign, it can never merge with this world. The notion of intentionality indicates that there is no such thing as the pure consciousness envisaged by essentialist philosophies. Consciousness is always conscious *of* something; the idealized image is always conscious of and turned back toward the real. To dream of a pure consciousness without the difficulties of existence, or of a world of things without the complications of con-

[103]Sartre, *The Psychology of Imagination*, pp. 214–215, 228–229.
[104]De Man, "The Intentional Structure of the Romantic Image," p. 69.

sciousness, is to ignore—in opposite but ultimately similar ways—
the ambiguous mediation that must always take place between the
two. Existentialism follows idealism in defining the sign as a mental
(or imaginary) rather than a natural structure. But the very fact
that the divergence of the imaginary from the real is described by
idealist aesthetics in terms of a transcendental vocabulary, and by
existentialist aesthetics in terms of the nothingness of the imaginary, is evidence that the latter sees the sign as submitting to the
judgment of the real world. In this regard, existentialism simply
discloses a view of imagination already latent in the aesthetics of
Romantic idealism. The distance between the two is, in fact, less
than might appear at first sight. In the aesthetic theories of Derrida and de Man, the designation of the sign as intentional results
in a radical deconstruction of signifying structures, which would
seem to limit the usefulness of such theories to the student of
Romanticism. At the same time, however, existentialist *metaphysics*
shares with idealist aesthetics a recognition which it fails to accommodate within its aesthetic theory: the recognition that the
imaginary, insofar as it is able to deny the real and imagine something not physically present, is an essential factor in human liberation. "If it were possible to conceive for a moment a consciousness
which does not imagine," Sartre comments, "it would have to be
conceived as completely engulfed in the existent. . . . crushed in
the world, run through by the real."[105]

The philosophical debate over whether imagination simply re-
combines impressions received from the senses (as Hobbes
thought),[106] or whether it is able to construct things "perhaps
more beautiful, than any, that exist in nature,"[107] raises an essentially similar question about the Apollonian capacity of the mind
to transcend the empirically given. So also does the frequent critical distinction between history and poetry.[108] Nineteenth-century

---

[105]Sartre, *The Psychology of Imagination*, p. 244.

[106]Hobbes defines imagination as *"decaying sense"* and notes that it is "only of
those things which have been formerly perceived by sense" (*Leviathan: Parts I and
II* [1651; rpt. Indianapolis: Bobbs-Merrill, 1958], p. 28).

[107]William Gilpin, *Observations on the River Wye* . . . (London, 1782), p. 45. Cf.
also Edward Young, *Conjectures on Original Composition*, p. 37; William Duff, *An
Essay on Original Genius*, pp. 7, 89.

[108]Distinctions by Aristotle, Sidney, and Bacon are too well known to need

definitions of Romanticism, in fact, identify the movement with a refusal to be limited to the present and with a longing for something nonexistent. It is the link between the imaginary and human freedom, explicitly made by Fichte in his distinction between imagination and cognition,[109] that represents the continued challenge of Romantic idealism to recent existentialist aesthetics, which might seem to limit man to a recognition of his own nakedness.[110] The basis for a response to this challenge exists in existentialist epistemology—something which should not surprise us in view of the fact that existentialism is a contemporary revision of Romantic idealism which retrospectively clarifies and tempers the latter. The aesthetic theory of Sartre, and of such post-existential writers as Derrida and de Man, fails to respond to the challenge.[111] However, it has been the purpose of this book to suggest that precisely such a response was constructed by Nietzsche, who is often (and inaccurately) hailed as the ancestor of deconstruction, but who combines an insight into the limits of an Apollonian Romantic idealism with a respect for the liberating power of aesthetic representation sanctioned by existentialism, though not by absurdism.

The dilemma of a Romanticism that attempts the subjective transformation of the objective world through feeling—the dilemma to which Nietzsche responds—is summed up by Schelling. In his work on a system of transcendental idealism he raises the question of how the mind can avoid necessitation and determine the real world "through a (freely projected) representation in us," and yet find its representations in conformity with objective fact.[112] This problem—the problem of how to create a world in which "the product of nature" and "the product of freedom" are

---

citing. More recent discussions of the problem include the one by Alexander Gerard, *An Essay on Taste (1759), Together with Observations on the Imitative Nature of Poetry* (1780; rpt. Gainesville: Scholar's Facsimiles and Reprints, 1963), pp. 282–284; and Shelley, "A Defence of Poetry," p. 281.

[109]J. G. Fichte, *Science of Knowledge* (1795), trans. Peter Heath and John Lachs (New York: Appleton Century Crofts, 1970), p. 6.

[110]Thus according to de Man imagination "does not result from the absence of something, but consists of the presence of a nothingness. Poetic language names this void with ever-renewed understanding" (*Blindness and Insight*, p. 19).

[111]See Appendix B for further discussion of Sartre's relation to Romantic aesthetics.

[112]Schelling, *System des transzendentalen Idealismus*, pp. 15–16. Translation mine.

seen to be the same[113]—has been a central preoccupation of both aesthetic and philosophic idealism, which seek to relate rather than segregate desire and existence. Yet as we have seen, poetic experience tends to refute Schelling's belief that in some miraculous way there exists "a *pre-established harmony*" between "the ideal and real worlds."[114] Dionysos and Apollo, the god of Experience and the god of Innocence, can never be identical.

Although the connection may seem fanciful, it is precisely the relationship between the Apollonian and the Dionysiac halves of the psyche, between transcendence and temporality, which is the subject of Coleridge's rather cryptic poem "Time Real and Imaginary":

> Their pinions, ostrich-like, for sails out-spread,
> Two lovely children run an endless race,
>   A sister and a brother!
>   This far outstripp'd the other;
> Yet ever runs she with reverted face,
> And looks and listens for the boy behind:
>   For he, alas! is blind!
>
> [3–9]

The blind boy, listless and silent, is wholly limited to the actual, while his sister, able to see and run far beyond him, represents the subjective power of the imaginary to deny the real and project itself into the future. In his notebook plan for the poem Coleridge had seemed to oppose the two states, and to see the imaginary as a shutting out of the real.[115] In the conversation poems, which also related a sentimental and real self to a naive figure, he had claimed the fusion of the two worlds. But the two children in this poem, though unable to overcome their duality, are indissolubly linked together—like other Romantic siblings such as Shelley's "twin babes" of life and death (*Epipsychidion*, l. 303) or the truth

---

[113]Ibid., p. 280.

[114]Ibid., p. 16.

[115]E. H. Coleridge cites a notebook entry of 1811: "How marked the contrast between troubled manhood and joyously-active youth in the sense of time! To the former, time like the sun in an empty sky is never seen to move. . . . To the latter it is as the full moon in a fine breezy October night, driving on amid clouds of all shapes and hues, and kindling shifting colours. . . . This I feel to be a just image of time real and time as felt, in two different states of being" (*Poetical Works*, I, 419–420).

and counterfeit of "The Pang More Sharp Than All." Thus the
liberation that the mind achieves through its capacity to imagine is
at best equivocal, because the imaginary remains conscious of the
real. The girl runs with reverted face and remains genetically
linked to the brother who is, in a sense, her own other half. Indeed, her ability to outstrip him and possess the future is constantly put into question by the peculiar backwards direction of
her gaze, through which she almost seems to share his blindness.

Nevertheless, the mood of this poem, in contrast to that of
poems such as "Limbo" or "Dejection," is strangely hopeful as well
as despairing. Unlike Asra, who exists completely outside the
world of the speaker, the sister in this poem guides her brother
and prevents him from being engulfed in the real. Through her
he too runs an endless, if illusory, race on the hill, instead of
remaining motionless and despondent as in the notebook entry. If
he is her other half through whom the epipsyche becomes exposed to the afflictions of the real world, then she too is his other
half: the sister and playmate through whom the speaker of "Frost
at Midnight" had hoped to know things denied to him in the real
world, and to feel the working of the potential within the actual.
The two children, in other words, emblematize the process of imagination as a flight from nothingness which circles back on itself.
Through its construction of an imaginary, childlike self, the mind
seems to escape itself, only to discover that the imaginary faces
back toward the real. This discovery, however, does not mark the
end of the race. Imagination is seen as both prospective and retrospective, visionary and limited.

The doubtful character of the unbinding that poetry claims
from the real world is evident in the odd comparison between the
children and ostriches (l. 3). Coleridge had once used a similar
image to distinguish his own poetry from the poetry of genius:
"Like the ostrich, I cannot fly, yet have I wings that give me the
feeling of flight." There is in "Time Real and Imaginary" a certain
self-deprecation, but also a certain irony toward the naiveté that
identifies the flights of imagination with those of eagles or
skylarks, not recognizing that poetry is a "bird of the earth."[116]

---

[116]Marginalia in Heinrich's *Commentary on the Apocalypse*, quoted in Bate, *Coleridge*, p. 41.

But it is a bird of the earth, and not a reptile. The equivocal victory won by this poem is apparent if we compare it with "Psyche," which also reflects on the duality of the human spirit, as butterfly and caterpillar, potentially free yet actually imprisoned. In "Psyche," hope exists in a transcendent and therefore unreal realm. Though the poem, by using an image of biological evolution, seems to guarantee the unity of the real and the ideal, the emphasis is rather on the impossibility of resacralizing a present emptied of value. Because the claims made for imagination in poems such as "Time Real and Imaginary" and "Constancy to an Ideal Object" are so tempered, the possibility of a mediation between the two orders is more real. The ostrich, as a bird which cannot fly, embodies the paradoxical creativity that is born only when "Hope and Despair meet in the porch of Death!" ("Constancy to an Ideal Object," l. 10). Like Wordsworth, in his encounters with mute and solitary figures, the imagining self in Coleridge's poem sees through its own illusions to the blindness at the heart of vision, yet does not renounce a certain power of vision that remains within the dreariness of life.

Shelley, in his exploration of the subterranean links between the two Shapes in *The Triumph of Life,* and Keats, in his reenactment of the Greek theogony, both discover the impossibility of decoupling Apollonian desire and the knowledge of life. Both acknowledge this difficulty in entrusting their poems to crippled, or somehow flawed, guides. It is tempting to see in the brother and sister of Coleridge's poem a similar emblem of the paradox against which Romantic poetry comes up in its attempt to transform existence through the guidance of the imaginary. Because the unreal, in Sartre's words, "is produced outside of the world by a consciousness which stays in the world,"[117] the work of art must be a product of the mutual heteronomy of nature and freedom. The blind boy in Coleridge's poem can imagine, regardless of presence, a world in which he runs an endless race on a fairy hill. But because he is blind, he is always compelled to envisage this counterworld as absent and incapable of vicariously delivering him from what he is. In a way, the poem is a deconstructive one, which goes behind the innocent picture of two children racing on

[117]Sartre, *The Psychology of Imagination,* p. 243.

a hill, to reveal how the imaginary self is only the mask worn by the real self. But in another way, the significance of the poem lies in the fact that the real self, like Camus' Sisyphus, is able to wear the mask of Apollo. Perhaps Coleridge's poem can provide us with our final instance of the treaty that the Romantic mind forges between desire and existence. The mind is never wholly blinded by reality, because it can imagine and thus become more than itself. But in the dialogue between experience and innocence envisaged by Schelling, it discovers depths and ambiguities that reveal as impossible the miracle of a silent dialogue: a dialogue without doubt, which makes the ideal present in the real world while closing out reality.

At the end of this long chapter, a postscript is perhaps in order. In discussing Coleridge we have been looking at a poet whose literary oeuvre makes a statement considerably less complete than those of Shelley and Keats. The resolution reached in "Mont Blanc" is first sketched in a moment of lyrical abstraction, but is also sustained in Shelley's final poem, a poem which is reflectively withdrawn from life through its dream mode, but also narratively engaged in the world outside the self. Keats's odes rehearse in miniature the modes of awareness present in his poetry as a whole. But the lyric, like the letter, is private, occasional, and essayistic; and the tragic aesthetics tentatively drafted in "Ode on a Grecian Urn" and "Ode to Melancholy" lacks authority until tested and consolidated in Keats's narrative poetry. Coleridge, however, is a different case. Although the dialectical development present in the other two poets also occurs in his work, it does so only in the mode of lyric, which is partly why this chapter on one of the major Romantic poets is so restricted in its focus. He abandons the narrative mode early in his career, and the major narrative poems therefore remain sentimental works which stand only on the threshold of a new awareness.

Christabel is considerably less ironic than *Isabella,* and even late in his life Coleridge continued to imagine for it the happy ending which he himself saw through when he abandoned the poem at its nadir with the rejection of Bard Bracy. The Baron's refusal to accept the Bard's interpretation of his dream functions as an intratextual allegory of the defeat of Coleridge himself, in his attempt to impose a redemptive poetics on the nightmare of his poem. But Coleridge sidesteps the radical implications of this crisis, by construing it as misunderstanding rather than defeat. *The Rime of the Ancient Mariner* resembles *The Triumph of Life* in its dreamlike rendition of events. It also foreshadows the later poem in its use of a journeying protagonist who narrates in retrospect the destruction of his illusions, and in its use of a *spectator ab extra* who is inoculated with the knowledge of life and whose presence in the poem enables the text to reflect on the effect of its own transmission. But the addition of the gloss establishes a repressive relationship between text and supertext, and substitutes the transcendental immunity of omniscient commentary for the discourse of dream-vision, in which the creative voice stands apart from experience but not above it. It is not until later in his career that an increasing self-consciousness forces Coleridge to experiment with irony, and it is only in two late lyrics that he cuts through a continuing vacillation between sentimentality and irony. These lyrics, moreover, are occasional poems and lack the climactic authority that they would have if they were the culmination of a sequence or a planned collection. The resolution reached by Coleridge assumes added importance because he is the only practicing poet who studied and contributed to the theory of Romanticism. Yet it remains a resolution rehearsed rather than performed, one that Coleridge reflects on in the privacy of lyric but never acts out in the more public mode of narrative or drama.

Conclusion

Romanticism, in the words of Arnold Hauser, "represented one of the most decisive turning-points in the history of the European mind," and was also "perfectly conscious of its historical role."[1] It was because of this epochal awareness that the period not only produced so many texts concerned with their own status but also, to a large extent, supplied the theoretical vocabulary for its own analysis. The purpose of this book has been to trace, through the poetry which lays the experiential groundwork for more explicit philosophical reformulations, the tension in Romanticism between a conventional vocabulary and an emergent self-understanding. Although Romantic philosophy tries, as Abrams argues, to construct a metaphysics of integration, it also anticipates the recognitions of existentialism and of a radical modernism.[2] The resulting shift in the mind's sense of its relation to external reality and to itself makes inevitable the change in the Romantic sense of the function of aesthetic structures which eventually occurs.

It is not simply the tension in Romantic *poetry* which declares the need for such a change. In a transitional work such as Mrs. Radcliffe's *Mysteries of Udolpho,* which begins and ends as a novel

[1] Arnold Hauser, *The Social History of Art,* III, 165.
[2] The continuity between the Romantics and the Moderns has often been recognized by critics such as Bloom and Frye, who have compared twentieth-century poets like Yeats and Stevens with the major Romantics, and by Robert Langbaum in *The Poetry of Experience.* My emphasis, however, is not on Modernism as a more ambivalent continuation of the Romantic quest for traditional sanctity and loveliness, or of the Romantic celebration of the constructive power of imagination. It is rather on Romanticism as an anticipation of the ambivalences of Modernism.

of sentiment but is not quite able to account for the core of Gothic and Freudian horror in its middle sections, we find the same problematical duality of surface and depth characteristic of much Romantic poetry. The rise of the Gothic novel and the increasing awareness of the irrational testify to a growing awareness that a rationalized and innocent language cannot signify the full truth of things.[3] The figure of the double, already implicit in Shelley's two Shapes and of increasing importance in the nineteenth century, acknowledges a gap between the conscious representation of the self and its unconscious identity. Also of interest is the presence of works like Coleridge's *Christabel,* which seem to invite a psychoanalytic interpretation and thus to make evident a tension between a conscious reading of the self and a subconscious knowledge that reflects on works of art which incorporate a tension between surface and depth. Romantic poetry does not end by embracing the nihilistic aesthetics of disclosure and depth favored by writers like Poe and Hogg. But its awareness of the discontinuity between aesthetic surfaces and the trauma of existence is both radical and irreversible.

Where previous periods saw literature as not permanently subject to temporality, as the unmediated or (in the case of Milton) mediated expression of a transcendent language, the Romantic period recognizes that the discourse of innocence is spoken from within experience. The simultaneously liberating and mimetic nature of art, arising from the fact that the unreal is created to free us from the world by a consciousness which stays in the world, makes of art a dialogue between illusion and its deconstruction. The Romantic poets, in certain moments, realize this fact and move beyond literary structures that prove self-frustrating in their desire either to surrender to illusion or to be rid of its burden. The organization of this book, in terms of an evolution from models of discourse that are more or less self-contradictory to ones that are less so, may seem to confer a certain teleological priority on the view of discourse that emerges from the "culminating" Romantic texts. This priority, however, exists only within the

---

[3]On the significance of the Gothic and the melodramatic to the theory of the literary sign, see Peter Brooks, *The Melodramatic Imagination: Balzac, Henry James, Melodrama, and the Mode of Excess* (New Haven: Yale University Press, 1976).

specific dynamics of the Romantic period. Although it is *possible* to extract from the biography of the Romantic imagination traced here a theory of imagination in general, the resulting model of discourse does not describe every literary text. The individual terms of a dialogue between illusion and its deconstruction exist in all works that are reflexively concerned with their own nature as signifying structures. Such works include those that draw attention to the problem of aesthetic representation by using "ecphrastic" images (which refer to the sister arts), texts within texts, or narrators, as well as those that thematize the problem of reading a text through the inclusion of prefaces, proems, "Arguments," or didactic and allegorical commentaries. But the manner in which the terms of the dialogue are related will differ from text to text, and the kind of relationship regarded as most satisfying will vary from period to period. In the larger context of literary theory it is possible only to speak of positions on the function of imagination, which the work may assume consciously or unconsciously, and of which the one taken by Nietzsche is one possibility.

The theory of literary discourse elaborated here is, therefore, offered only as one which resolves the tensions peculiar to the Romantic period. Moreover, the movement through sentimental and ironic to tragic or lyrical models of discourse provides a psychological sequence in which it is helpful to view Romantic poetry as a whole, and not necessarily a chronological sequence found in its entirety in the work of every Romantic poet. If the careers of both Keats and Shelley provide examples of a definitive movement toward a revised view of the power of art, it is only Keats whose work includes instances of the evasively and defiantly sentimental poem, as well as the ironic and tragic work. Irony is not a mode which seems to have held much attraction for Shelley. In works such as *The Cenci* and the Gothic romances he deals with narratives that are grotesque in subject matter, but (unlike a writer such as Hoffmann) he does so in a manner that is not ironic so much as melodramatic, and therefore sentimental.[4] Coleridge

---

[4]Northrop Frye speaks of the "polarised characterisation of romance, its tendency to split into heroes and villains. Romance avoids the ambiguities of ordinary life, where everything is a mixture of good and bad" (*The Secular Scripture*, p. 50). Insofar as melodrama shares this polarized characterization, it can be seen as an inverted form of romance: it adheres to the sentimental and escapist morality of

is sentimental in his early lyric poetry, and tries to be ironic in his later poems. But it must be said that his resolution of the tension thus established is intermittent and lacks the climactic authority that similar resolutions possess in the work of Keats and Shelley. A more problematical case is Wordsworth, the subject of much recent critical scrutiny. The two mountain-top ascents are attempts to affirm the transcendental and prophetic status of a vision of the continuity between the mind's representations and the external world celebrated throughout *The Prelude*. The Dionysiac imagery of abyss and ocean used in the Snowdon passage, however, exposes an element of sublimation in the Wordsworthian sublime that the poetry, at this point, seems to resist. This repression of tragedy in favor of apocalypse has been analyzed by David Ferry who, in effect, deconstructs Wordsworth's claim to have ascended to a summit of vision beyond doubt,[5] and to have attained the kind of complex naiveté assumed by Abrams. *The Prelude* becomes, in this reading, a self-frustrating work. Yet, as we have seen, Wordsworth at other points grows aware of the possible intentionality of his words, as he communicates them to ruined figures who disclose to him the potential death of his own vision. The implications of these moments in which the poem confronts its own subtext are sometimes repressed and sometimes openly faced, with the result that *The Prelude* is a work which at times is sentimentally optimistic, and at other times is dialogical in the manner suggested by Nietzsche in his analysis of lyric. Unlike Keats and Shelley, Wordsworth does not move firmly toward a revised sense of the status of his own vision. Yet these momentary insights which make his work something more than a poetry of sublimation are too frequent to be considered accidental, and suggest the centrality of an ambivalent view of the imagination to Romantic poetics.

The examples of Coleridge and Wordsworth suggest that the early Romantics were perhaps too committed to the legacy of a transcendental poetics to complete the process of self-revision which they begin. The career of Blake, the earliest of them, re-

---

romance, though it shows this morality submitting to defeat at the hands of the real world, where villains unjustly triumph over the innocent.

[5] David Ferry, *The Limits of Mortality* (Middletown, Conn.: Wesleyan University Press, 1959), pp. 169–171.

veals an increasing defiance of his own initial insights, brought about largely by his vatic conception of the function of the poet. In *Songs of Innocence and Experience* sentimental and ironic poems are placed in dialogue with each other, within a structure which allows a plurality of significations to be unendingly opposed to one another. The poems of Experience function ironically to alert the reader to "gaps" in the poems of Innocence that call into question the sentimental fiction of a transcendental or original innocence, which the Piper sees it as his function to re-present through poetry. But the poems of Innocence function in similar fashion with reference to the poems of Experience, to reveal that irony itself may be fiction of disillusion. Implicit in this juxtaposition of text and countertext is a view of imagination as an entry into ambivalence and dialogue. Though the Bard tries to resolve the debate in favor of a revolutionary sentimentalism of the imagination, he is himself implicated in the ambivalence he denies, because his invocation is part of a dialogue with Earth that puts his authority in doubt. Yet the later Blake, who abandons dialogue in favor of vatic monologue, increasingly reifies the logocentrism of the Bard. He uses the futuristic and therefore intentional language of prophecy. But he puts this language forward as myth and not as fiction, as transcendent and not as human discourse.

Wordsworth may seem more equivocal. It is not simply that in *The Prelude* he submits epic pretensions to the humility of conversation. His language tends to be epistemological rather than mythic, and therefore invites doubt and permits scrutiny. He is, in fact, the Romantic poet most frequently discussed by critics who question the assumptions of the organicist school.[6] And it is significant that throughout *The Prelude* prophetic epic, the expression of a transcendental poetics, alternates with meditative lyric, the product of an aesthetics of dialogue and doubt. Yet the logocentric legacy of a post-Miltonic poetry is once again evident in the fact that Wordsworth, when he speaks in a public voice, feels compelled to put his poem forward as a kind of secular scripture.

[6]See in particular de Man, "The Intentional Structure of the Romantic Image"; Helen Regueiro, *The Limits of Imagination: Wordsworth, Yeats, and Stevens* (Ithaca: Cornell University Press, 1976); Frances Ferguson, *Wordsworth: Language as Counter-Spirit* (New Haven: Yale University Press, 1977).

The moments of skepticism are never structurally climactic; they are always interludes, which therefore produce little revision in Wordsworth's idealism. They occur, moreover, in solitary encounters, when there is no one to overhear.

Although a historical discussion of the evolution of Romanticism has not been one of my purposes, it seems appropriate to conclude by suggesting that such an evolution did occur. The early Romantics are characterized by a more unbending commitment to a transcendental poetics, by a reluctance to follow through on their own insights, and most significantly, by the absence of that radical irony which makes it impossible to turn back to illusion. But more important than these differences is the essential continuity of concern between early and late Romanticism. The career of Byron, the Romantic poet who comes closest to a radical modernism, confirms the extent to which the later Romantics have moved beyond their predecessors, but also brings out the reasons why the break is not total. There are few subtexts in Byron's work. At first sight it seems that where Wordsworth and Blake are sentimental, he is almost continuously ironic. Indeed Camus has described Don Juan as the first existentialist, because he submits to the randomness of existence without craving the illusion of a transcendental truth.[7] But the point about Byron is that he too cannot be satisfied with irony, and approaches Juan through the eyes of a narrator whose occasional lapses into sentimentality keep unsettling the poem's commitment to realism. Implicit in Byron's abandonment of visionary narrative (the preferred mode of the Romantic long poem) for the narrative realism of *Don Juan* is a deconstruction of the logocentric assumptions of his predecessors. The same irony is apparent in his use of the middle rather than the high style of discourse, and in his reduction of the narrator from the status of author and prophet to one who merely interrupts and digresses. But it is significant that Byron's last poem, *The Island*, is a romance: a form through which he declares (though with embarrassment) his unwillingness to give up the notion of the poet as mythmaker.

This paradox should give us pause as we contemplate the ap-

---

[7]Albert Camus, *The Myth of Sisyphus* (1942), trans. Justin O'Brien (London: Hamish Hamilton, 1955), pp. 59–61.

parently anti-Romantic direction of Byron's career, from *Childe
Harold's Pilgrimage,* which renounces the sentimental illusions of
quest-romance and realizes the nothingness of human endeavors
before the power of the ocean, to *Don Juan,* which tries to subsume the nihilism of *Childe Harold* by replacing Romantic irony
with pragmatic irony.[8] One suspects that Byron's crucial work is
not *Don Juan* but *Cain,* a play in which he experiments with a
tragic model that he cannot quite work out, but which might have
offered him something between the ruthless exposure of Cain's
Promethean illusions in Act III and the sentimental vindication of
Cain's descendants in *Heaven and Earth.* The failure of Cain to
become a tragic rather than an ironic hero precipitates Byron
toward a repressive abandonment of Romantic humanism. In
Don Juan he tries to become a modern poet and to make irony into
a *modus vivendi.* But he succeeds only in raising to a self-conscious
level the cyclical oscillation between the ironic and the sentimental
pervasive in his work. Through the changing attitude of the narrator toward his fiction of a character completely committed to
the standpoint of irony, Byron dramatizes his own inability to
resolve a dialectic which forces him to continue his poem endlessly
and to no purpose. In that very process he declares the need for
the resolution forged by Keats and Shelley, whose final poems
reach beyond Byron's precisely because they do not reach as far,
and allow the poet to remain the maker of his own unmaking.

---

[8]Kierkegaard discusses this form of irony, in which the angst-producing inability to find a final truth becomes the freedom to live without the burden of
truth: to live purely in the present moment without the responsibility of the past or
the fear of the future (*The Concept of Irony,* pp. 296ff.).

Deconstructive Theory in Relation to Existential Phenomenology

Although Derrida is often seen as a structuralist in terms of his method, he has also been linked in terms of his metaphysics to existential phenomenology.[1] The connection between Heidegger and Derrida is well known, and is most evident in the latter's use of the term *différance*,[2] which derives from Heidegger's similar concept in the essay "Language."[3] Equally obvious is their common derivation from Nietzsche (noted by Derrida himself[4]), who anticipates the notion of a text as something which "differs" from itself and which, in its inability to become self-identical, denies the claim of literature to be a locus of meaning. In all three cases, a semiotics of "differance" and temporality follows logically from a larger analysis of man, the producer of signs, in existential rather than essentialist terms.

More unorthodox is my inclusion of Sartre as one of the philosophical predecessors of deconstruction. Sartre is significantly different from Heidegger, and lacks what Derrida calls "Heideggerian *hope*."[5] Without wishing to minimize the influence of Heidegger, I would argue that the emotional coloration of Derrida's language and his use of a hermeneutics of suspicion

---

[1] Robert Scholes, *Structuralism in Literature* (New Haven: Yale University Press, 1974), pp. 211–212; Robert Detweiler, *Story, Sign, and Self: Phenomenology and Structuralism as Literary Critical Methods* (Missoula: Scholars Press, 1978), pp. 187–191.

[2] Derrida, "Differance," *Speech and Phenomena*, pp. 129–160.

[3] Martin Heidegger, "Language," *Poetry, Language, Thought*, trans. Albert Hofstadter (New York: Harper & Row, 1975), pp. 189–210.

[4] Derrida, "Differance," p. 159.

[5] Ibid.

make it useful to consider him within the French as well as the German existential tradition. An intense sense of angst, alienation, and nothingness is characteristic of Sartre, in a way that it is not of Heidegger, for whom the denial of a "transcendental signified" allows man to express the courage to be. Also, a sense of the text as unreliable and of language as deception and void seem logical extrapolations from the aesthetics of Sartre and a postwar French literature which is much in his debt. Sartre, unlike Husserl and Heidegger, does not focus upon problems in semiotics. But it is possible to draw a useful contrast between assumptions about the status of imaginative discourse implicit in his discussion of the nature of *imagination* on the one hand, and in Heidegger's discussion of the nature of the *sign* on the other hand. While Heidegger does not take a logocentric view of language, he looks on it constructively as a "rending that divides and gathers . . . [and] joins the rift of the difference."[6] Intellectually Heidegger is deconstructive, but emotionally he is humanistic, and emphasizes the extent to which language, though caught in the paradox of *différance,* is still a naming of Being. Sartre's emphasis is almost the reverse. For him, language is a projection of nothingness, an attempt at being which knows itself principally as an unsuccessful flight from nothingness. Derrida is, of course, interested in semiotics, whereas Sartre is interested in aesthetics. But my feeling is that the Derridean concept of language, as something which deconstructs itself because it makes us conscious of the absence of an object that would not have to be re-presented if it were present, is similar to the Sartrean concept of imagination as a projection of nothingness.

The link between Sartre and de Man is, if anything, stronger. Because of Derrida's influence on him, de Man has been thought to derive from Heidegger. His interest in the semiotics of literary modes, moreover, is not characteristically Sartrean. His vocabulary, nevertheless, reflects the emphasis on nothingness characteristic of Sartre. We are told, for example, that "poetic language names the void," and that imagination "asserts itself as pure nothingness . . . stated and restated by a subject that is the agent of its own instability."[7]

[6]Heidegger, "Language," p. 204.
[7]De Man, *Blindness and Insight,* pp. 18–19.

Sartre's Theory of Imagination in Relation to the Romantic Tradition

One of the assumptions of this book is that modern philosophical movements such as existentialism are often useful in illuminating nineteenth-century philosophy, because they bring to the surface certain insights which are only latent in the latter. Since this general principle does not seem to hold true for the recent aesthetic theorists mentioned in this book, some discussion of their relationship to the Romantic aesthetic tradition is in order. That the anti-logocentric view of language urged by Derrida is too limited for a movement that remains humanistic even on the threshold of the Absurd has already been suggested. Derrida is ruthlessly modern, a theorist for the generation of Robbe-Grillet and Beckett. The case of Sartre is very different, and can be summed up by saying that his aesthetic theory is *too* logocentric for his epistemology, with the result that he has to make of art a special case which he regards with some dubiousness. The paradox is that Sartre's characterization of art is more complex than he realizes, and does allow the imagination to survive in the modern world without being the euphemism for escape that he takes it to be. In defining art in a manner that is regressive in relation to his own epistemology, and in then expressing doubts about such an art, Sartre mirrors rather than goes beyond the confusion of the Romantics before Nietzsche.

It seems clear, both in *Being and Nothingness* and in *The Psychology of Imagination,* that Sartre sees consciousness itself as always *positioned* in the real world. The idea of a consciousness existing permanently in an imaginary world is self-contradictory. Thus it must be in the nature of consciousness to be dual: to imagine (i.e., to see the unreal) and also to perceive (i.e., to see the real). Sartre's statements on the imaginative act suggest that it shares in the dual nature of consciousness: the unreal, for instance, "is produced outside of the world by a consciousness which stays in the world."[1] The imagining consciousness, in other words, simultaneously transcends itself toward the unreal and stays within itself: in denying reality it constitutes itself according to the criteria of what Sartre calls "imagination," but in seeing through this denial it also constitutes itself according to the realistic criteria of "perception." Nevertheless, because he cannot conceive of imagination and perception as simultaneous, but only as successive and mutually exclusive activities, Sartre himself polarizes the imaginary and the real, and identifies the work of art wholly with the former. What he says, in effect, is that even though consciousness cannot *become* a shut imaginary structure, it can *produce* a shut imaginary structure (the work of art). This structure will not in itself contain any consciousness of the real world, but the consciousness which produces it will then have to deconstruct it from the vantage point of the real world, because it is precisely in the nature of consciousness that it cannot escape from the real world.

It seems logical that if human consciousness itself cannot close out the real world, then it also cannot produce an aesthetic structure which does so. There is no such thing as pure imagination, whether we define it as pure being (in line with Romantic idealism) or as pure nothingness (in line with Sartre, and the earlier figures such as Novalis and the Decadent poets who have influenced his aesthetic theory). The consequence of the Sartrean polarization of Beauty (or Value) and Reality is a familiar one in terms of nineteenth-century literature. In *What is Literature?* Sartre is forced to introduce a deep cleavage between poetry (which is purely imaginary) and prose (which accepts a realistic perspective), and thus ambiguously to devalue poetry from the perspective of the real, from which it appears as both an *Adonais*-like martyrdom and a socially irresponsible act. Sartre differs from the Decadent poets in seeing the yielding of construction to deconstruction as a desirable and necessary thing, but he also perpetuates their tendency to exile poetry from the mainstream of the world.

[1] Sartre, *The Psychology of Imagination*, p. 243.

Sartre, it seems clear, is not really able to get beyond the problem that faced the Romantics themselves: the problem of how to account for the fact that consciousness is "positioned in the world" and yet is free. By identifying art with the imaginary he emasculates it, differing from the early Romantics only in that he identifies it with an angel of death rather than a beautiful soul. Yet, plainly, Sartre's philosophy provides, on a systematic epistemological level, a basis for the kind of resolution of the Romantic dilemma achieved by Nietzsche on a mythographic level. It is also apparent that Sartre is extremely useful for a study of Romanticism, indirectly because of his influence on critics such as de Man, but more centrally because Sartrean existentialism as a philosophy of consciousness is a direct development of Romantic idealism by way of Hegel and Nietzsche: it recognizes that man is a creature who both exists and dreams, and it tries to respond (though from a more overtly pessimistic perspective) to the Romantic sense that the imagination is the locus of man's transcendental freedom.

The solution lies perhaps in not equating the *imaginary* with the more complex phenomenon of *imagination*. The fact that Sartre must define the imaginary in terms of nothingness indicates that he cannot disengage his definition of it from the criteria of reality. But even if there were a purely imaginary state, completely removed from reality, the temporal and noninstantaneous character of literature would prevent the latter from coinciding with it. In other words the imagination must embrace both the imaginary transcendence of the world, and the necessity to relate fiction back to reality, which arises from man's existence in a perceptual (i.e., real) world. The creative act is a complex, double act, in which the imaginary and the perceived are simultaneously present and transparent to each other, rather than successively present as ecstasy and disillusion. In using various polar terms (transcendence/immersion, surface/depth, idealization/deconstruction, fiction/mimesis, presence/absence, Apollo/Dionysos) I have tried to suggest the kinds of accommodations that Romanticism develops between the freedom and the limitation of aesthetic signs. Sartre's aesthetic theory, animated by a recognition that art is something more than a structure of the real world, fails to develop such an accommodation and thus ends by making it less than the structures of the real world.

Selected List
of Works Cited

Pre-Romantic and Romantic Sources (English)

Addison, Joseph. *The Spectator* (1753). Ed. Donald F. Bond. 5 vols. Oxford: Clarendon, 1965.

Blake, William. *The Complete Writings of William Blake.* Ed. Geoffrey Keynes. Oxford: Clarendon, 1966.

Coleridge, Samuel Taylor. *Aids to Reflection* (1825). Ed. Thomas Fenby. Edinburgh: John Grant, 1905.

———. *Biographia Literaria, with his Aesthetical Essays.* Ed. John Shawcross. 2 vols. Oxford: Clarendon, 1907.

———. *Collected Letters of Samuel Taylor Coleridge.* Ed. E. L. Griggs. 6 vols. Oxford: Clarendon, 1956–1971.

———. *The Complete Poetical Works of Samuel Taylor Coleridge.* Ed. E. H. Coleridge. 2 vols. 1912; rpt. Oxford: Clarendon, 1966.

———. *The Notebooks of Samuel Taylor Coleridge.* Ed. Kathleen Coburn. 3 vols. London: Routledge & Kegan Paul, 1957–1973.

De Quincey, Thomas. *The Collected Writings of Thomas De Quincey.* Ed. David Masson. 14 vols. London: A. and C. Black, 1897.

———. *The Posthumous Works of Thomas De Quincey.* Ed. A. H. Japp. 2 vols. London: Heinemann, 1891.

Duff, William. *An Essay on Original Genius* (1767). Gainesville: Scholars' Facsimiles and Reprints, 1964.

Hazlitt, William. *Complete Works of William Hazlitt.* Ed. P. P. Howe. 21 vols. London: J. M. Dent, 1930–1934.

Keats, John. *The Letters of John Keats 1814–1821.* Ed. Hyder E. Rollins. 2 vols. Cambridge: Harvard University Press, 1958.

———. *The Poems of John Keats.* Ed. Miriam Allott. London: Longmans, 1970.

Shelley, Percy Bysshe. *Poetical Works.* Ed. Thomas Hutchinson. 1905; rpt. Oxford: Clarendon, 1967.

———. *Shelley's Prose or The Trumpet of a Prophecy.* Ed. David Lee Clark. 1954; corrected ed. Albuquerque: University of New Mexico Press, 1966.

_____. Shelley's "Triumph of Life": A Critical Study. Ed. with introduction and
commentary by Donald Reiman. Urbana: University of Illinois Press,
1965.

Wordsworth, William. The Poetical Works of William Wordsworth. Ed. Ernest de Selincourt and Helen Darbishire. 5 vols. 1949; rpt. Oxford:
Clarendon, 1966.

_____. The Prelude (1850 version). Ed. Ernest de Selincourt and Helen
Darbishire. 2nd ed., Oxford: Clarendon, 1959.

Young, Edward. Conjectures on Original Composition (1759). Leeds: Scolar
Press, 1966.

Pre-Romantic and Romantic Sources (German)

Eckermann, J. P. Conversations with Goethe (1836–1848). Trans. Gisela C.
O'Brien. New York: Frederick Ungar, 1964.

Hegel. G. W. F. Aesthetics: Lectures on Fine Art (1835). Trans. T. M. Knox.
2 vols. Oxford: Clarendon, 1975.

_____. The Phenomenology of Mind (1807). Trans. J. B. Baillie. Revised ed.
1931; rpt. New York: Harper, 1967.

Kant, Immanuel. The Critique of Judgment (1790). Trans. J. H. Bernard.
1892; rpt. New York: Hafner Press, 1951.

Kierkegaard, Søren. The Concept of Irony (1841). Trans. Lee M. Capel.
1965; rpt. Bloomington: Indiana University Press, 1971.

Nietzsche, Friedrich. The Birth of Tragedy (1872), in The Birth of Tragedy
and the Genealogy of Morals. Trans. Francis Golffing. New York:
Doubleday, 1956.

Richter, Jean-Paul. Horn of Oberon: Jean-Paul Richter's "School for Aesthetics" (1812). Trans. Margaret R. Hale. Detroit: Wayne State University
Press, 1973.

Schelling, F. W. J. The Ages of the World (1854). Trans. F. de Wolfe Bolman. New York: Columbia University Press, 1942.

_____. System des transzendentalen Idealismus (1800). Hamburg: Felix Meiner
Verlag, 1957.

Schiller, Friedrich. Naive and Sentimental Poetry (1800), in Naive and Sentimental Poetry and On the Sublime. Trans. Julius A. Elias. New York:
Frederick Ungar, 1966.

_____. On the Aesthetic Education of Man, in a Series of Letters (1801). Trans.
Reginald Snell. New York: Frederick Ungar, 1965.

Schlegel, A. W. A Course of Lectures on Dramatic Art and Literature (1809–
1811). Trans. John Black. 1815; revised ed. A. J. W. Morrison. London: Henry Bohn, 1846.

Schlegel, Friedrich. Dialogue on Poetry and Literary Aphorisms (1797–1800).

Trans. Ernst Behler and Roman Struc. University Park: Pennsylvania State University Press, 1968.

Schopenhauer, Arthur. *The World as Will and Representation* (1819; 2nd. ed. 1844). Trans. E. F. J. Payne. 2 vols. 1958; rpt. New York: Dover, 1969.

Modern Critical and Philosophical Works

Abrams, M. H. *Natural Supernaturalism: Tradition and Revolution in Romantic Literature*. New York: Norton, 1971.

Artaud, Antonin. *Le théâtre et son double*. 1938; rpt. Paris: Gallimard, 1969.

Blackstone, Bernard. *The Consecrated Urn*. London: Longmans, 1959.

Bloom, Harold. *The Ringers in the Tower: Studies in the Romantic Tradition*. Chicago: University of Chicago Press, 1971.

———. *Shelley's Mythmaking*. 1959; rpt. Ithaca: Cornell University Press, 1969.

———. *The Visionary Company: A Reading of English Romantic Poetry*. New York: Doubleday, 1961.

Bostetter, Edward. *The Romantic Ventriloquists: Wordsworth, Coleridge, Shelley, Keats, Byron*. Seattle: University of Washington Press, 1963; revised ed., 1975.

Butler, E. M. *The Tyranny of Greece Over Germany*. Cambridge: Cambridge University Press, 1935.

De Man, Paul. *Blindness and Insight: Essays in the Rhetoric of Contemporary Criticism*. New York: Oxford University Press, 1971.

———. "Genesis and Genealogy in Nietzsche's *The Birth of Tragedy*." *Diacritics*, 2, no. 4 (1972), 44–53.

———. "The Intentional Structure of the Romantic Image." *Romanticism and Consciousness*. Ed. Harold Bloom. New York: Norton, 1970. Pp. 65–77.

———. "Political Allegory in Rousseau." *Critical Inquiry*, 2 (1976), 649–675.

———. "The Rhetoric of Temporality." *Interpretation: Theory and Practice*. Ed. Charles Singleton. Baltimore: The Johns Hopkins University Press, 1969. Pp. 173–209.

Derrida, Jacques. *Of Grammatology* (1967). Trans. Gayatri Spivak. Baltimore: The Johns Hopkins University Press, 1976.

———. *Speech and Phenomena, and Other Essays on Husserl's Theory of Signs* (1967). Trans. David B. Allison. Evanston: Northwestern University Press, 1973.

Dickstein, Morris. *Keats and His Poetry: A Study in Development*. Chicago: University of Chicago Press, 1971.

Evert, Walter. *Aesthetic and Myth in the Poetry of Keats.* Princeton: Princeton University Press, 1965.

Frye, Northrop. *The Secular Scripture: A Study of the Structure of Romance.* Cambridge: Harvard University Press, 1976.

———. *A Study of English Romanticism.* New York: Random House, 1968.

Hartman, Geoffrey. "Toward Literary History," *Beyond Formalism: Literary Essays 1958-1970.* New Haven: Yale University Press, 1970. Pp. 356-386.

James, D. G. *The Romantic Comedy.* London: Oxford University Press, 1948.

Sartre, Jean-Paul. *Imagination: A Psychological Critique* (1936). Trans. Forrest Williams. 1962; rpt. Ann Arbor: University of Michigan Press, 1972.

———. *The Psychology of Imagination* (1940). Trans. Bernard Frechtman. 1948; rpt. New York: Washington Square Press, 1968.

Sperry, Stuart. *Keats the Poet.* Princeton: Princeton University Press, 1973.

Stillinger, Jack. *The Hoodwinking of Madeline and Other Essays on Keats' Poems.* Urbana: University of Illinois Press, 1971.

Wasserman, Earl. *The Finer Tone: Keats' Major Poems.* 1953; rpt. Baltimore: The Johns Hopkins University Press, 1967.

———. *Shelley: A Critical Reading.* Baltimore: The Johns Hopkins University Press, 1971.

Wilson, Milton. *Shelley's Later Poetry: A Study of His Prophetic Imagination.* New York: Columbia University Press, 1959.

Index

DARK INTERPRETER

Designed by Richard E. Rosenbaum.
Composed by The Composing Room of Michigan, Inc.
in 10 point Baskerville V.I.P., 2 points leaded,
with display lines in Baskerville.
Printed offset by Thomson/Shore, Inc. on
Warren's Number 66 Antique Offset, 50 pound basis.
Bound by John H. Dekker & Sons, Inc.
in Joanna book cloth
and stamped in Kurz-Hastings foil.

Library of Congress Cataloging in Publication Data

Rajan, Tilottama.
   Dark interpreter.

   Based on the author's thesis, University of Toronto.
   Bibliography: p.
   Includes index.
   1. English poetry—19th century—History and criticism. 2. Romanticism—
England. I. Title.
PR590.R27 1980   821'.7'09   80-14476
ISBN 0-8014-1292-7